GR8 PL8S

THE BEST OF AMERICA'S VANITY PLATES

GR8 PL8S

Sam G. Riley

New Chapter Press

POUND RIDGE, NEW YORK

All inquiries should be addressed to New Chapter Press Inc., Old Pound Road, Pound Ridge, New York 10576.

First printing February 1991

Library of Congress Catalog Card Number: 90-091942

ISBN 0-942257-25-1

Cover Design by Carole Anne Clarke

MANUFACTURED IN THE
UNITED STATES OF AMERICA

To Becky, who helped me dream up the idea for this project and encouraged me to do a book rather than merely a column on it, and to Heather and Dan, who, like Becky, were frequently in the car with me and had to suffer my cries of ''Hey! There's a good one! Write it down, will you?''

Acknowledgments

The author extends sincere thanks to the many persons from departments of motor vehicles and similar governmental units who provided material for this book. Those whose names appear below, arranged alphabetically by state, are officials with whom the author corresponded. Thanks also to the many others contacted by phone whose names were not recorded.

Johnny L. Newman (AL), Jay N. Dulany (AK), Charles Beaver (AR), Marie Lenze (AZ), William N. Gengler and Elizabeth Smith (CA), Linda J. Haynes (CO), Rosmary H. Savino and Paul R. Oates (CT), Robert J. Voshell (DE), Jack Pelham (FL), Clint Moye (GA), Lawrence K. Hao (HI), Herbert A. Kinney (ID), Linda J. Becker (IL), Vickie Bender and Tom Siersdale (IN), Dennis Ehlert (IA), Thomas W. Skinner (KS), Mildred Carter and

Jerome L. Lentz (KY), John J. Politz (LA), Monica W. Fortier (ME), James P. Lang (MD), Kerry Conard (MA), Lee W. Schmitz (MI), Joseph Bowler (MN), John A. Lucks (MO), William F. Furois (MT), Margaret L. Higgins (NE), Judith A. Feliz (NV), Robert K. Turner (NH), Rudolph L. Torlini (NJ), Frank A. Mulholland (NM), Ellen F. Catalano and Frank J. Conley (NY), Betty Lewis and William S. Hiatt (NC), Bruce Larson (ND), Anne Crowley Warner (OH), Natalie S. Barnes (OR), John A. Pachuta (PA), Thomas M. Harrington (RI), J. S. Hicks (SC), Norman Edwards (TN), William D. Pool (TX), Sherrie Wignall (UT), William H. Conway and Naomi Decker (VT), Jerry Canada and Jeanne Chenault (VA), Jack L. Lince (WA), Glenn O. Pauley (WV), Norbert K. Anderson (WI), and Earl Kabeiseman (WY).

CONTENTS

Introduction

One day a couple of years ago, a throaty-sounding car zipped past me in traffic. I think it was a BMW. Quite unintentionally, I noticed its license plate: **WHOOSH**. How perfect, I thought. It was then I began to take notice of a phenomenon that has swept America in the last twenty years: the personalized or "vanity" license plate.

Like a lot of other people, I had never thought it necessary to apply for any sort of special message on my license tags. I simply took whatever the gods of random order handed me. I had, of course, always entertained vague hopes of being given a series of letters and numbers that would be easy to remember — ABC123, for example — but I had never been so lucky.

Then, my son Dan became the happy owner of the massive, gas-sucking 1971 Buick that in the years of reasonable fuel prices had belonged to his grandparents. It was essential, he assured me, that he get personalized plates that would mark this wonderful, freedom-generating milepost in his life. He spent days deep in thought, forsaking all homework, to come up with . . . The Perfect Plate. Finally, inspiration came as he reflected that like the Buick, he himself had been born in 1971. His plate, then, was **TWO7T1S**. I was proud of his originality, and this, too, made me think twice about what personalized plates have to offer.

To be sure, many such plates aren't so clever. Countless thousands do no more than display their owner's name or initials, or the make of the car, which is obvious enough without a license plate that underlines it for you by spelling out **FORD** or **CHEVY**. But let us not dwell upon such as these. Even the car owner's name or identity can be of some interest if presented in an unusual way, as in **BORG 9**, the California plate of movie actor Ernest Borgnine, or even better, and more abstract, Lawrence Welk's California plate: **A1ANA2**.

The fact is, many car owners have seized upon this tiny bit of space — a 12 × 6-inch metal tag — to tell us something interesting, or funny, or revealing. One- or two-word poets of the road, these motorists have shown a remarkable ability to squeeze meaning into a small format.

The first form of car-carried expression was the bumper sticker. A beat-up junker might display an announcement that read, "My Other Car's a Porsche." A more recent bumper sticker read, "Looking For Love But Will Settle For Sex." Similarly, students have been fond of buttons as a form of self-expression. Buttons told the world that Chip was a Lover, Not a Fighter, and proclaimed Muffie's undying loyalty to the latest rock group. Every St. Patrick's Day, the familiar "Kiss Me, I'm Irish" buttons appear (and occasionally, something more original, such as "Quiche Me, I'm French").

Buttons and bumper stickers are all right in their limited way, but personalized plates are better. You want buttons and stickers, you buy them. But with personalized plates, you must *create* your own message.

Here's how it works. You decide what you'd like to say to the rest of us on your plate, and then you visit your local office of the Department of Motor Vehicles and fill out an application. The people at the DMV will type it into their computer to see if it's already been taken by someone else in your state. If the message you want is available, you pay a fee ranging between $10 and $100, usually on top of the standard fee for a non-personalized plate. Prison inmates will stamp out the actual plates, an activity far more fun than fashioning knives out of mess-hall spoons, and within a month or so your message will be bolted onto your car for all to see. You get the satisfaction of original self-expression; the state gets some unbegrudged revenue. Not a bad deal all the way round.

Now, the license plate is one of those utilitarian objects of everyday life that most of us tend to take for granted — so much so that its origins are less than clear.

No individual has emerged as the "father of the license plate," but New York is thought to have been the first state to require automobile registration, in 1901. In the early years of the twentieth century, car owners had to make their own license plates, out of square or rectangular pieces of heavy leather to which large metal letters were riveted. Connecticut, another of the states that pioneered license plate use, introduced state-issued plates in 1905. These porcelain-covered metal plates were used there through 1916. Incidentally, Montana's DMV reports that because of wartime steel shortages, its 1944 plates were manufactured from pressed soybeans. Very interesting. If you got tired of your plate, you could have it for a snack.

As for personalized plates, Connecticut was the first state to issue them — way back in 1937. To get one of these plates, a driver had to have a good driving record, and he or she could use only four letters for its message. If not for World War II, Connecticut's innovation no doubt would have caught on more quickly in other states, but it wasn't until 1956 that the second state, North Dakota, followed suit. The only additional state to begin issuing personalized plates in the 1950s was New Hampshire, in 1957.

A fair number of other states got in on a good thing in the '60s: Vermont in 1962; Oklahoma in 1963; Ohio, Pennsylvania and Texas in 1965; Massachusetts and New Mexico in 1966; Arkansas and Maine in 1967; North Carolina in 1968; and Delaware, Georgia and Nevada in 1969.

Most of the remaining states began their

own personalized plate programs in the 1970s: California, Oregon and Wyoming in 1970; Nebraska, South Carolina and Washington in 1971; Arizona, Florida and Idaho in 1972; Louisiana, Michigan and Montana in '74; Iowa, Kansas, Minnesota, South Dakota and Utah in '77; Indiana and Kentucky in '78; and Missouri and Wisconsin in '79.

The 1980s saw four more states adopt the personalized plate: Illinois and Maryland in 1980, my own ever-conservative Virginia in '81, and, finally, West Virginia in 1982. Now it is unanimous: every state uses these plates. Furthermore, personalized plates appear to be an American invention. Most other countries requires that their plates use a numerical code or letter designations to identify the vehicle's locality, which precludes personal messages.

Our state governments also rake in a great deal of annual revenue from these plates. Virginia, for example, has made up for being next to the last state to adopt personalized plates by actively promoting their use, calling them "CommuniPlates" and keeping their cost among the lowest in the nation: $10, in addition to the fee that is charged for a standard plate. In 1990, only a few years after the program's inception, more than 10 percent of registered Virginia vehicles sport these plates: 563,170 out of a total of 5,145,700. At $10 each, this translates into more than $5 million a year in extra revenue.

The cost of getting a vanity plate varies from state to state. Like Virginia, North Carolina and Wisconsin have kept the annual cost low at $10. Oklahoma charges $12. At the high end are Alabama and New Jersey at $50, and Illinois and Texas at $75. This higher cost undoubtedly reduces the number of people willing or able to pay this much for their plate, yet out of a total of 13 million registered vehicles in Texas, 200,000 (roughly 1.5 percent) have nevertheless coughed up the necessary money. Illinois pulls in even bigger bucks, with 550,000 drivers willing to pay the stiff $75 fee for a plate of their own choosing. Minnesota gets the most up-front, $100 (though renewal is only $10).

Whatever the fee, most states allow the motorist to use a maximum of either 6 or 7 characters to construct the plate's message. Wyoming allows only 4. The generous states are Florida, Montana, and North Carolina, each of which allows 8 characters per plate. Quite a few states have made changes in the number of characters allowed, and the trend is decidedly upward.

Dependable figures on numbers of personalized plates in the various states are hard to come by, but certainly California has the largest number, around 1,200,000. In 1988, California reported that the fund built up from the sale of personalized plates had since 1970 expended a total of $220 million. The money is used to fund environmental projects.

To gather material for this book, I began with my local DMV office, where a helpful gent named Jerry Canada gave me a current list of the principal DMV offices in each state. I wrote to all of them, asking for samples of their personalized plates, minus the owners' names, of course. A few offices sent the complete computer printout of all the personalized plates in their state: Alaska, Iowa, Mississippi, Washington and Wyoming. Twelve other states offered to sell me a printout, at prices ranging from $10 for Texas (on microform) to Arizona's $4,000. Others sent samples of their states' more unusual plates, and a few sent nothing at all. Most of the more than 10,000 plates in this collection, then, came from these materials. The rest I collected here in Virginia and on my own travels here and there.

As my collection grew, I was able to group the plates into those categories represented by the chapters that follow. I hope that you, like myself, will enjoy eavesdropping in this unusual manner on what we Americans have on our minds. By our plates ye shall know us.

— **Sam G. Riley**
Blacksburg, Virginia
February, 1991

CHAPTER 1

Mine All Mine

The kind of plate for you if your car is AWESOME.

A lot of personalized plates show their owner's delight in his or her car's power or speed. **ADRNLIN** (WA) says it well, as does **AHK SHN** (TX). Just as creative is **ALLHEL** (WA), as in "faster'n all hell." The Iowa plate **BBEEP** seems to say, move over! I'm comin' through!

FSTRNU (KY, MS) issues a challenge. **CIFUCAN** is one Alabamian's way of saying, just see if you can pass me, smart guy! **CMEPASSU**, a North Carolina plate, goes at the same idea from the opposite direction. **IDSMOKU** and **QUIKRNU** (WA) smugly challenge other drivers, and **I8UUP** (WA),

UR8UP (MS), **U8DUST** (MS), **IPASTYA** (WA), **BLEW BYU** (ID), and **AHED A U** (TX) celebrate after the fact.

One can almost hear the rumbling, throaty exhaust in **EAR JAR** (IA), feel the rush of wind in **FLYBYU** (MS). The confidence in **EAT DST** (VA), **4 SMOKN-U** (VA), **2MUCH4 U** (IA, ID), **2QUIK4U** (KY), and **PASS N U** (TX) can't be missed. **HOS PWR** (MI), meet **MOR HP** (VA).

HRTBEAT (IA) has the same connotation of pride in speed, as do **LIVWIRE** (WA), **MSLCAR** (IA), **PHAST** (AK), **PHLASH** (AK), **QKSLVR** (AK), and **TNT** (AK, KY). Reeking of muscle-car macho is **150MPH** (IA), and somewhere driving the roads of Washington state is **DRZOOM**.

Very popular are plates that depict "speed noises": **VAAROOM** (ID, IN, WA), **VAROOM** (IA, KY, MI), **VAVOOM** (IA, MI), **V ROOM** (KY, ND), **VROOMM** (IA, MS, TX), for instance, or **RROARR** (ND), **RRRRRM** (MI), **RRRRR** (AK, TX), and **RRRRRM** (MI).

WHOOSH (IA, MS, VA) and **WOOSH** (IA, ID, TX) also sound like something zooming past you, as do, of course, **ZOOM** (AK, ID, MI, MS), **ZOOMMM** (IA, MI, MS), **ZOOOOM** (IA, ID, IN, MI, MS), **ZZOOM** (IA, MI, TX), **ZZOOMM** (IA, MI, TX), and **ZZZOOM** (IA, ID, KY, MI), not to mention **ZZZZZP** (VA) and **TZINGG** (VA).

Less speed-oriented motorists prefer to point out their chariot's sleek lines and dreamy curves, as in the Alaska plates **ABUTY** and **AQTPI**, Louisiana's **DUBLTAK**, North Dakota's **SO CUTE**, Wisconsin's **ITSA10**, Virginia's **O2SUAVE**, Delaware's **PZAZZ**, Iowa's **2SEXY**, North Carolina's **B14 ALL2C**, South Carolina's **2SMOOTH**, and Washington's **CHROME**, or **LAVISH**, or **KNOCKOUT**, or **SLIQUE**.

Variations on the word "looker" appear in many states. The best of these use Q's in place of the O's, giving the appearance of eyelashes: **LQQKER** (AK, IA, IN, LA, MI, SC).

Some prideful plates are more general in nature; on-lookers won't know for sure whether the car's speed or beauty inspired, for example, the almost limitless variations of "awesome": **AASOME, AHHSOM, AHHSUM, AHSUM, AHSUMM, AUHSOM, AUSOME, AUSUM, AWESOM, AWESOM, AWESUM, AWSOM, AWSOME, AWSUM, AWSUME, AWSUMM, AWWSUM**, and **2 AWSUM** — all of which appear in Iowa alone. One Virginian managed another variation not used by the awe-inspired Iowans: **AWHSOM**, and an Oregonian came up with **2AHSUM**.

ACEHI (IA), **AMAZIN** (IA, ID), **AONE** (ID, WA), **APLUS** (IN, WA), **CATSPJ** (VA), **DAZLER**

(AK, WA), **DILLE** (AK), **DIVINE** (AK), **GROOVY** (AK, IN, MS), **GR8EST** (OR), **HALCYON** (ID), and **HMDINGER** (WA) also express a general happiness about one's whole car, as do **ILUVIT** (IA), **INX2C** (CO), **ITSGRT** (VA), **KLASACT** and **KLASAKT** (WA), **LYMLITE** (WA), **ONAIR** (MI, TX, WA), **SUMCAR** (WA), **22 COOL** (IA), and **222 CUTE** (VA). Reminiscent of Billy Crystal's "Fernando" comedy routine ("E-e-e-you rook mahvlus") are **MARVLOS** (VA), **MARVLUS** (AL), and **MAVLUS** (MS)

Pleased yet plaintive plates are **MYFRIEND, MY1LOVE, MY1LUV**, and **MY1WISH**, all from the state of Washington. A Delaware resident's car is his **SHATZI** — German for "sweetheart"; an Iowan's car is a **WOWZER**; a North Carolinian drives **1KLASY#**; a Connecticut motorist is in **7 HEAVN**.

GLAD2BME (NC) and **GILOVIT** (LA) tell all who pass that the car is a real **GEM** (IA) — just **PHNOMNL** (ID). A real **PLEASR** (TX) with **PIZZAZZ** (TX). A **PZACAKE** (WA).

Satisfaction in ownership is just as plain in **ALLMINE** (IA, OR); **CMYCAR, CMYVAN**, and **DONGOOD** (VA); **EZ2BME** (OH); **FYNALY** and **GOTIT** (AK); **IGOTIT** (DE, IA); **IOWNIT** (IA); **IAMD1** (AK); **ITSMINE** (on a New York Mercedes); **JUSMYN** (AK); and **A14ME** (VA).

Putting a special spin on pride of ownership are **YUWISH** (IA) and **4U2NVY**, which is on a New Mexico Porsche.

Pleasure in that great American summum bonum the bargain is seen in **BARGUN** (OR), **SWTDEAL** (WA), and **TRUVALU** (WA). **BAAAD** (AK, IA, ID, MI), **BAAD** (IA), **BBBADD** and **IBBAD** (AK) make use of teenage slang, as do **GNARLY** (IA) and **NARLEY** (WA).

HAUTEUR (WA) is prideful, indeed, and **JOYOJOY** (VA) isn't merely symmetrical, but expresses pure happiness. **ITLDO** (IA) would be best used on a Rolls Royce or something comparably expensive. **NOGOSLO** (WA) is a plate for a car that's **PAWRFUL** (SC), and has its own southern accent. **MOSOUL** (AK) is hard to figure; maybe it has more soul than it can con-trol.

Recalling the original ads for Mazda ("Mazda engine goes hmmmmmmm . . ."), one wonders if **HMMMMM** (IA) is on that make of car, or if **SMLWNDER** (WA) is on a tiny sportscar. **STWISE** (WA) is an interesting way to describe one's car, as is **THGOODS** (WA). **THUNDR** (AK) puts one in mind of Robert Mitchum tearing along a back country road as a moonshiner one step ahead of the law in the movie *Thunder Road*. And let us trust that **VETYGD** (AK) is on a Jaguar or some other suitably British make.

All in all, a lot of American drivers seem to consider their car, as one Virginia driver put it, **2RIFIC**.

AAHH (WY)
AAHSUM (ID)
AAWSOM (TX)
ABABE (CO, ID)
A BALL (TX)
ABEAUTY (IN)
ABLAZE (TX)
ABOMB (IA)
ACES (ID)
A DANDY (TX)
A DEAR (TX)
A DOLL (TN)
A DREAM (AK, IA, TX)
AFEAST (NH)
AGEM4U (VA)
AGOODE (NH)
A HOT 1 (TX)
AHSOM (ID)
AHSOME (IN, MI)
A JEWEL (TX)
A JOY (ID)
ALLHIS (IA)
ALLMIN (ID)
ALLMYN (ID)
ALLOUT (MI)
ALL4ME (KY)
ALMINE (ID)
ALOOKR (KY)
A LULU (MI)
AMAZIN (IA, ID)
AMAZN (VA)
AMBIANZ (WA)
AM FAST (TX)
AOK (ID)
A PEARL (ID)
ASSET (AK)
AWSSUM (IN, KY)
A ZIP (VA)
A11 MINE (VA)
BAD (ID, WY)
BADBOD (ID)
BADNEWS (IA)
BADNUZ (IA, WI)
BEAUTY (ID)
BFAST (IA)
BGTIME (MI)
BLACK TY (VA)
BUG OUT (CT)
CAR 4 ME (KY, TX)
CHICK (KY)
CLASIC (AK)
CLASSC (VA)
CLASSY (AK, IA, KY, MI)
CMEEGO (IN)
CMEFLY (ID, IN)
CMEGO (CO, ID)
CMOMGO (IA)
COOL (MI, WY)
COOL DEAL (NC)

CARAZY (MI)
CATCHME (IN)
COSTLY (KY, MI)
CREMPUF (ID)
CRMPUF (AK, ND)
CUTIPY (VA)
CYCLONE (IA)
DANDY (DE, ID)
DANDY 1 (MI)
DBEST (AK, KY, MI)
DBLTRBL (ID)
DCEPTV (AK)
DEBEST (ID)
DELITE (AK)
DELUX (AK)
DELUXE (KY)
DEVLSH (AK)
DINAMO (ID)
D LISH (MS)
D LITFL (MS)
DPLUM (AK)
DRMCAR (MI)
DYNAMO (IA, IN)
EAT DST (TX)
ECSTASY (IA)
EPIC (CA)
EPITOME (CA)
EQUIPT (VA)
EXCLLNT (VA)
EXLENT (KY)
EXOTIC (TX)
EXPNSV (AK, IA)
EXTASE (AK)
EZ2LUV (KY)
EZ4U2NV (ID)
FANCEE (ID)
FANTAZ (ID)
FAROUT (MI)
FASCAR (MI)
FASST (MI)
FAST (ID)
FASTCAR (IA)
FASTNUF (IA)
FASTOY 4 (CA)
FASTRNU (OR)
FASTRAK (ID)
FAT CITY (VA)
FFFAST (MI)
FIERCE (IA)
FINALLY (IN)
FINALY (IN)
FINECAR (IN)
FIREBAL (IA)
FITSME (TX)
FLASH (AK, MI)
FLYINBY (ID)
FLYNHI (AK, MS, ND)
FLYNLO (AK)
FOXY (AK, IN, KY)
FRISKY (AK, TX)
FSTRIP (DE)
FUN (WY)
FUN CAR (MS)
FUNKY (TX)
FYRBAL (ID)
GOODY (IA)
GOOD 1 (IA)
GORGIS (MI)
GORJUS (AK, MI)
GOZFAST (CA)
GRAN-FUN (VA)
GRREAT (ID)
GRRR8 (ID)
GR8EST (ID)
HEVEN (IA)
HEVNLY (IA)

HGHLIFE (IA)
HI CLAS (MS)
HI COTN (MS)
HI CTTN (MS)
HI-PER (KY)
HIPURR (KY)
HOT (MI)
HOT CAR (MI)
HOTENUF (WA)
HOTFOOT (WA)
HOTNUF (IA)
HOTONE (AK)
HOTROD (AK, IA)
HOTSTUF (IA)
HOTTOY (AK, IA)
HOTWAD (IA)
HVY CHV (WI)
HYCLAS (WA)
HYKLAS (IN)
IBFAST (AK, ID)
IBGONE (AK)
IGNITION (NC)
IGOTIT (DE, IA)
I GOT 1 (MI)
II BAD (IA)
II HOT (IA)
II MUCH (DE, IA)
II WILD (IA)
IMAJOY (MI)
IMAQT (MS)
IM DVINE (VA)
IM FUN (MI)
IM LEADN (VA)
IMNTUNE (WA)
IN STYL (MI, ND)
INXTC (IA)
ION-1 (NC)
I PAS U (VA)
I PURR (MS)
I QUIKR (MS)
I R BAD (MS)
IRFLYN (MI)
IR FUN (VA)
ISNEAT (IN)
IT DO GO (IA)
IT FINE (VA)
IT FLYS (IA)
ITGOES (CT, IA)
ITGOZ (IA)
IT HUMS (OH)
ITLFLY (IA, MI)
ITLGO2 (VA)
ITS A PET (IN)
ITSBAD (IA, IN)
ITS FAST (IN)
ITSFUN (IA)
ITSGR8 (AK)
ITSHOT (AK, WA)
ITS MEAN (IN)
ITSMYN (AK)
ITSOFUN (WA)
ITSO ME (MS)
I XLER8 (MS)
JET FIRE (VA)
JSDUCKY (WA)
JUICY1 (DE)
JUSBAD (AK)
JUS RITE (IN)
KEY2XTC (WA)
KLASIK (ND)
KLASSIC (IN)
KLASSIK (IN)
KLASSY (IA, IN, MI)
KOOOOL (IA)
LANDYAT (WA)
LANDYHT (WA)

LANDYOT (IN, WA)
LANYAHT (WA)
LANYOT (WA)
LAVISH (WA)
LE BEST (TX)
LIKENU (IA)
LILDEVL (IA)
LIT NIN (MS)
LIVNEND (IN)
LIV WIR (MS, TX)
LKGD 2ME (VA)
LNDJET (WA)
LNDYAHT (WA)
LNDYCHT (WA)
LNDYOT (IA, ID)
LOADED (IA, WA)
LOKNGD (KY)
LOKNGUD (ID)
LOOKER (IA, MS, TX)
LOOKNGD (WA)
LOVELY (KY, MI, TX)
LOWCUT (WA)
LOWLQQK (WA)
LQQKR (VA)
LUKN GD (TX)
LUKY ME (MS)
LUNKER (IA)
LUSHUS (TX)
LUV IT (ND)
LUVTHIS (WA)
LUXURY (KY)
LYTENIN (WA)
MEGABUX (IL)
MENT4ME (ID)
MIGHTY (IA)
MINT (IN)
MOPOWER (IN)
MPRESV (TX)
MYBABY (CT, WA)
MYBAG (WA)
MY BOMB (VA)
MY BONUS (WA)
MYDFINE (WA)
MYHTRD (AK)
MYKAR (AK)
MYLILQT (WA)
MYPET (CT, TX)
MYSTCL (TX)
MYSTYLE (WA)
MY TEE-1 (TX)
MYTFINE (ID)
MYTYPE (IA)
MYWISH (IA)
NARLY (IN)
NARRRLY (ID)
NEAT (DE)
NEW CAR (TX)
NEW LOOK (WA)
NFASHN (VA)
NFLITE (WA)
NFLYTE (WA)
NICE (DE)
NIFTY (AK, IA, ID, TX)
NOCKOUT (ID)
NOCOUT (WA)
NOFAKE (IA)
NOKOUT (WA)
NOTBAD (IA, MS)
NOTOY (IA)
N STYLE (ID, TX)
NU LOOK (ID)
NULQQK (KY)
NUN BTR (IL)
O C MEGO (TX)
OKBYME (KY)
OK4ME (IA)

ONADIME (WA)
ONEDRFL (WA)
ONERFUL (WA)
OPULENT (WA)
ORGAZMC (WA)
OSOFAST (ID)
OSOFINE (ID, IN)
OSOFUN (ID)
OUCH-HOT (VA)
OVRKIL (IA)
O2BXLR8N (NC)
O2SUAVE (VA)
PAMPRD (ID)
PANACHE (ID, IN, WA)
PANASH (WA)
PASSD U (MS)
PAYD4 (MI)
PEACHE (VA)
PEACHY (IA)
PERFECT (IA)
PERKY (IN)
PHANCY (AK)
PIZAZZ (IA)
PLUSH (AK)
POSH (AK, IA, KY)
POWRWGN (WA)
PREMO (WA)
PRETTY (KY)
PRIMA (DE)
PRIMEAU (WA)
PRIMO (WA)
PRRRFKT (VA)
PUREJOY (NC)
PURFECT (IA, ID)
PURRR (DE)
QKSLVR (AK, TX)
QT (AK)
QTEE (AK)
QTPI (AK, IA)
QTPIE (AK, IA, OH, TX)
Q-T-PY 2 (TX)
QUICKIE (TX)
QUICKY (TX)
QWIKIE (TX)
QWKENUF (TX)
RAD (TX)
RADICAL (IA)
RADICL (IA)
RADIKL (IA)
RADNBAD (WA)
RADROD (AK)
RAKISH (TX)
RARE (IA)
RARN2GO (IA)
RDHOT (VA)
REDHOT (IA, NJ)
REDHOTT (IA)
REWARD (AK)
RITZII (IA)
RITZY (IA, MS)
ROCKET (AK)
ROCKIT (AK)
RODCAR (AK)
RTSTUF (AK)
RUGGED (AK)
SASSY (IA, MI)
SAVAGE (IA)
SCHNEL (MS, TX)
SCHNELL (ID, WA)
SEEMIGO (ID)
SELECT (IA)
SEXY (KY, TX)
SEXXY (TX)
SEXZ (AK)
SGOOD (DE)
SHATZY (TX)

SHINEON (WA)
SHINY (MI)
SHI SHI (MS)
SINFUL (KY)
SIZZEL (IA)
SIZZLE (IA)
SIZZLIN (IA)
SLEEEK (IA, MS)
SLEEK (AK, IA, ID)
SLICK (AK, ID, MI)
SMASHIN (WA)
SNAPPY (MS)
SNAZY (IA)
SNAZZY (AK, IA, MI)
SNUG (MS)
SO BAD (ID)
SO BADD (MS)
SO CUTE (MI, ND, TX)
SOFINE (KY)
SOFYNE)ID)
SO GOOD (MI)
SO HOT (MI)
SO NICE (AK)
SO RARE (K)
SOOSEXY (MI, VA)
SO SEXY (MS, TX)
SPEEDO (MS)
SPIFFE (WA)
SPIFFY (IA, MI, TX)
SPORTY (AK, IA, MI)
SPUNKY (AK, IA, MI)
STAR (IA)
STNNING (ID)
SUMFUN (AK)
SUPER (MI)
SUPERB (MI)
SUTZ ME (TX)
SUZOOM (VA)
SVELTE (MI)
SWEET (AK)
SWET RYD (VA)
SWOOSH (ID)
SWTDEAL (WA)
SZLNHOT (WA)
S1DRFL (OR)
S1DRFUL (WA)
S1RFUL (WA)
TAD2FST (ID)
TAK IT IN (TX)
TENPLUS (CA)
THE LOOK (ID)
THE RITZ (IN)
THEROD (IA)
THE YAHT (VA)
THISLDO (ID)
THRILL (AK, IA)
THRUST (IA)
TIP TOP (CT, MS)
TOCOOL (IA)
TOGOOD (AK)
TOOBAD (AK, IA)
TOOBADD (IN)
TOO COOL (IN)
TOO FAST (IN)
TOOHIP (AK)
TOOHOT (IL, VA)
TOOMUCH (IA)
TOPFCT (GA)
TOPNOCH (WA)
TO THE T (TX)
TOTOBAD (VA)
TOWILD (AK)
TRIFIC (IA)
TRIFIK (IA)
TUF CAR (IL)
TUTUF (VA)

U B MINE (TX)
UDLOOZ (MI)
UDLOSE (MI)
UDLUUZ (MI)
UDLUZ (MI)
U JELUS (MS)
U LIK IT (TX)
ULTIM8 (MI)
ULTMIT (KY)
U-LUST-4 (TX)
UNEAK (MS, WA)
UNEEK (ID, KY, MI, MS, VA, WI)
U-NEIK (TX)
UNEQUE (MI)
UNIQUE (AK, ID, MI, WI)
UNREAL (IA, MI)
UPBEAT (WA)
UPGRADE (KY)
UPTOWN (AK, IA, ID, MI)
UP2PAR (IA, ID)
URLOOKN (ID)
U4EA (IN)
U4EAH (MI)
VERYBAD (IA)
VISION (IA)
VIVACHE (VA)
VOLATLE (VA)
VRMM (CA)
VRMMM (CA)
VRMMMM (CA)
VRMMMMM (CA)
VROOM (CA)
VROOMER (CA)
VROOMIN (CA)
VROOMM (CA)
VROOOM (KY)
VRROOM (CA, KY)
VRROOMM (CA)
VRROOOM (CA)
VRROUM (CA)
VRRRMM (CA)
VRRRMMM (CA)
VRRROOM (CA)
VRRRRM (CA, KY)
VRRRRMM (CA)
VRRRROM (CA)
VRRRRRM (CA)
VRRUMM (CA)
VRUUMM (CA)
VRUUMMM (CA)
VRUUUMM (CA)
VRUUUUM (CA)
VRYBAD (MI)
VRYBEST (CA)
VRYBST (CA)
VRYBST1 (CA)
VRYCHIC (CA)
VRYCMFY (CA)
VRYCOOL (CA)
VRYCUTE (CA)
VRYDEAR (CA)
VRYFAS (CA)
VRYFINE (CA)
VRYGOOD (CA)
VRYHOT (CA, VA)
VRYJAZY (CA)
VRYMRRY (CA)
VRYNICE (CA)
VRYNIIC (CA)
VRYPEPY (CA)
VRYPREP (CA)
VRYPURE (CA)
VRYQCK (CA)
VRYQWIK (CA)
VRYRARE (CA)

VRYSEXY (CA)
VRYSHRP (CA)
VRYSLCK (CA)
VRYSPCL (CA)
VUROOM (KY)
VWOOM (TX)
VWOOOM (TX)
WAYBAD (IA)
WACOOL (IN)
WATFUN (IN)
WAYCOOL (IA, ID)
WAYHOT (IA)
WAYOUT (IA)
WAY2BAD (IA)
WAY2FAS (IA)
WAY2SLO (IA)
WE BAD (TX)
WE BAD 2 (TX)
WEFLYLO (ID)
WE LOVE IT (IL)
WEOSOM (ID)
WHAMMY (IA)
WHISH (VA)
WHTEHOT (ID)
WHTHOT (AK, IA, MI)
WICKED (AK, IA)
WILD (IA)
WINSUM (MI)
WIZBANG (IA)
WLDFYR (FY)
WONDAFL (NC)
WOOOSH (ID, MI)
WOOSHH (TX)
WRLWND (AK)
WRTFIN (KY)
XCELENT (IL)
XCELNT (AK)
XCELR8 (MI)
XCLENT (KY, MI)
XCLUSIV (IN)
XCPTNL (TX)
XITING (IA)
XITMNT (IA)
XLENT (KY)
XLLENT (IA)
XOLENT (TX)
XPENSIV (ID, IN)
XPENSV (IA, KY, MI, TX)
XPENZV (TX)
XPLOSV (KY)
XPNSIV (AK, DE, MI)
XPNSV (IA)
XQUIZIT (AK, TX)
X SAL NT (TX)
X TA C (OH)
XTACEE (IA)
XTASEE (IA)
XTASY (IA)
XTC4ME (ID)
XTRAFUN (IN)
XTRFUN (AK)
XZOTIC (IA)
X2C4US (IA)
YACHT (AK)
YUMMY (MS)
ZBEST (IA, IN, MI)
ZCUTE1 (IA)
ZDEMON (IA)
ZFINEST (WA)
ZIPNBY (ID, WA)
ZIPNBYE (ID)
ZIPNBYU (WA)
ZIPPIN (IA)
ZIPPY (IA, MI)
ZITGO (IA)
ZKAR4ME (WA)

ZKR4ME (KY)
ZLOOK (KY)
ZOOMER (AK)
ZOOOM (MS)
ZOOOMM (KY, MI)
ZWAY2GO (ID)
ZZZIP (MS)
ZZZP (MI)
1ANONLY (KS)
1BADTOY (IA)
1BAD10 (KY)
1BEAST (IA)
1DERFL (IA, MI, MS)
1DERFUL (IA, IN, MS)
1DRFUL (ID)
1FAST1 (KY)
1HOTNO (VA)
1HOTTOY (IA)
1-N-FLT (VA)
1NONLY (ID)
1OFA KND (VA)
1OFBST (VA)
1QUIKKV6 (VA)
1QT PIE (VA)
1TOGO (IA)
1TORUN (KY)
1-2-BEAT (TX)
10 PLUS (TX)
2AWSUM (KY)
2BAD (IA)
2COOL (IA)
2CUL4U (KY)
2CUTE (IA)
2FAST (AK, KY, MI)
2FAS 2C (MS)
2FAS4U (AK, ID, MI, MS)
2FINE (AK, KY, MI)
2FINE4U (LA)
2GOOD (AK)
2GOOD4U (ID)
2GR8 4U (MS)
2HIP 4U (ID, MS)
2HOT (AK, KY)
2HOT4U (KY)
2KOOL (AK, MI)
2 KUHL (KY)
2MUCH (AK, CT)
2MCH4U (IA)
2NARLY (AK)
2ND2NUN (IA)
2NICE (AK)
2NICE4U (ID)
2QCK4U (KY, WI)
2QK4U (VA)
2QT 2KAR (VA)
2QUICK4U (IA)
2QUK4U (IA, TX)
2QWK2C (KY)
2QWK4U (IA, OH)
2 SEXXY (KY)
2SHARP (KY)
2-SLIC (KY)
2WILD4U (IA)
4KEEPS (KY)
4 TUN IT (VA)
4U2C (KY)
4 U2NV (KY, TX)
7 HEVEN (MS)
90S LOOK (VA)
200MPH (KY)

CHAPTER 2

Hard Luck Stories

If your car is SHOTBAD.

If you think your old **CLUNKER** (IA) is **2 GOOFY** (VA), **A LEMON** (AK, MS), **A CROCK** (WA), or a **BUMMER** (AK), then this sort of plate might be just right for you.

A Washington driver chose **DTH TRP** for his car; an Alaskan graphically labeled his **DODO**; an Iowan called his an **EYEZOR**. **GAUCHE** (AK, IA), **GOOFY** (IA), and **GAUDY** (TX) are equally deprecating. A Washington motorist has proclaimed that his vehicle is **HAUNTED**; an Iowa owner said his is **II UGLY**; an Idahoan went a step further and nicknamed his car **OLUGLY**; and an Alaskan has used his tag to send out a perpetual **MAYDAY** because his car is **OVRDHL** (AK).

KAPUT (German for "broken"), **HAZRDUS**, **HEYWIRE**, **HEHWIRE**, **HELLISH**, **ICKEY**, **IMAREK**, and **IMRUSTY** all adorn Washington cars. Alaskans say they have cars that are **LOUSY**, **ORNERY**, **ROTTEN**, **RUINED**, **RUSTIN**, **SCRUBY**, **SOBAD**, **TERIBL**, and **XRATED**. A Virginian, making a **CATTY** (WA) comment about her car, labeled it **AMEWZING**. A North Carolinian proclaimed that his car is **JUS2LOUD**; a fellow Tarheel considers his car to be **SHOTBAD**.

A few owners damn their cars with faint praise, as in **DUZRUN** (AK); **ITGOES** and **ITWORKS** (DE); **ITLDO** (VA); **NUTOME** (AK); **OK4NOW** (IA), **OK4A4DR**, **OK4BN4N**, and **OK42DAY** (WA); and **THS L DO** (TX). A plate that reads **4 TIRES** (ND) seems to carry with it an implied "and that's about all!"

As if that's **NOTENUF** (SC), why not go the whole hog and admit your car looks like it has **LEPROSY** (IA), that it's just about **DONFUR** (AK), that it's a **LOTECH** (IA), **MAKEDO** (IA) **NHTMARE** (WA). Go ahead. So far as your car is concerned, admit it's a **RDHAZRD** and a **RATTRAP** (WA), a **PWRLSS** (CT, TX) **RATMBLE** (WA) that was a **RIPOFF** (IA) when you bought it and has been an **UNSAFE** (WA), **MPOSIBL** (WA) **TRAUMA** (IA) for you ever since. You won't always have to drive a

TACKY (MI, MS), **TRASHY** (TX, WA), **RAGTAG** (MI) old **OILBRNR** (WA), but for now it's just something you'll have to **SETL4** (IA) while you're **RUFFNIT** (KY, LA).

So if your auto **WUZGOOD** (WA), if it sounds **2NOISY** (VA) or looks **2FRGON** (MS), if it's **WEIRD** (IA) or **WASTED** (IA, MS) or plain **UGLY** (AK, IA, ID, TX, WA), and it has you **ONDEDJ** (VA), then why not get yourself a plate that says **MYWRECK** (WA), or **SUBPAR** (WA), or even **MYSOB** (AK)?

Or maybe you could be more subtle, as were drivers in Idaho and Virginia who chose **THE RUB**. Presumably, when onlookers see these two cars rattling down the road, they can pause reflectively, stroke their chins, and declaim: "Aye, there's the rub."

A BOMB (TX)
ABSURD (AK, MI)
ABUSED (DE, IA, OH, MI)
A DEBIT (WA)
A DINK (TX)
AGEING (TX)
AGONY (TX)
ALLBAD (KY)
ALL WET (ID)
A MESS (MS)
A NOY N (MS)
ART BRN (ID)
ATE UP (MS)
AWFUL (MI)
BAD ACT (MI)
BAD APL (ID)
BADNUF (AK, MI)
BADNUZ (ID)
BAD TOY (AK)
BAD WAY (VA)
BD DREAM (VA)
BEDLAM (AK)
BG PYMT (MS)
BOOBOO (ID, IN, MI)
BRDBOX (AK)
CLAMITY (WA)

CLINKR (WA)
CRAPPY (WA)
CROCK (MI)
CRUD (MS)
CRUMBY (ID, MI)
DATANK (IA)
DECENT (AK, KY)
DIRTY (IN, KY, MI)
FILTHY (IA, TX)
FOR NOW (MS)
FUELISH (WA)
GAS GUZ (MS)
GASHOG (IA, IN, MS, OR, TX)
GAS PIG (TX)
GOKART (IA)
GON BAD (ID, MS)
GREASY (IA, MS)
GROSS (ID)
GRUBBY (IN)
GRUNGY (TX)
GUZLER (ID, MI, MS)
HAFACR (NH)
HAFCAR (NH)
HAYWRE (MI)
HAZARD (AK, MI)
HELLCAR (WA)
HEX (AK)
HEYWIRE (WA)
HOPELUS (VA)
HY RISK (TX)
H2OLOO (KY)
I AM 8UP (IN)
ILEGAL (IA)
IM SLOW (MI)
ITLRUN (KY)
ITUGLY (VA)
ITYBIT (IA)
ITYBTY (IA)
JALOPY (WA)
JINX (KY)
JINXED (MI, TX)
JUNK (KY, MI, TX)
JUNKER (CA, IA)
JUNQUE (MS)
KLUNKER (WA)
KLUNKY (WA)
LEMON (IA, IN, OR, VA, WI)
LOBLOW (MI, WA)
LODOWN (IA)
LOENUF (IA)
LO-LIFE (TX)
LOWRENT (WA)
LOWTECH (WA)
MAKN DO (TX)
MATCHBX (IA)
MIHEEP (WA)
MISQUE (WA)
MTCHBOX (IA)
MT 1 (V)
MY DEBT (ID)
MY FOLY (MI)
NAASTY (IA)
NASTY (AK)
NITMARE (ID)
NO ACCT (IL)
NOCURE (IA)
NOGAS (AK)
NOGOOD (WA)
NOISY (MS)
NOTA-10 (TX)
NOT SAFE (WA)
NOXCUSE (AL)
NUT BUS (TX)
OILEE (VA)

OK4NOW (KY)
PLNCRZY (ID)
RABBID (ID)
RATNEST (WA)
RAUNCHY (ID)
RD HOG (TX)
RECHED (TX)
RISKY (IA)
ROTTER (AK)
RUNT (IA)
RUSTY (MI)
RUSTY 1 (AK)
SHAKY (IA)
SHLOMO (IA)
SHPREC (MI)
SHPWRK (MI)
SHUBOX (IA)
SKIDROE (WA)
SKIDROW (ID, WA)
SLIME (AK)
SLO-POK (LA)
SMFRY (IA)
SNAFU (AK, MI, TX)
SO-SO (KY, TX)
SQUAT (IA)
SQUIRT (IA)
SQURRT (IA)
STOLEN (DE, ID, IN, KY, MI, OR)
TANK (IA)
TEACUP (IA)
TEECUP (IA)
TERRIBL (ID)
THE RUT (VA)
TINNY (MS)
TO SLACK (VA)
TRASH (MS)
TRAVESTY (NC)
UGLYBUG (WA)
UGLY 1 (KY)
UNCLEN (IN)
UNLOVD (TX)
UNPAID4 (IL)
VRYSCRY (CA)
VRYSKRY (CA)
VRY SLO (CA)
VRY SLOW (CA)
VRY UGLY (CA)
VULGAR (MI)
WRECK (IA)
WRECKED (CA)
XRATID (MI, VA)
1 JUNKER (CA)
1 JUNK R (MS)
1 JUNKY 1 (CA)
2FUNKY (KY)
2HUGE (IA)
2HYPER (IA)
2LANGSAM (NC)
2SHORTT (VA)

If we're an AIRHEAD or a DWEEB.

AIMLESS, AIRHEAD, A WINO and **A WITCH** are all from Washington State. Virginia drivers apparently admit they are **AROGNT** or **DMNTED**; an Iowa motorist admits he's a **BOOZER**.

Rugged Alaskans bill themselves as **BADGUY**, **BADMAN**, **HELRAZR**, **IMRUDE**, **LKHOLIC**, **MRRUDE**, a **SLEAZ** or **SLEAZE**, **UNCIVIL**, **UNRULY**, a **WILDMAN**, **YDBIRD**, and **XNICEGY**. In Washington State a few less macho-minded residents agree to being a **BUFOON**, **CHUMP**, **CNILE**, **CRYBABY**, **DINGBAT**, **EGGHEAD**, **GEEK**, **GULIBL** or **GULLIBL**, a **HASBIN**, **NOBODY**, **MRPOOP**, **OLCROW**, **PBRAIN**, **TWIT**, and even a **WHIMP**. A Virginian claims he's a **WUSSIE**, and the Mississippi plate **BRDLGS** makes one wonder if the owner's legs are so skinny she's suing them for nonsupport.

Other plates are admissions of running short of cash: **BNKRUPT** (WA), **BROKE** (AK, ID, MI, WI), **HOBO** (IA, TX), **IMAHOBO** (WA), **IMNDEBT** (WA), **INDEBT** (IA, IN, MI, MS, TX, WI), **INHOC** (IN, MI, MS, WA), **INHOCK** (MS, WA), **INTHRED** (WA), **IOALOT** (TX, WA), **IOLOTS** (ND), **IOUDAD** (IA), **IO2MUCH** (SC), **IO4IT** (IA, MS), **IRPOOR** (WA), **MYDEBT** (AK, TX), **N DEBT** (MI), **NO BUX** (PA), **NO MONEY** (IN), **NOMUNY** (VA), **N2DEEP** (ND, TX), **OHIOWE** (ND), and **POBOY** (AK, MI, MS, TX).

It appears, in fact, that drivers are willing to confess virtually anything. An Alaskan chose **AK JADE**, Washington residents **BARFLY**, **BIGOT**, and **DOXIE**. Virginia motorists label themselves **CRZNUT**, **DUM KOPF**, **MISFIT**, and **REDNCK**. **IDOIT**, proclaims one Virginian; **IDONT**, protests another.

Iowans seem particularly fond of variations on the word ''crazy'': **CARAZY**, **CRAAZY**, **CRAZED**, **CRAZEE**, **CRAZIE**, and **CRAZY**, as well as **KRAZED**, **KRAZEE**, **KRAZI**, **KRAZIE**, **KRAZY**, and **KWAZY**. Others here and there flaunt their size: **FATBOY** (IA, ID, MS, TX), **FAT BROAD** (VA), **FATMAN** (IA, ID, MS), **FATN40** (IA, OR, TX), and **FATS** (IA). Washington plates read **I82MUCH**, **PORCINE**, and **SLOB**; a Connecticut tag, **SKINNY**.

A few deprecating plates take a religious approach: **CINFUL**, **CYNFUL** and **CYNNER** (WA); **HEATHN** (TX); **NO ANGL** (ND); and **SINNER** (WA).

In Iowa lives **DGRUMP**, in Washington **DMOOCH**. A North Carolinian is an **EZ-TOUCH**, a North Dakotan **GAGA**, a Delaware resident a **GADFLY**. Someone in Washington State is **FULABUL**; an Oregon driver is a **LEDFUT**. A New Jersey car owner says he is **SENILE**; a Washington woman nicknames herself **OLDILOX**; an Ohio motorist is **WAY2HI**; and another Washingtonian calls himself an

OLPOOP, what Katharine Hepburn calls Henry Fonda in *On Golden Pond*.

Virginia has a **BSYBDY** and a **WISEGY**, Washington State a **CRMUDGN** and a **DINGBAT**, Iowa a **GOON** and a **LOUT**, Alaska a **MOONER** and a little **SQUIRT**, Idaho an old **SEWNSEW**. A Californian labels herself **DE TWIT**.

Others inclined to let it all hang out have opted for the likes of **GLDDIGR** (WA), **IMGROSS** (WA), **IM NUTS** (IN, MS, OH), **INSANE** (DE, IA, IN, TX) **KEPT** (WA), **LOONEY** (DE, MS, TX), **SATYR** (WA), **SHMUCK** (IA), **STUPID** (DE, MS), **THIEF** (ID, MS, ND), **TWERP** (AK, IA), **SAFCRKR** (WA), and **WACKO** (IA, ID).

Though some of these plates might strike you as a trifle **GROSS** (AK), you're no **DWEEB** (MS) or **GWEEDO** (IA) if you can laugh at yourself to this extent.

A FOOL (AK)
A HOOD (MS)
AIRHED (WA)
A KRAUT (MS)
ALKY (MI)
AMUCK (MI)
A PATSY (CA)
APFOOL (WA)
ASLEEP (OR)
AWOL (MI)
BADASU (MS)
BADAWG (MS)
BADBOY (AK, ID, IN, MS, ND)
BADBOYZ (ID)
BADBRO (AK)
BADGAL (MS)
BAD GIRL (IN)
BADGRL (KY)
BADR NU (MS)
BAG LADY (ID)
BAG MAN (ID)
BEERFAT (WA)
BEZERK (IL)

BIMBO (ID, MI)
BO LEGS (MS)
BONEHED (WA)
BORED (IA)
BOSSY (AK, DE, IA)
BRDLEGS (CA)
BRDLGS (CA)
BRN WLD (MS)
BUFFOON (IN)
BUM (KY, MI)
BUMKIN (MS)
BUSTED (MS)
CONMAN (IA, MI)
CNFSD (VA)
CNFUSD (MS)
CPYKAT (IA)
CRABBY (IL)
CRAFTY (IA, MS)
CRANK (IA)
CROOK (MI)
CRUDE (MS)
CRUMB (MI)
CURMUJN (VA)
DECADNT (WA)
DESPOT (CA)
DNGBAT (ID, KY)
DOGHAUS (WA)
DRUNKY (DE)
DULIFE (IA)
DUMB (WA)
DUMBUNY (WA)
DUMDUM (WA)
DUMMY (CT)
DYEHRD (IA)
EL MEANO (ID)
ETCROW (WA)
EVEL 1 (WA)
EVIL (MI)
EZ HUMP (OH)
EZ PREY (MS)
FAIRY (MS)
FAT (ID, MS)
FAT BOI (ID)
FATSO (TX)
FATTY (IL)
FEISTY (ID, TX)
FLAKEY (MS)
FLAKY (MS)
FLIRT (ND)
FLOOZY (AK, VA)
FREEKY (MS)
FRUMP (AK, ID)
FRUMPEE (WA)
FRUMPY (OR, WA)
GEEK (WA)
GEEZER (WA)
GET N BY (ND)
GON DEF MS)
GON MAD (MS)
GOUT (CA)
GOZDWN (CA)
GREEDY (IA)
GRINGO (AK, IA)
GROUCH (IL, MI, MS)
GRUMP (AK, DE, IA, ID, IN, MI, MS)
GRUMPE (MS)
GRUMPI (MS)
GRUMPY (AK, IA, IN, MI, MS)
GUIDO (AK, MS)
GUILTY (AK, IN, MI, MS)
GUTLESS (WA)
HAG (WA)
HALF-WIT (NC)
HARDUP (IA)

HAYSEED (ID, WA)
HELCAT (WA)
HELLCAT (WA)
HEYSEED (WA)
HNGOVR (TX)
HOBO (IA, MI, TX)
HOOD (KY)
HUSTLER (WA)
HYPER (IA)
I AM BAD (TX)
I AM BLU (TX)
I AM LO (MS)
IAML8 (CT)
I AM OLD (OH)
I AM SHY (OH)
I AM SLY (TX)
I AM VAIN (IL)
IBGKID (VA)
IBLATE (IN)
IBLUIT (WA)
IM BROKE (IL)
IMCRAZY (IA)
IMCRZY (MI)
IMEEEZZ (MS)
IMEZ (MS)
IM HIGH (WA)
IM LATE (IN, MS)
IM LA8 (KY)
IM LOST (IA, MI, MS, TX)
IM LOST2 (IA)
IM L8 (VA)
IM N DEBT (IN)
IMNOZEE (WA)
IM NUTZ (DE)
IM POOR (TX, WA)
IMSICK (DE)
IM 1 UP (TX)
IM2L8 (VA)
IN A DAZ (TX)
IN DET (MS)
INDETT (MI)
IN D RED (TX)
IOA TON (MS)
IOGMAC (NM)
IOIOIO (MS)
IOMUCH (VA)
IOSUM1 (VA)
I 4GET 2 (MS)
JAPSAP (WA)
JARHEAD (WA)
JERK (IA, MI)
JINXED (AK)
JUSAHIK (VA)
KARNUT (IA)
KRAZEE (AK)
KRAZY (AK)
KRAZY ME (IL)
KRUDE 1 (WA)
KUNFUZD (VA)
LEAD FT (MS)
LEDFOOT (IA, WA)
LEDFT (IA)
LOAFER (DE, IA, TX)
LOCO (IA)
LO LIFE (MS)
LONELY (IA)
LONER (IA)
LOWCLAS (WA)
LOWFUN (WA)
LOWLIFE (IA, WA)
LOWNUF (IA)
LUNATIC (DE)
L8AGAN (MS)
L8AGIN (ID)
L8AGN (MS)
MADMAN (DE, MI, TX)

MANIAC (DE, IA, ID, KY, MI)
MEAN (AK, MS)
MEANIE (AK, IA)
ME KRAZY (CA)
MINDLES (VA)
MISER (MS, WA)
MONO (AK)
MPOTNT (AK)
MRGRUMP (AK)
MRSDUD (WA)
MRSHOBO (WA)
MRSOB (AK)
MRYUCK (WA)
MRYUK (WA)
MSFIT (MI)
MY EGO (AK)
MY1VICE (ID)
MZBHVN (ND)
NASTY (IN, MI)
NASTY ME (IN)
NDCENT (AK)
N DEBT (OH)
N ESCRO (MS)
NITWIT (MI)
NOBODY (CA)
NO HERO (WA)
NO HOME (IA)
NO LUCK (IA)
NO MUN E (TX)
NSANE (DE, KY, MS)
N TRUDR (IA, VA)
N2 AMESS (VA)
OALOT (VA)
OBNXUS (AK, TX)
ODDBALL (IN, WA)
OHSOSO (WA)
OLCOOT (MS, WA)
OLDGOAT (WA)
OLDKOOT (WA)
OLGRUMP (WA)
OLLGOAT (WA)
OUTSIDR (VA)
PEST (IL)
PEZANT (MS)
PICKY (WA)
PIEFACE (WA)
PIFACE (WA)
PIGLIPS (WA)
PINHEAD (IA, WA)
PINHED (AK)
PLMCRZY (IA, WA)
PLMKRAZ (WA)
PLMKRZY (WA)
PLMLOCO (WA)
PO FOLK (MS, TX)
PO FOLX (TX)
PO GAL (MS)
PO MAN (MS)
PRISSY (IA)
PROWLR (TX)
PSYCHO (AK, MI, MS, TX, WA)
PSYCO (MS)
PUNCHI (IA)
PUNCHY (TX)
PUNK (MS)
PWRLSS (AK)
RATFACE (WA)
RATFINK (WA)
RDHAWG (ID)
RECLUSE (WA)
REDNCK (WA)
REDNEC (WA)
REDNECK (WA)
REDNEK (AK, WA)

REMISS (WA)
RIFRAF (WA)
RIFRAFF (MS, WA)
RIPPED (DE)
RISQUE (AK)
ROGUE (ID)
RONCHY (AK)
ROUNDR (IA)
ROWDIE (IA, MI)
ROWDY (AK, IA, MI)
RUBE (WA)
RUDE (KY, MI)
RUDEBOY (WA)
RUMRUNR (WA)
RUNT (MS)
RUTHLES (ID)
SAPSTOY (WA)
SCHMUK (WA)
SCREWY (IA)
SCROOGE (IA)
SCRUFFY (IA)
SHAM (AK)
SHESPLD (WA)
SHIFTY (IA)
SHOOFF (IA)
SHOWOFF (IN, LA, MS)
SHYBABY (IA)
SHYONE (IA)
SICKO (IA)
SIMP (MS)
SIMPLE (MS)
SINFUL (ID)
SISSY (AK, MS)
SKYGEEK (WA)
SLEEZ (AK)
SLOPOKE (IA)
SLOPPY (AK, IA)
SLY 1 (OH)
SNEAKY (IA, MI, MS, TX)
SNEEZY (IA)
SNIFFY (IA)
SNOB (IN, KY)
SOB (MI)
SO SO (MS)
SO VAIN (MS)
SPOILD (MI, MS)
SPOILD 1 (VA)
SPOILED (ID)
SPOILT (MI)
SPOYLD (ID, MS)
SPOOKY (MS)
SPOKED (MI)
SQIRMY (IA)
STINKR (KY, MI)
STLCRZY (ID)
STONED (ID, MI, WA)
STUFFY (DE)
STUMPY (MS)
TAXDUE (IA)
TEASER (AK)
THE BUM (ID)
THEHAG (IA)
THEWINO (WA)
THEWOP (WA)
TIGHT (DE)
TIPLER (TX)
TOO OLD (MS)
TRAMP (AK, WA)
TRCULNT (WA)
TR1CKY (MS)
TRIXTR (MS)
TWISTED WA)
UNKUTH (KY)
UPPITY (AK)
VARMIT (AK, IA, ND)
VILLAIN (ID)

VRRRAGO (CA)
VRY RUDE (CA)
VULGAR (MS, WA)
WACKO (IA, ID)
WACKY (DE, IA)
WARPED (ID, TX)
WEBHIGH (WA)
WEIRD (AK)
WEIRD 1 (CT)
WENCH (WA)
WE R EASY (IL)
WHACKO (WA)
WHIMPY (IA)
WICKED (IN)
WIMP (DE, KY)
WIMPY (IA, MS)
WINO (ID, MS, WA)
WITCH (ID)
WLD MN (VA)
WLD WMN (MS)
WOP (WA)
WRATH (ND)
XCTABL (MS)
XENTRC (VA)
XNTRIK (MS)
X RATED (MS)
YLD MAN (MS)
YSGUY (IA)
ZEDUCED (WA)
Z FREAK (IN)
ZOMBIE (WA)
ZONKED (AK)
1BADBOY (IA)
1BUM (IA)
1CLOWN (IA)
1 CROOK (ID)
1GRUMP (IA)
2BROKE (MS)
2 COCKY (MS)
2 COKY (MI)
2CRAY Z (MS)
2HOBOS (IA)
2LOUD (IA)
2LUNLY (VA)
2NASTY (ID)
2 RUDE (KY)
2TALL (ND)
2 TIPSY (ID)
2 TIRED (IA)
2WILD (IA)
2XPNSV (IA)
5THWHL (AK)

CHAPTER 3

It's A Living

Doctor, Lawyer, Merchant, Chief

Since most of us spend a good third of our day at work, it's hardly surprising that a lot of us use our license tag to proclaim what we do for a living. We want the world to know us not just for who we are, but for what we do.

Some of these plates are entirely straightforward, as is the case with **ACTOR** (TX, WA) and **ACTRESS** (WA), **ACTUARY** (IA, WA), **BAILIFF** (WA), **BELBOY** (IA), **CABBIE** (IA, MI), **FARMER** (IA, IN), **RABBI** (MI, WA), **PRIEST** (AK), or **UMPIRE** (AK, IA, IN, MI, MS, TX).

Other job plates ask a little more of our imaginations: **ABACUS** (AK, IN, MI), is probably the license of mathematicians or math teachers. (Although, the first **ABACUS** in California, twenty years ago, belonged to the senior vice-president of a computer magazine.) **ADDUMUP** (IA) is likely an accountant or bookkeeper; **ABCDEF** (AK, WA), **ABCD123** (IN), and **AEIOU** (MS, WA) are probably elementary school teachers.

BOOKEM (NC) is likely a cop, and **EMBALM** belongs to the owner of an Ohio funeral home. No doubt policemen are the owners of **DAFUZ** in Iowa and Ohio, **DAHEAT** in Washington State, and **DFUZZ** in Louisiana. **PHLYBOY** (WA) is probably an airline pilot, **ILUSTR8R** (WA) a commercial artist, **I MIXEM** (VA) a bartender, **INTWORK** (VA) a commuter of some sort, and **POLLYA** (ID) a pollster.

HFRRRR belongs to the owner of an Iowa ranch; **HIBID** to a construction company in the same state; **OLDAGE** to a Washington retirement home; **TENHUT** (IA), **A10SHN** (PA), and **HUP234** (OR) to members of the military, possibly drill instructors; **UROUT** (IA), **YEROUT** (IA), and **YUROUT** (IA) to umpires; **WEBONDU** (WA) to a bail bondsman; **ZINGERS** (WA) to a comedian; **BAUHAUS** (WA) to an architect; and **IFOTOU** to an Oregon photographer.

Some job plates reveal the company their owner works for: **AMWAY** (AK), **AVON** (DE),

MARAKA and **MARYKAY** (IA), and **TUPRWR** (VA), for instance.

Most, however, show only what job the plate owner holds, or what function he or she performs. **ABOSS** is in Iowa, **HAIRDU** an Ohio hairdresser, **GRO-BIZ** a Virginia florist, **ARIST** in Arkansas, **GROCER** in North Dakota. **BACKHO** and **BACKHOE** (IA) must be real operators. **BIUSED** (DE) is very likely a car salesman, **BLT2GO** (NC) a short-order cook, **BOMSQD** (WA) one of the bravest of employees. One suspects that **BYER** (OR) or **DSPLAY** (IA) work for department stores and that **BYAHOME** and **BYLAND** (WA) are realtors. **SHOD2GO** is a California blacksmith; **ONTHJOB** (CA) a vocational counselor.

Iowa has custom plates reading **COWBOY**, **COWGRL**, **COWMAN**, and **COWPOK**, plus the more unusual **COWPUNK**, who we can only picture as riding the range in purple, studded chaps, his spiked hair stampeding the livestock.

Some of these plates are a little harder to figure than others. **CROBAR** (IA) may be a wrecker, **DEBIT** (IA) an accountant, **ENZYME** (AK) a researcher, **DR PLAY** (VA) a physical education teacher or a coach, **HWYBLUZ** (WA) a road-weary trucker, **ICTHRUU** (WA) an x-ray technician, **GREASE** (AK) a mechanic, **HOTTAR** (OR) a roofer, **I CARAT** (IA) a jeweler. **IDGDIRT** (IA), **IDIGDRT** (WA), and **IDIGIT** (IA) probably own or work for construction companies. **IFIXIT** (OR), **ILFIXIT** (IA), and **IFIXM** (CT) are doubtless repairmen of some sort. **JOEPRO** (AK) is possibly a teacher of golf or tennis, **I SCRUB** (CT) a housecleaner or a surgeon. **MUDMAN** (IA) might well work with concrete, **PONTIUS** (WA) by all rights should be a pilot. **SAYCHZ** (VA) must be a photographer, **SENDU** (OR) a travel agent, **SNAPON** (DE) a hardware salesman, **SPOOK** (WA) a member of some not-so-secret intelligence operation.

Is **TRASH** (DE) a sanitation worker? Is **TROWEL** (IA) a mason? Is **TUGDOC** someone who repairs tugboats, a dentist, or an obstetrician? Is **LABOR** (DE) another o.b. specialist, or a union representative?

Hold that thought, because medical doctors appear to be the profession most likely to sport a personalized plate. Obstetricians have such plates as **CME4OB** (WA), **DLVIRY** (WA), **LBR DOK** (ID), **D STORK** (WA), **IDELIVER** (WA), **IDLIVER** (ID), **IDELIVR** (WA), **STORK** (AK, DE, OR), and **THE STRK** (NC). One wonders if the Oregon plate **NO OB** belongs to a former o.b.-gyn doctor who gave up the obstetrical part of his or her practice due to the enormous cost of malpractice insurance for that specialty.

Surely **BABYMD** (LA), **BBXMNR** (OR), and **KID DOC** (MI) are pediatricians, and it is likely that **BABY DOC** (IN) refers to the former, and not the deposed head of state in Haiti.

BACKDOC (IA, ID), **BACKDR** (TX), **BACMAN** (MI), **BACKFXR** (WA), **BONEDOC** (IN, WA), **BONEDOC** (IN, WA), **BONEDR** (WA), **FIX BAX** (IN), **DR BONZ** (VA), and **I FIX BAX** (IN) must belong to either orthopedic surgeons or chiropractors. It's anybody's guess whether **BONDOC** (WA) refers to "bone doctor" or "boondocks" — a country doctor. **FRAXUR** (VA) is more than likely an orthopedist.

AH CHOO is a Minnesota allergist; **MDUC2P** (NJ) and **IC2ITUP** (NV) are urologists who have active senses of humor, which a person would need for that line of work. One dares not speculate about the Washington State tag **DKDOC**.

GIEN DR (gastro-intestinal enterologist), **LADYMD**, **EAR DOC**, and **GYN DOC** are Virginia plates. **EARS2U** has been on the road in both Indiana and Michigan for many ears. Iowa has **EYEDOC** and **EYEDR**, Michigan **DR EYE**, Indiana, Utah and Connecticut **FOOTDR**, Iowa and Texas **FTDOC**, Delaware **GYN**, Mississippi **I DO GYN**, and Washington **IMAIDOC, JOCKDOC, HEADDOC, BURNDOC**, and **DRCGOOD**, the last presumably an eye specialist.

Other medical plates are Arkansas' **KID-DOC** and **KIDDR, FAM DOC** (ID), **LABDOC** (WA), **LUNG DR** (TX), **MIND MD** (WI), the generic **MEDICO** (TX), **ROCNDOC** (WA), **SAWBONZ** (LA), **SAYAAH** (IA, IN, MI, MS), **SAYAHH** (IA, IN, MI, MS, TX), **SHRINK** (MI, MS, TX, WI), **SHRYNK** (WA), and **X RAY MD** (MI).

SURGEON (WA) and **SCALPEL** (ID) are quite clear, but what of **STITCHR** (WA)? Surgeon or seamstress? Is **FACEMD** (WA) a plastic surgeon or a cosmetologist? What about **TLCDOC** in Iowa? Does **SOLE DR** (MD) refer to feet or fish?

Three plates that require a moment's reflection are **12 IN DR** (12 inches = a foot) for a Virginia foot specialist, a Texas anesthesiologist's **AH-GAS, 2020 MD** for an Iowa eye doctor, and similarly **2020** (SC). Is **HELIDOC** (WA) a physican who must make housecalls in remote places? **LAZYMD** (WA) must specialize in golf, and **FISIKAL** must be a general practitioner or internist.

Finally, there are **XRAYDOC** (WA) and **ZIT DR**, a Virginia dermatologist. Physicans in training choose the likes of **DR TO B** (VA), **MD2B** (NC), **MD TO B** (MS), and **INTERN** (MI).

Veterinarians get in their licks with **CAT-DOC** (WA), **DAWGDOC** (ID), **DOGDOK** (WA), **FIX-PETS** (WA), **K9DOC** (CO), **PETDOC** (IA, ID, IN, MI), **PETCARE** (WA), and **PETDOK**, **PETDR**, **PETSVET**, **PETVET**, and **PETVETT**, all from the State of Washington, plus **VETDR** (IA) and **PURRFECT** (NY).

Not to be outdone, dentists have come up with plates like **CAVITE** (WA), **D KAY** (WA), **DR2TH** (MI, WA), **IDIGDK** (UT), **IMADDS** (IA), **KID DDS** (TX), **PAINLSS** (VA), and **OPNWDE**, **OPNWIDE**, **OPNWYDE**, and **OPNWYD**, all of Washington State. Also there are **TEETH** (DE, IL, KY, MI, WA), **TOOFDR** (ID, NJ), **TOOTHDR** (IA, ID, IN), **TUTHDOC** (WA), **TUTHDR** (WA), **2THDOC** (AL, SC, WI), **2THDR** (IA, ID, IN, LA, MS, ND, TX), and **2THFXR** (MI, OR, TX). **SMILEDR** (WA), **GRIN DR** (MS), and **BRACES** (MI) must be orthodontists, **JAW DOC** (VA) an oral surgeon, **GUM DR** (TX) a periodontist.

People in ancillary medical jobs have their own plates, as well. **BEDPAN** (WA) must surely be the heartfelt sentiment of a **NURSE** (IA, ID, MS, WA). **ONURSE** (IA) sounds a little tired of being summoned.

Dental hygienists are the probable owners of **CLNTETH** (WA), **FLOS-EM** (ID, TX), and **FLOSSM** (MI, TX). Optometrists probably account for **EYE** (DE), **EYECARE** (IA, ID, TX, WA), **EYEXAM** (WA), and **ISIGHT** (WA). **MIND MD** (WI) and **MINDOC** (ID) are probably psychiatrists, or perhaps psychologists. **HYPNTST** works in Washington, **MEDIC** in Indiana and Texas, **MIDWIFE** in Iowa, and **MIDWIF** in Alaska. Is **LUVDR** just someone from Washington who is bragging about his prowess, or the plate of a marriage counselor? Is **TALKDOC** (WA) a speech therapist? Also on the road are **PARAMED** (IA), **PHARMCY** and **PILROLR** (OR), **REXALL** (IA, MI, TX), and in Washington **RXMAN**, **RXPERT**, **RXPROF**, and **RX4U**.

Where medical people go — to hear them tell it, at least — can lawyers be far behind? **BARISTR** (WA), **ASST DA** (MS), **ESQ** (IA), **ESQUIRE** (WA), **LITIG8R** (IN), **PATENTS** (IN, WA: presumably a patent attorney), and **TAX-LAW** (ID, WA) are among the more innocent-sounding examples of lawyer tags. More ominous are **CME2SU** (OR), **I SU** (IN), **ISUEM** and **ISUYU** (WA), **SHYSTERR** (ID, IN, WA), **SHYSTR** (AK, MS, TX), **SUEM4U** (WA), and **2SUCME** (KS). Could it be that **WHPLASH** (WA) also belongs to a jocular attorney? Or **PLNTIFF** (IA)? Or **ACQUIT** (TX)? **I OBJECT** (IN)? **DFENDR** (IN)? **I APPEAL** (VA)?

Even judges occasionally turn playful and purchase their own personalized plates, as in **DJUDGE** (IA, MI, WA: Remember *Laugh-In*'s routine about "Here come de judge"?); **HIZONER** or **HIZONOR** (WA); **ALLRISE** (IN, WA); and **YRHONOR** (IA).

There is no accounting for what CPAs and other members of the accounting fraternity pick for their vanity plates. **ACCNT** (CO) and **A CPA** (CO, MI) are the plainer sort, but **BADCPA** (WA) makes you wonder. Also **I ADD4U** (ID) and **I CALQL8** (IN) are a credit, not a debit, to the profession.

CPASAM (AK), **CPACLU** (WA), **CPA 4U** (VA, TX), **IMACPA** (IA, LA), **IDOTAX** (OR, MS), and **IDOTAXS** (WA) are others. **MRTAX** (IA) possibly belongs to someone with the Internal Revenue Service, as must **REVENU** (CT) and **AUDIT** (IA). A few more in this category are **TAXCPA** (AK), **TAXHELP** (IN, WA), **TAXLADY** (WA), **TAXMAN** (AK, IA, ID, MI, MS, WA), **TAXPRO** (IA, MI, MS, WA), and **TAXTIPS** (WA).

In our institutions of learning, the occasional teacher manages to summon up the creativity normally demanded only of students to produce such plates as **ALGEBRA** (IN, SC), **ARTTCHR** (WA), and **ET TU**, a Virginia English teacher's plate. Others are **HISTORY** (IA), **HISTWY** (VA), **ITUTOR** (WA), **LENSGUY** (WA), **LUV2TCH** (IA), **MRCHIPS** (WA), **N LITEN** (MI), **PHD** (OR), and **PHDNERD** (OR).

BEOWULF (WA), **SONETT** (AK), **SYNTAX** (IA), and **VERSE** (IA) must surely be English teachers, and **SCIENCE** (WA) is probably a teacher. More direct, though less inventive, are **TCHUR** (VA), **TICHUR** (NC), **TEACHER** (IA, ID, IN), **TEACHR** (AK, IA, ID, IN, MI, MS, ND), and **TEACHU** (IA). **ITEACH** (AK, IN, KY) is also clear in meaning, but what about **I MOLD** (IA)? Could be a potter?

Those of us who work in the mass media have made our own small contributions to the poetry of the open road, as well. **ADMAN** (IA, IN, KY) meet **ADWOMAN** (WA). Others are **ADMAKER** (WA), **AIRWAVE** (IA, IN), **AIRTIME** (AK), **DISCJK** (VA), **EDITOR** (WA), **IDONEWS** (IA), **IEDIT** (WA), **IWROTE** (WA), **KAR2NST** (WA), **NEWSGUY** (ID), **ONLIVE** (IA), **PAGEONE** (WA), **PBLSHR** (WA), **PBLSHR** (VA), **PRESS** (AK, GA, KY, SC), **REUTERS** (WA), **REWRITE** (WA), **SCOOP** (IN), **THE NEWS** (IN), **VEEJAY** (IA, ID), and **WRITER** (IA, ID, IN, MI, MS, TX). **WEATHER** (WA) is probably a tv weatherperson or a meterologist, or both, as is **TV4CAST** (WA).

The most dreaded of callings, insurance, is responsible for the likes of **ADJUSTR** (WA), **CME4INS** (ID, WA), **INSURE** (AK, IN, KY, MI), **NYLIFE** (OR), **N SURE** (TX), and **RUINSRD** (VA).

Some apparently job-related plates are teasingly obscure. Is **ANVIL** (WA) a blacksmith? Is **DSTPAN** (WA) a housekeeper? Is **IBRIKIT** (VA) a brickmason, **I-UN-LOC** (TX) a locksmith, or **IWIR4U** (VA) an electrician? And what of **FARMBO** in Indiana? One imagines that somewhere in the enormous, rich fields of that state, a muscular, fatigue-clad Rambo-style farmer pounding the heck out of his chores.

Are Washington's **HDHNTR**, **HDNUNTR**, and **HEDHNTR** employment consultants? Is **KWK STP** (ND) a military drill instructor, as in "quick-step, march"? Is **ISIGN** (WA) the plate of someone who signs for the deaf?

ONTAP (DE) is probably a tavern owner, **PLAN4U** (IA) a financial planner, **SCRIBE** (WA) either a court steonographer, a secretary, a reporter, or a whimsical-minded writer. **UNYUN** (WA) is probably an onion grower.

BANANA is a Delaware banana importer, **CRAZED** an Oregon novelty wholesaler,

OFUDGE an Oregon candy shop owner, **SAWDST** and **SAWDUST** vehicles belonging to an Iowa construction company. **PNO2NR** (MI) is clear enough once you sound it out.

One doubts the literal application of **AGIGALO** (WA), **BOOKIE** (AK), **GUN4HRE** (WA), **HOOKER** (AK, KY), **MOBSTER** (IA), and **SHYLOCK** (WA). But who knows?

AA MUVR (TX)
ABC-AN-D (TX)
ABC DEE (TX)
ABC-DOC (TX)
ABC-VET (TX)
A BONES (TX)
ACHOO (TX)
A CHEF (TX)
A CLOWN (IA)
ACQUIT (KY)
ACTANT (TX)
ACTN UP (TX)
ACTRES (TX)
ACTS4U (TX)
ACURATE (IA)
AD-ART (TX)
ADDMUP (KY)
ADITUP (KY)
ADJUST (MS, TX)
AD LADY (IN, TX)
AD LIB (TX)
ADMIRAL (ID, IN)
ADMIRL (AK, TX)
ADS MD (IN)
ADVIZ4U (ID)
ADVRTZ (KY)
AERONOT (ID)
AEROSPC (WA)
A FT DR (TX)
AF-RET (NH)
AFUR4U (NH)
AGENT (NH)
AHMEE (NH)
AIRBNE (NH)
AIRBRN (MI)
AIRCRU (NH)
AIRMAN (KY, MI)
AIRTIME (ID)
AIRWIK (NH)
AKEEMAN (WA)
ALCHMST (WA)
ANALOG (DE)
ANCHOR (ID, MS)
ANG DOC (MI)
ANML DR (VA)
ANURSE (IA, MI, MS)
APILOT (ID)
APRAIS (VA)
APRAZR (ID)
APRSR R E (VA)
ARCATEK (VA)
ARCHTEC (VA)

ARCHTEK (VA)
ARCITEC (SC)
ARKTEK (MI, VA)
ARMY LT (MS)
ART BIZ (WA)
ATTNY (MI)
ATTRNY 1 (IN)
ATTY (IN)
ATTYMD (MI)
ATURNY (MI)
A YCHER (MS)
AVIATOR (IA, ID, IN)
AVIATR (IA)
AVIATUR (AK)
AV8ER (ID)
AV8OR (KY, MS)
AV8R (ID)
AV8TOR (ID, IN, MI)
AV8TR (ID)
BABY DR (MS)
BABY RN (MS)
BAC DOC (TX)
BAC-DR (TX)
BACKHO (IA)
BACK MAN (IN)
BAGBOY (KY)
BAGELS (AK, MI)
BAKDOC (ID, MI)
BAKER (MI)
BAKMAN (KY)
BARBEQ (IA)
BARBER (IA, ID, MI)
BAR BIZ (MS)
BARBQ (IA, IN)
BARMAN (KY)
BDYFXR (MI)
BEARDOC (ID)
BEDMAN (MI)
BEEPER (IN, MS)
BENEFITS (NC)
BG CROP (ND)
BIG MAC (MI)
BIKE-DR (OR)
BILDER (KY)
BILDOR (MI)
BILD4U (MI)
BIOTEC (MI)
BISTRO (MI)
BKEEPR (IN)
BKSMD (IN)
BLDG4U (IA)
BLK GLD (IN)
BLKSMTH (IN)
BLKTOP (IN)
BOATDOC (IN)
BONEFXR (CA)
BONE MD (ID)
BOOKEM (ID)
BOOKIE (ID)
BOOK'M (NC)
BOOKMAN (IA)
BOOKUM (KY)
BOOZE (KY)
BOSMAN (IA)
BRN2SHP (ID)
BRACES (MI)
BRCKLYR (CA)
BRCKMAN (CA)
BRDCSTR (CA)
BRDGWRK (CA)
BRDMKR (CA)
BREAD4U (CA)
BROKER (ID, IN, MI)
BUD REP (VA)
BUGABU (KY)
BUGMAN (KY, MI)

BUGMUG R (VA)
BUGOUT (KY)
BUILDER (ID, IN)
BUILDR (ID, KY, MI)
BULMKT (IA)
BURKNG (VA)
BUYSTOK (WA)
BYABOAT (WA)
BYA HOM (MS)
BYHOME (KY)
BYMYRUG (WA)
BYPAPER (WA)
BYPASS (IN)
BYSOAP (WA)
BYSTOK (MI)
BYTERM (KY)
CABLETV (IN)
CABNBOY (VA)
CADDCTR (IN)
CALGAL (ID, MI)
CALQL8 (IN)
CANDMAN (WA)
CAR DOC (IA, MS, WA)
CARGUY (MI)
CAR HOP (MS)
CARPET (IN)
CARPTPRO (NC)
CARTUNE (WA)
CARWASH (WA)
CASHFLO (ID)
CASKETS (IN)
CATDOC (KY)
CATVET (KY)
CEMENT (KY)
CEMIST (MI)
CENATOR (WA)
CEO (WA)
CEO 2BE (VA)
CHAP V (VA)
CIA SPY (VA)
CLEAN4U (WA)
CLERGY (AK, IA, MS)
CLOCKDR (ID)
CLOCKS (MI)
CLOWN (IA)
CME2BUY (KS)
CME4AD (ID)
CME4TRX (WA)
COACH (AK, ID, KY, MI, MS)
CO AGNT (MS)
COBBLER (ID)
CO COLA (MS)
COINOP (AK)
COLUMN (MI)
COMEDY (MI)
COMM LAW (VA)
CONDO (AK)
CONDOS (MI)
CONSLT (IA)
CONSUL (MI)
COOK (MI)
COPIER (VA)
COPYCAT (ID)
COPYFAX (IN)
COPYTYM (ID)
COP2BE (KY)
COWGIRL (IN)
COWHAN (MS)
CPA (KY, MS)
CPA2B (KY)
CRABBER (WA)
CRFTSMN (WA)
CTCLRK (MI)
CURATOR (WA)
DABOSS (AK, MS, VA)

DAIRYMN (ID)
DALAW MI)
DA MAN (MS)
DANCER (ID)
DATA PRO (IL)
DAYCARE (IA)
D-BOSS (KY)
DEALER (MI)
D BOSS (MS)
DBUGMAN (ID)
D COOK (MS)
DCOR8 (MI)
DEALS (ID)
DE BOSS (MS)
DEJAY (AK)
DEKUK (MI)
DENTAL (MI)
DENTST (TX)
DEPUTY (ID)
DERCHEF (WA)
DESELMD (CA)
DESIGNR (CA)
DEZINER (WA)
DEZYNER (ID)
DIGDRT (KY)
DIRTMAN (WA)
DISPLAY (WA)
DKAY (WA)
DMD MD (IN)
DOC (ID)
DOC DDS (IN)
DOCKTR (MI)
DOCENT (MI)
DOC VS (MI)
DOGTRNR (ID)
DOKWRKR (WA)
DOLMKR (VA)
DONUTS (ND)
DOORMAN (WA)
DR AUDIO (IN)
DR BONES (IN)
DR DENT (IN)
DR FOOT (ID, MI)
DR MUSIC (IN)
DR PIKY (VA)
DR XRAY (IN)
DRYDOC (KY)
DRYICE (WA)
DRYWAL (AK, KY, MI, MS)
DRYWALL (ID, IN)
DR2BE (MI)
DSIGNER (IA)
DSIGNR (ID, MI)
DZINER (ND)
DZYNER (ID, KY)
EARBIZ (IA)
EAT-DR (KY)
EDUKTR (KY)
EGGMAN (AK, IA, WA)
EL TEACH (VA)
EN DOC (TX)
ENGINER (WA)
ENTRPNR (IN)
EPIDMCS (CA)
EPIDMIC (CA)
EQTYMAN (CA)
EQTYMGT (CA)
EQUAKES (CA)
EQUITEE (CA)
ER DOC (IN, MS)
ET TWO (TX)
EXEC (MI, TX)
EX WAC (VA)
EXWAVE (VA)
EY DUDE (MS)
EYE BIZ (MI)

EYEDOC (KY)
EYE DOK (ID, TX)
EYE GUY (ID, MI, TX)
EYE MAN (TX)
EYE MD (MS, TX)
EYE VET (VA)
FARMER 1 (IL)
FARMIN (ID)
FAXMAN (WA)
FBIGUY (MI)
FENCE (DE)
FILMAKR (WA)
FILR UP (MS)
FINE RX (MS)
FIREMAN (IA, WA)
FIREMN (VA)
FISH DOC (ID)
FISHRUS (WA)
FIXIT (AK)
FIXMUP (AK)
FLIER (MI)
FLORIST (IA, IN)
FLOSS UM (VA)
FLY BOY (CT, MI)
FLYER (MI)
FOTOS (MI)
FONE DR (IN, MS)
FOTOG (TX)
FRY GUY (MS)
FRISUR (VA)
FST FOOD (ID)
FUZZ (AK, KY, MS)
GAS MAN (MS)
GDPR4U (VA)
GENERIC (WA)
GENERIK (WA)
GEN MGR (WI)
GESTALT (IN)
GI DOC (TX)
GI JANE (MS)
GLAZIER (IN)
GLF PRO (MS)
GMAN (KY, MI)
GOLFMD (KY)
GOLF PRO (IN)
GRASS (TX)
GROCER (IN, KY)
GUARD (IN)
GUIDE (AK)
GUM DR (TX)
GUN DOC (TX)
GUN DR (MS)
GUNMAN (MS, OR)
GUNSMTH (WA)
GUTTER (ID)
GYNO (CA)
GYNPHYS (CA)
GYNSURG (CA)
GYNTKLR (CA)
GYRO (CA)
GYROS (VA)
GYROTRK (CA)
HAIR (AK)
HAIR DO (KY, MS)
HAIRDOC (CA)
HAIRDR (IN)
HAIR DU (OH, MS)
HAIR HQ (IA)
HAIR4U (KY, MI)
HANGMAN (WA)
HARDHAT (IA)
HATLADY (WA)
HATMAN (WA)
HDWARE (VA)
HEAL (MI)
HEALER (ID)

HEARING (ID)
HEAT MAN (VA)
HITECH (IA)
HITS4U (KY)
HIYIELD (IN)
HOME PRO (IN)
HOMES 4U (IN)
HORS DOC (VA)
HOSSDOC (WA)
HOSSDR (WA)
HOTTUB (IA)
HOUSE4U (WA)
HUCKSTR (WA)
HUT ONE (MS)
HUT 1 (MS)
HUT 2 (MS)
HWRDJNS (WA)
HWYHERO (WA)
H2OBOY (IA)
IADJUST (WA)
IBUILD (IA, KY)
IBLD4U (ID)
IBUY4U (ID)
ICFEET (ID)
I CLEAN (MI)
ICLOWN (IA)
IDESIGN (IA)
IDLIVER (ID)
I DLIVR (KY)
I DLVR (KY)
IDEZIN (VA)
IDOC (IN, KY)
IDO GYN (MS)
I DO HAIR (IL, WA)
IDR (KY)
IEDUC8 (KY)
IEXPORT (WA)
IFENCEU (WA)
IFIXVWS (WA)
I FLOSS (IN)
I FLY 4 U (OH)
IHULA4U (WA)
IINSURE (IN)
IINSURU (IN)
ILFXIT (IA)
ILL SUE (MS)
IMOVE4U (WA)
IMOW (WA)
INK BIZ (TX)
INK MAN (TX)
INNKPR (IA)
INSURE (ID, TX)
INSUREU (IN)
INSURIT (IN)
INSURU (IN)
INVEST (KY, MI)
INVSTR (TX)
ILFXIT (IA)
ILLSU4U (IN)
ILOG4U (VA)
ILSTR8R (WA)
IMAREF (WA)
IMOE4U (VA)
I MOVE (IA)
INKEEPR (WA)
I OBJECT (ID)
I PAPER (IL)
I PAVE (ID)
IPLN4U (VA)
I PRINT (ID, MI)
I PLUMB (TX, WA)
IPLUM4U (WA)
IREBILD (WA)
I REPO (KY)
IROOF (WA)
IROPE (WA)

I SELLM (MS)
ISELSTF (WA)
I SEL4U (KY)
ISUEEM (IN)
I SURVEY (VA)
I TEACH (ID, MS)
I TOW (VA)
I TYPE (ID)
I VEND (MS)
I WELD (KY)
I WRITE (ID, IN, MI, MS, WA)
JAW DOC (ID)
JEEPMAN (CA)
JET-DR (KY)
JET M.D. (TX)
JEWLER (IA, MS)
JEWLUR (MS)
JOB 4 U (TX)
JOC DOC (TX)
JOCKDOC (WA)
JOCKY (MI)
JOINUP (AK)
JONLAW (AK)
JPROF (CA)
JRNLST (MI)
JUDGE (ID, IN, MI, MS)
JUKBOX (IA)
JUKEBX (IA)
JUSTICE (IN)
KEYMAN (IN)
KEY ONE (SC)
KEYS (IN, VA)
KIDCARE (WA)
KIDDR (MI, TX)
KILBUGS (WA)
KLNRUG (WA)
KNDRGTN (IN)
KOREA 4X (VA)
KRZY MD (TX)
KWK STP (ND)
K9 CLIP (TX)
K9 DOC (MS, TX)
K9 TUTR (KY)
LAB DR (KY)
LADIE RX (VA)
LADY DR (TX)
LAND 1 (VA)
LANFIL (IA)
LANDMAN (IN, WA)
LANDPRO (ID)
LAW (ID, IN, KY)
LAWBKS (IN)
LAWCPA (ID)
LAW DR (MI)
LAWMAN (MI, MS)
LAWNDR (WA)
LAWNS (IN)
LAWNS4U (WA)
LAW PRO (TX)
LAWSERV (IN)
LAWYER (ID, KY, MI, MS, TX)
LAWYR (TX)
LAWYR 2B (VA)
LAWYR4U (ID)
LAW Z (TX)
LE BOSS (MS, TX)
LE CHEF (MS)
LECOP (IA)
LEVRAGE (WA)
LIBRARY (WA)
LITG8R (KY)
LITTG8 (KY)
LMBRBIZ (WA)
LMBRGUY (WA)

LNDSCPR (VA)
LOANS (IN)
LOANS4U (WA)
LOC DOC (IN, TX)
LOC DR (VA)
LOCK DOC (IN)
LOGGER (AK, KY, MS)
LOGIN (MS)
LOGMAN (MS)
LOGO (WA)
LOVE MD (TX)
LT. COL. (TX)
LUMBER (KY)
LUVTRKN (WA)
LUV2LOG (WA)
LUV2SHO (WA)
LUV2TYPE (WA)
MA BELL (IL)
MAC TOOLS (NC)
MADCOOK (WA)
MAESTRO (IN)
MAILMAN (IN, WA)
MAIL RM (VA)
MAIL4U (MS, WA)
MANAGR (KY)
MBALMR (IN)
MD LAW (MI)
MEATCTR (IN)
MEDIATE (IN)
MEDOC (TX)
MEDTEC (IN)
MEISTRO (CA)
MEKANIC (CA)
MEKANIK (CA)
MEKANIX (CA)
MIDWIFRY (ID)
MILKMAN (IA, ID, WA)
MILKMN (WA)
MINER (AK)
MIXERS (VA)
MKANIK (AK)
MOMDOC (ID)
MONY MKT (VA)
MOO DOC (ID)
MOONLTR (WA)
MOVER (KY, TX)
MOW 1 (VA)
M-PRINT (TX)
MRBEEF (IA)
MRBONZ (KY)
MR COPY (IN)
MREXEC (AK, MS)
MRFAX (WA)
MRHEAT (IA)
MR LUBE (MI)
MRNEON (WA)
MROZONE (WA)
MRPOOL (IA)
MRPORK (IA)
MR ROOF (MI)
MR TUX (WA)
MR UMP (KY)
MR UPS (IL)
MR WOOL (VA)
MR XRAY (MI)
MS BEEF (IA)
MS BOSS (OR)
MS BROKR (ID)
MS CPA (IN)
MS DONUT (IN)
MS EXEC (WA)
MS FOTO (TX)
MS PHD (WA)
MS PRO (AK)
MUSIC4U (VA)
MUZAK (AK, TX)

MXERS (VA)
MYSTRO (AK)
NAVYCB (KY)
NEON (AK)
NEONART (WA)
NEURO 1 (NC)
NEWS (IN, MI)
NEWSGUY (ID)
NFL REF (MI)
NGNEER (MI)
NL UMP (KY)
NO-BUG (KY)
NOT GLTY (IN)
NO WORK (TX)
NO.1 DJ (TX)
NO.1 DOC (OH, TX)
NRV DOC (MS)
N SPECT (CT)
NSURES (KY)
NTRPRZ (IA)
NVESTR (KY)
N2HAIR (WA)
OFFSET (WA)
OILMAN (KY, MI)
OLECARS (VA)
OPNWYD (MI, WA)
ORGNIST (WA)
PAPARER (WA)
PARSON (CA, IA)
PARTS4U (CA)
PASTA (CT, DE)
PASTOR (AK, TX)
PAVER (ID, IN, WA)
PAVING (GA)
PAWNIT (MI)
PBBDOC (ID)
PEDDLAR (WA)
PEDDLER (WA)
PER4MER (WA)
PESTPRO (ID)
PETDOC (KY)
PET DR (IN)
PETFOOD (WA)
PETSHOP (WA)
PETSITR (WA)
PETSRUS (VA)
PETSVET (WA)
PETS4U (VA)
PETVET (KY)
PGA PRO (OR)
PHLYBOY (WA)
PHOTOG (AK)
PHOTOS (TX)
PHUT-DR (TX)
PIANIST (IN, WA)
PIG BOY (ID)
PIG MAN (ID)
PILOT (ID, TX)
PIPE DR (ID)
PIZAHUT (WA)
PIZZA (KY)
PLAN4U (ID)
PLMBER (IA)
PLOWBOY (IA)
PLUMBER (IA, ID, IN)
PLUMBOB (ID, IN)
PLUMBR (IA)
PLUMER (MI)
PLUMMR (AK)
PODMED (IN)
POSE 4ME (VA, IN)
PRE MD (TX)
PRE-MED (TX)
PRINTER (ID, IN)
PRINTR (KY)
PROGMR (VA)

PROGOLF (ID)
PROPMAN (WA)
PRSPCTR (WA)
PURSER (WA)
PVTEYE (IA, MI, VA, WA)
Q-AND-A (TX)
RADIO (ID, MI)
RAIDU (VA)
RANCHER (WA)
RANCHR (ID, TX)
RDTAPE (TX)
REALTOR (IA, ID, IN)
REALTR (ID, IN, KY)
REALTY (ID)
REF4EE (MS)
RENTALS (ID, IN)
REPAIRS (ID)
RENT DU (TX)
RETIRED (IA, ID)
RETN-A (KY)
RETNAVY (ID)
REVERN (IA)
REV MD (IN)
REV RUN (MS)
RKTECT (MI)
RLEST8 (MI)
RMB MD (MI)
ROC DOC (MS)
ROCSTAR (CA)
ROOFER (IN, MI, TX)
ROOFING (ID, TX)
ROOFS (KY)
RSHACK (MS)
RTIST (ID, MS)
RUGDR (ID)
RUGMAN (DE, KY)
RX (MS, TX)
RX-AL (KY)
RX DOC (TX)
RX DUDE (TX)
RX GOLF (MI)
RX HEVN (VA)
RX I AM (MS)
RX IST (MS)
RXLNT (MS)
RXMAN (ID)
RXPERT (MS, TX)
RXTACY (MS)
RX VETT (MS)
RX4RNR (MS)
RX 4 YOU (TX)
RX7HVN (ID)
SAILOR (ID)
SAILR (AK)
SALOON (TX)
SARGE (AK, KY)
SARGENT (ID)
SARGNT (TX)
SAWLOG (MS)
SAWMIL (AK, MS)
SAY AH (KY, TX)
S-BROKER (VA)
SCH MRM (TX)
SCHOLAR (ID)
SCOOPS (IN)
SCOOPUM (CA)
SCRAP (TX)
SCRIBE (WA)
SEABEE (TX)
SEALS (IN)
SELL4U (KY)
SENATOR (IA)
SENSEI (AK, MS, WA)
SGTMAJ (MI)
SGTMAJR (WA)
SGTSGT (MI)

SHAMAN (AK)
SHAMUS (KY)
SHERIF (IN, KY)
SHERIFF (ID, IN)
SHOFER (IN, MI, WA)
SHOFIR (ID)
SHOFEUR (WA)
SHOFUR (IA, ID)
SHOWBIS (CA)
SHOWMAN (MI, WA)
SHRIFF (TX)
SHRLCK (ID)
SHTMTL (MI)
SHUBIZ (KY)
SHU FIXR (VA)
SHYSTR (IN)
SIGNBZ (KY)
SIGNKNG (WA)
SKIBIZ (MI)
SKI COP (NC)
SKI*DOC (MI, TX)
SKIFUZ (ID)
SKI LFT (CT)
SKI PRO (IA)
SKYCAP (MI)
SKYCOP (IL)
SKYDOC (ID)
SLEUTH (AK, MS)
SMOKEY (WA)
SMPERFI (WA)
SMPRFI (WA)
SMPRHRFI (WA)
SMYLMKR (ID)
SNEEZE (KY, TX)
SNOMAN (IA)
SOFTH2O (ID)
SOUL DR (ID)
SPINALS (IN)
SPUD (ID)
SPUDFMR (ID)
SPUDMAN (ID)
SPUDS (ID)
SPUD4U (ID)
SPY (DE)
STATZ (WA)
STOCK (AK)
STOCKS (AK)
STRINGR (ID)
STUCCO (ID)
STYLIN (TX)
STYLIN U (VA)
STYLIST (IA, ID, IN)
STYL IT (TX)
STYLST (IA, ID, KY, TX)
STYLYN (TX)
SUBS (CT)
SUBSRUS (WA)
SUE EM (ID, TX)
SWEEPER (IL)
SWMTCHR (WA)
TACOMAN (WA)
TALK DR (TX)
TAPKEG (KY)
TATOOU (WA)
TATTOO (MI)
TAXES (ID, KY)
TAXGUY (ID)
TAXXMAN (ID)
TBILL (IA)
TCHR (MI)
TEACH (KY)
TEETH (KY)
TEEVEE (MI)
TEND BAR (CA, VA)
TENSHUN (CA)
THE BOS (MS)

THE BOSS (ID)
THE COOK (ID)
THE FED (MS)
THE FUZ (MS)
THELAW (IA, KY, MS)
THEMAN (AK, MS)
THE MOB (TX)
THE REV (MS, SC)
THE PRO (ID)
THE UMP (IA, MS, WA)
TH-FUZ (TX)
TH FUZZ (MS)
TIC DOC (MI)
TIMBER (AK)
TMBRRR (AK)
T-MITE (KY)
TOC DOC (TX)
TOE DOC (TX)
TOE DOK (TX)
TOP COP (MS, TX)
TORTS (KY)
TOT DOC (MI)
TOTH DR (TX)
TOWBIZ (KY, MI)
TOW MAN (MS)
TOYBIZ (IA)
TOY MAN (MS)
TOY MKR (IN)
TOYSRME (IA)
TOYSRUS (IA, IN)
TOYS4U (IA)
TRADER (NC)
TRAPPER (IA)
TRAPPR (IA)
TRAVEL (KY, MI)
TRAWLER (WA)
TRAWLR (WA)
TREDOC (ID)
TREE DR (ID, MS, WA)
TRETOPR (WA)
TRIALS (ID)
TRKDRVR (WA)
TROOPR (IA, MS)
TRUCKN (ID)
TRUSTEE (IN)
TRUCKER (ID)
TSHIRTS (ID)
TURISM (ID)
TUX (IA)
TUXEDO (AK, IA)
TUXMAN (KY)
TUXRUS (IN)
TVL AGT (MS)
TV FIXR (VA)
TV GNUS (NC)
TV MAN (AK, MI, MS, WI)
TV NEWS (MI)
TV NOOZ (MI)
TV PROD (MS)
TV SPOT (MS)
TXDRMY (ID)
TX. LWYR (TX)
TYPIST (WA)
TYPSET (IA)
UHAUL (IN)
UMDOC (MI)
UMPREF (MI)
UNDRTKR (ID, IN, WA)
UPS MAN (IN, MI)
UROL (ID)
UROLOG (TX)
UR OUT (KY)
USAIR (TX)
USA-RET (TX)
US HIST (MS)
USMAIL (IA, IL)

USMALE (IA)
USNAVY (KY)
USNRET (KY)
VAC DOC (IN)
VAN DOC (MI)
VENDEUR (IN)
VERDICT (IN)
VETFUN (IA)
VICAR (AK, IA)
VOCALS (ID)
WAITER (MI)
WALMART (IA)
WALL DOC (IN)
WALL ST (MI, VA)
WALPAPR (WA)
WASFUZ (WA)
WATER DR (IN)
WE COPY (ND)
WE DRAW (TX)
WE FARM (IL, IN)
WE FIX (ID)
WE FOTO (ID)
WE HAUL (IN)
WELDER (AK, IN, WA)
WELDIT (IA)
W*MELON (TX)
WE MOW (ID, KY, VA)
WE PAVE (WA)
WE ROOF (ID)
WE TOW (MI)
WE TYPE (IL)
WHP LSH (MS)
WIPLASH (ID)
WIPLSH (MI, TX)
WTRBED (WA)
WTRBEDS (IN)
WTRBOY (VA)
WUZFUZ (IA)
XAMINR (CO)
XLOGGER (WA)
XMAYOR (WA)
XMODEL (WA)
X PAWSUR (VA)
XPLORER (WA)
XRAYDR (KY)
XSEABEE (WA)
XSHERIF (IN)
XTRMN8R (WA)
YARDPRO (WA)
YERDOC (ID)
YEROUT (KY)
ZAMBONI (WA)
ZIP IT (VA)
ZOO DOC (TX)
Z*STORK (TX)
ZTVMAN (MI)
ZZZ DOC (MS)
1COACH (IA)
1CPA (IN)
1GMAN (IA)
1JUDGE (KY)
1 MAD MD (ID)
1 MDGAL (VA)
1NURSE (IA)
1 PASTOR (VA)
1RX (KY)
1*STORK (TX)
1ST SGT (MS)
10SPRO (IA, MI, MS)
10SUMP (ID, MI)
2BY CME (MS)
2 CURE (VA)
2THDK (IN, KY)
2THDOC (KY)
2TH DOK (CA)
2TH-DR (KY)

2THFXR (KY, MI, OR, TX)
2THMAN (ID)
2THVET (ID)
4CAST (IN)
20-20 (KY)

CHAPTER 4

I Am What I Am

BOY1DR,
and other modest self-revelations.

ABIT-YSR (a bit wiser), claims the plate of a Pennsylvanian who, like a great many other U.S. motorists, uses her license tag to make a public statement about her own condition, status, age, mood, or appearance.

Some of these plates refer to a person's physical looks: **A BLONDE** (WA), **ADONIS** (MS, OR, WA), **A HUNK** (MS), **BALDY** (IA), **BIGOX** (AK), **BICEPS** (AK), **DIMPLS** (IA, MI, MS), **FIT** (IA, TX), **FUZFACE** (WA), **GD BUNS** (ND), **HAIRY** (AK), **HVYWGT** (IA), **MUSCLS** (AK), **NSHAPE** (WA), **IM7FT** (IA), **OVR 6FT** (MS), **6FT GAL** (AK), **5 FOOT 2** (IN), even **7 FOOT 2** (AK).

Many a plate reveals something about weight, from **CHUBBY** (MS), **FATTBOY** (NC), or **FATNFIT** (WA) to **FATNOMO** (WA), **LOST WT** (IA), **SKINNY** (MI, MS, WA), **SLIM** (AK, IA), **SLIMER** (IA), and **THINMAN** (WA).

Other plates report the car owner's age, as in the optimistic **EVER 39** (TX, VA) and **39 4EVR** (WI), the somewhat more accurate **I40ISH** (VA), the much more exact **IAM 60** (IA, MS), and the plaintive **O 2B 21** (AZ, OR).

General admissions of the passing years are **OLD** (DE), **OLDBOY** (IA. Question: Has he a network?), **OLD MAN** (IA, ID, MI), **OLLADY** (IA), and **OLWOMN** (AK). **MY 50TH** (ND) proclaims a major birthday. Let's hope it's on a red Porsche.

One wonders if **SEXY 60** (WA) refers to the owner or to the car. Combining age and looks is **1FAT 40** (VA). An Iowa driver is **30ISH**; another in that state says he or she is **27 AGIN**. An Alabaman is **30 SUMPN**, drivers in both Alaska and Mississippi are **40 PLUS**, another Mississippian tells the world that **40 IS OK**, and a Washington state resident is **PUSHN50**. An aging Tar Heel complains, **I HATE 51** (NC).

A few drivers use their plate to proclaim their race or national origin, sometimes even using less than flattering terms. **AGREEK**

(WA), **BLK GAL** (MS), **CAJUN** (IA), **D ARAB** (IA), **ESKIMO** (AK), **EL DAGO** (MS), **IMA WASP** (WA), **ITALIANO** (NC), **MRS WOP** (WA), **TOPWOP** (WA), **4 TOP WOP** (CA), and **SIOUX** (AK) are examples. Just this sort of plate has set Italian-Americans against one another in San Francisco, where Dominic Troncale's plate proclaims that he is **A DAGO 2**. In the fall of 1990, the Sons of Italy Grand Lodge of California, based in San Francisco, petitioned the California DMV to recall all plates bearing the words "dago" or "wop." Mr. Troncale maintains that he has a right to call himself anything he wishes and has had to defend his plate in an administrative hearing.

Plates such as **ADMSLDY** (WA — admiral's lady), **BACHELR** (WA), **CINGLE** (WA), **DIVORCE** (LA, WA), **FTLOOSE** (WA), **FREEMAN** (WA), **IB SNGL** (WA), **IM FREE** (AK, ID, MS), **IMTAKEN** (ID, TX, WA), **IM TOOK** (MS), **JST MARYD** (NC), **MARYED** (AK), **NOWIFE** (ID, MS, WA), **ONMYOWN** (WA), **SENGUL** (VA), **SPINSTR** (IA), **UNWED** (VA, WA), **WIDOW** (IA, WA), and **X HUBBY** (MS) declare their owner's marital status.

Other plates using "Ex" or "X" tell us about their owners' former condition, as in

EX EXEC (WA), **EXPOW** (IA), **EXWINO** (WA), **XDRUNK** (ID, WA), **X MAYOR** (IA), or **X SLAVE** (MS). A disgruntled car owner in Washington has **XGMFAN**. One wonders if **X MAN** and **X MEN** in Mississippi have had sex-change operations, or if there is a simpler explanation.

AGRUMP (IA), **AMUSED** (IA, ID, TX), **CHIRPY** (DE), **DROLL** (IA), **ENVIOUS** (WA), **FEISTY** (IA, MI), **FRAZZLD** (WA), **FRISKY** (IA, MS), **HAPPY** (AK, MI, TX), **IMBLUE** (IA, IN), **LKYLDY** (IA, MS), **MELLOW** (AK, IA, MS, TX), **NERVUS** (IA, TX), and **ON EDGE** (MS) tell us something about their owners' state of mind. So do **PERPLXD** (WA), **REFINED** (WA), **RELAXD** (MS), **RESTLES** (IA), **SASSY** (MS), **SAUCY** (AK), **SHAKEN** (IA), **SNTAMNTL** (NC), **XCITED** (CO, MS), and **XENTRK** (WA).

ANGST (WA) would make a perfect plate for Woody Allen, **BOY1DR** (OR) for Vice President Dan Quayle, **HI ROLR** (MS) for Telly Savalas, **HOLYRNU** (WA) for any tv evangelist — take your pick. **ASNDANT** (WA) sounds like the plate of a hard-charging young businessperson climbing the corporate ladder, as do **HEDNUP** (AK), **MOVNUP** (AK, IA, IN, MI), and **ONMYWAY** (IA).

GODESS (OR), **GENTRY** (WA), **HI IQ** (CT), **CLOUD 9** (AK), **HICLASS** (WA), **IM BOSS**

(IA), **IN LOVE** (IA, MI, MS), **IN STYL** (AK), **INTHPNK** (WA), **LUCKYME** (IA), **MRBIG** (DE, IA), **NHEAVN** (WA), **NRAR4M** (PA: in rare form), and **RIDNHI** (AK) sound like the plates of people who are happy with their lot in life.

Less so are **DAZED** (MI, NJ), **FEDUP** (IA), **HYNDRY** (WA), **H8 2BBLU** (VA), **I DNTKNW** (WA), **ISOLNLY** (WA), **JETLAG** (IA, MI), **LUMBAGO** (WA), **MISLED** (AK, MI, WA), **NUTNNU** (IA), **NVRHOME** (WA), **RIPTOFF** (IA), **SADSACK** (WA), **STARVIN** (WA), **TIRED** (IA), **UNDRDG** (AK), **UPNDAIR** (WA), **UPNDOWN** (WA), **XLOVER** (IA), and **2BUSY** (AK).

Residents of cold climates have come up with **BRRRRR** (AK), **CHILLY** (WA), **FREEZIN** (AK), **ICECOLD** (WA), **IMCOLD** (AK), **ICFEET** (WA), **KKKOLD** (AK), **2COLD** (AK), and **2 KOLD** (AK).

Others proclaim their "cool" in a different sense of the word, as in **BNCOOL** (IA, MS), **ADUDE** (IA, MI), **IAMCOOL** (WA), **IMCOOL** (IA), **IM2COOL** (IA), **LECOOL** (IA), **MRCOOL** (IA: on the car of a Mr. Kuehl), **MRKOOL** (IA), and **WEBCOOL** (WA). Along the same line are **BNBAD** (AK), **BNWILD** (AK), **CHOTZPA** (WA), **IMBAD** (AK, IA), **IRBAD** (AK), **LAIDBAC** (LA), **LAID BK** (MS), **LAYD BK** (MS), **MR MOJO** (IA),

WEBAAD (WA), **WEBEBAD** (WA), **WLDBOY** (IA), and **WLDWMN** (IA, ID).

Perhaps **DEJAVU** (CT, MI) is the car owner's statement about having owned the same make of car once before. **FSHWFE** (WA) must either belong to the spouse of a commercial fisherman or to a weekend ''fishing widow.'' **GNTLMAN** (WA) and **GRANDAM** (IA) bear the stamp of almost old-fashioned elegance. **GUDOBOY** (WA) sounds more Southern than Northwestern.

FEMNIST (WA) and **HUMANST** (WA) are serious-minded proclamations, whereas **HOHUM** (AK) is completely bored with it all, as is **ENNUI** (WA). **IMATR2** (CT) and **DFIANT** (IA) sound rather defensive, as in a sense does **NUMONY** (IA).

Washington State is home to both **MRWRITE** (possibly an author) and **MRWRONG**, Virginia home to **MS RITE**. Does the North Carolina tag **MR NML** stand for Mr. Normal?

Some drivers say they are **DBONAIR** (WA), **SUAVE** (AK, MI, TX), **TWEEDY** (AK), **WEALTHY** (WA), a **PREYUPY** (WA) or a fullblown **YUPPIE** (AK, IA, MS). A Washington plate proclaims its driver is **NOYUPPY**; one wonders if the car is a BMW. Another Washingtonian is **NUWAVE**, still another an **OLHIPPI**. Oregon has **PUNK**, Virginia **PUNKE**. Another Virginian boasts of his or her **BARFEET**, an Iowan of **BARFEFT**.

Mississippians include **GAY** and **GAY 1**, and who is **PHAQUE**?

Whatever we choose to suggest or reveal about ourselves, you've got to admit we certainly are **CR8IF** (OR).

ACTNUP (MI)
AFRO (AK)
AGYPSY (WA)
A JOKER (IA)
AKMTMN (AK)
AKQTPI (AK)
ALBINO (MI)
ALLLEGS (WA)
ALONE (MI)
AMAZON (MI, MS)
AMOROUS (ID)
ANXPERT (ID)
ARASH 1 (VA)
A ROMEO (MS)
AARTSY (MI)
ARUFLYF (WA)
ASLEEP (IA)
AWOMAN (IA)
A YANK (MS)
A YANKE (MS)
BACHLER (WA)
BACHLOR (WA)
BACHLR (ID, MS, TX)
BACHLUR (WA)
BADBOY (MI)
BADLUK (AK)
BADLUV (AK)
BAK-OU (KY)
BAK4MO (MI)
BALDIE (IA)
BAREFT (ID)
BASHFUL (ID)
BEEFY (MI)
BENHAD (ID)
BENME (ID)
BETRNU (KY)
BGFISH (AK)
BGMAMA (IA)
BHAVIN (KY)
BIGBUT (KY)
BIGBUX (AK)
BIGGUY (AK, ID, MI)
BIGMAN (KY)
BGFELLA (WA)
BLOND (AK, MI)
BLONDE (KY)
BLUSTR (AK)
BNGOOD (AK, IA, MS)
BNLAZY (IA, MS)
BORED (MI, VA)
BOS LDY (ID, MS)
BOS MAN (MS)

BOSS (MI)
BOSSY (KY)
BOWTIED (WA)
BRDLADY (IN)
BRDWNER (CA)
BREDWNR (CA)
BRNEYES (IN)
BRN2WN (ID)
BULLISH (IN)
BYMYSLF (WA)
BZLADY (AK, ID)
BZYLDY (IN)
CANDO (AK)
CASUAL (AK)
CHI GUY (MS)
CITYFOX (WA)
CITYGRL (ID)
CLDNINE (ID)
CLOUT (DE)
CLSYLDY (ID)
CNTRFOLD (WA)
COMMUTR (WA)
COED (DE)
COPING (MI)
COQUET (KY)
COWBOY (ID)
COWGAL (ID)
COWGIRL (ID)
COWPOK (ID)
COWPOKE (ID)
CRUCUT (MI)
CUDDLY (MS)
CUTUP (MI)
CURIUS (VA)
CUTN UP (MS)
CUZN IT (MS)
DAINTEE (CA)
DAINTIE (CA)
DAINTY (CA)
DAINTY 1 (CA)
DAJAVOO (CA)
DAJAVU (CA)
DAYZED (VA)
DBLOND (AK)
DEAF (MS)
DECENT (MS)
DESRVED (CA)
DIMPLES (ID)
DOIN OK (TX)
DON JUAN (IN)
DREAMY (MS)
DUBIOUS (IN)
DUDE (WY)
DVORCD (KY, MI)
DVORCED (ID)
ECLCTIC (WA)
ECLECTC (WA)
ECSTAZ (IN, MI)
ELATD (IL)
ELATED (ID)
ENVIED (MI, MS, WA)
EQLUVR (CA)
ERLEBRD (WA)
EVEREDY (WA)
EVER 18 (TX)
EVILWMN (WA)
EXBUM (WA)
EXCOP (TX)
EX-JET (TX)
EX-NUN (TX)
EX-NYKR (TX)
EX POW (IA)
EX-WIFE (TX)
EXWINO (WA)
EZGOIN (KY, MI)
EZLIFE (AK, IA, MI)

EZLIVN (AK, MI)
EZLUST (AK)
EZMONY (AK)
EZ2LUV (AK)
FARMBOY (WA)
FASTLNE (WA)
FATCAT (AK, IA, KY, MI, MS, TX)
FATCATS VA)
FATCITY (WA)
FAT JAW (TX)
FAT KAT (MS)
FAT LESS (IA)
FAT LIP (TX)
FATTBOY (NC)
FICKLE (IA)
FIGARO (WA)
FIGHTER (WA)
FIT FAT (TX)
FIT TXN (TX)
FIXIN 2 (MS)
FLIRT (AK, ID, TX)
FLIRTN (MS)
FLYNHI (ND)
FOXEY (IL)
FOXY 40 (TX)
FRAGLE (VA)
FREE (MS)
FREED (VA)
FREEMAN (WA)
FREE2GO (WA)
FRNDLEE (WA)
FSHWYF (AK)
FTLOOSE (IN)
FUNNY (NJ)
FUN 42 (AK)
FXY LDY (AK, CT)
FXYMOM (IA)
GDKARMA (WA)
GDOLBOY (WA)
GEEZER (IN, MI)
GENIUS (MS, TX)
GENTLMN (KY, WA)
GETNBY (AK, ID, MI, MS)
GETN IT (MS)
GITINFIT (VA)
GITNBY (ID)
GLAM-R (KY)
GLDBBOY (WA)
GLDNGRL (WA)
GLUM (ID)
GOINDEF (ID)
GO-N-DEF (TX)
GONZO (IN, MS)
GOODGUY (ID)
GOTABME (LA)
GOTAWAY (SC)
GOURMET (WA)
GRAY OK (TX)
GRINGO (ID)
GRTFUL (MS)
GRUMPY (KY)
GR8FUL (AK, MS)
GR8FUN (AK)
GR8LDY (KY)
GUDCOOK (WA)
GUNSHY (WA)
GURU (KY)
GUTSIE (WA)
GUTSY (IA)
GUYTNO (MI)
GYPCBUM (CA)
GYPCE (CA)
GYPCEE (CA)
GYPCY (CA)
GYPSE (CA)

GYPSEA (CA)
GYPSEE (AK)
GYPSEY (CA)
GYPSIE (CA)
GYPSY (CA)
GYPZI (CA)
GYPZIE (CA)
GYPZLDY (CA)
GYPZY (CA)
HAF2LAF (WA)
HAIRY (AK)
HANDFUL (WA)
HANSUM (IA)
HAPPI (KY)
HAPPY (AK, MI, TX)
HAPPY 1 (TX)
HARDCOR (WA)
HARLOT (KY)
HARTHRB (WA)
HAVNFUN (ID, IN)
HDN OUT (MS)
HEALTHY (IN)
HEDNIST (WA)
HEPCAT (MI)
HERMIT (AK, MI)
HERO (AK, WY)
HHOBO (IA)
HIANUF (WA)
HICLAS (WA)
HIGH (MS)
HILBLY (IA)
HIP (AK)
HIPPI (IN)
HIPPIE (ID, KY, MI)
HIROLN (MI)
HLFBRD (MS)
HLFPNT (VA)
HMBOY (AK)
HOGWILD (IN)
HOMBOY (IN, MI)
HOMEBOY (IN)
HOMESCK (VA)
HOM4GD (KY)
HONEST (AK, MI, TX)
HOSTAGE (NC)
HOTBOD (IA)
HOTEMPR (WA)
HOTSHOT (IA)
HOTZ4ME (WA)
HOT4U (MS, WA)
HOT4 YOU (WA)
HPY LDY (TX)
HRDKOR (KY)
HRDROC (MI)
HRD2PLS (WA)
HARD2PLZ (WA)
HRD24GT (WA)
HRTBRKR (ID)
HUGABLE (ID, WA)
HUGBLE (KY)
HUMBLE (AK)
HUNGRY (AK)
HUNK (MS)
HVNFUN (WA)
HVNPHUN (WA)
HURTIN (KY)
HYPNTZD (WA)
H82BL8 (NC)
IADRWMN (WA)
IALADY (IA)
IAMAQT (DE)
IAMARTC (PA)
I AM DRY (TX)
IAMBLU (VA)
IAMBOSS (WA)
I-AM-EZ (TX)

IAMLATE (WA)
IAMNO1 (MI)
IAM OK (MS)
IAMRICH (WA)
IAM 21 (MS)
IAM40 (IA, MS)
IBEBAD (KY)
IBFAST (MI)
IBHAPPY (ID)
IBLOST (AK)
IBLUVD (ID)
I BN GOOD (VA)
I BOGGIE (VA)
IB SNEZN (WA)
IB FORTY (VA)
ICANCU2 (WA)
ICARE (AK)
ICARE2 (AK)
ICUCME (WA)
ICUTOO (WA)
IDNTKNW (WA)
IDOMN8 (KY)
IDZERVIT (NY)
I GET BY (MI, OH)
IGOTGAS (WA)
IH8RAIN (WA)
IH8SNO (MI)
IH82BL8 (WA)
II BLUE (AK)
I KNOW (IN)
ILANDR (AK)
I LUV ME (IN)
IMAPEPR (WA)
IMAPHD (WA)
IMATWIN (WA)
IM A 10 (MS, OH, OR)
IMBACK (DE, IA)
IM BHAVN (VA)
IM BEST (IA)
IM BIG (IA)
IM BROK (ID)
IM BROKE (ID, IN)
IM BUSY (MI)
IM CUTE (CT)
IM DRY (KY)
IMEZ (WA)
IM FINE (AK, LA)
IM GAME (IA)
IM GOLDN (WA)
IM GOOD (AK, IA, ND)
IM HAPPY (IN)
IM HIP (IN)
IM HIPP (IN)
IM HOT (AK, IA)
IM HSTRY (WA)
IM LEADN (VA)
IMLOST (KY)
IMLUVD (IA, KY)
IMNHEVN (WA)
IM NLOVE (VA)
IMNLUV (AK, IA, KY, TX)
IMNOT4U (IA)
IMNXTC (KY, MI)
IMOKUOK (WA)
IMOKUR2 (WA)
IMON2U (IA)
IM PHUN (MS)
IM RICH (ID, MS, TX, WA)
IM SINGL (TX, WA)
IMSOBER (WA)
IMSPCL (MI)
IM SURE (IA)
IM THE 1 (OH)
IM UNEQ (MS)
IM WILD (IA, KY)
IMZ14U (AK)

IM2POOR (ID)
IM4FUN (IA)
IM4PLAY (IA)
IM4TUN8 (WA)
INANOUT (WA)
INARUSH (WA)
INDEBT (AK, KY)
INEEDU (WA)
INHOC (ID)
INHOCK (AK)
INLIMBO (WA)
IN LUV (MS)
INOCNT (IA, ID)
INOSINT (WA)
INOSNT (WA)
IRNMAN (WA)
INTENSE (IA)
INTREPD (WA)
INTUNE (IA)
I NO 1 (MS)
IOKUOK (DE, MS)
IOUZIP (MI)
I POLKA (AK)
I ROCK (AK)
I ROLL (AK)
IRONMAN (ID, WA)
IRTIRED (WA)
IRUN (AK)
ISAYNO (MS)
I-WORK (KY)
JEALOUS (IN)
JINXED (ID)
JOECOOL (AK)
JOCOOL (VA)
JO KOOL (IN)
JSKDS (AK)
JSTTZN (KY)
JUSAKID (ID)
KIDFREE (WA)
KINKEE (WA)
KINKIE (WA)
KINKY (TX, WA)
LA-D-BLU (TX)
LASTLAF (WA)
LAYDEE (AK, TX, WA)
LAYINLO (WA)
LAYNBAC (VA)
LAYNLO (AK)
LAYNLOW (WA)
LAYZME (ID)
LA-Z-BOY (IN, TX)
LDYFAIR (WA)
LDYNRD (AK)
LEADER (IN)
LEAN (WY)
LEFTEE (MS, WA)
LEFTI (A)
LEFTY (TX, WA)
LILGUY (AK)
LILKID (AK)
LILONE (AK)
LITLFT (AK)
LITLGUY (WA)
LIVNLG (MI)
LKYWUN (IA)
LNDLBBR (WA)
LNGHAIR (IN)
LNGLEGS (WA)
LONWOLF (WA)
LOOKEN (TX)
LOOKIN (TX)
LOOKN4U (WA)
LOST (SC)
LOSTLUV (WA)
LOTO WIN (CA)
LOVER (IN, MS, NJ)

LOV GOD (TX)
LOWKEY (AK)
LRGFRY (IA)
LSTBOY (IA)
LTLLDT (VA)
LUCKEY (IA)
LUCKI (KY)
LUCKY (KY, TX)
LUCK 1 (AK)
LUCKYL8D (IN)
LUCKYME (IA)
LUVJOB (VA)
LUVNIT (AK)
LUVN 69 (MS)
LUVRGRL (AK)
LUVSICK (WA)
LUV2LAF (AL)
LV-N-LG (VA)
L8BLMR (TX)
L8WRK (MI)
MACHO (WA)
MAD CAP (TX)
MAD DAD (TX)
MAD LAD (MS)
MAD MAN (MS)
MAKINIT (LA)
MARIED (AK)
MARRIED (WA)
MBA (IA)
ME COLD (TX)
MEHUGGY (CA)
MELLLO (TX)
MELLO (IA, MS, TX)
MELLOW (KY)
MENSH (WA)
MIDAS (ID, WA)
MIDLIFE (WA)
MISTIC (MS)
MIXDUP (KY)
MOVNON (AK)
MPULSV (KY)
MR BUSY (IA)
MR HAPPY (WA)
MR LUCKY (IA)
MRPREP (IA)
MR TEASE (ID)
MR UGLY (IN)
MR WEIRD (WA)
MRSWOP (WA)
MRSZOOM (WA)
MSBAVN (MI)
MS BUSY (IA)
MS RITE (VA)
MS SEXY (MS)
MSINGLE (IN)
MT MAMA (TX)
MTMAN (IA, MI, TX)
MTNEAR (VA)
MTNEER (MI)
MUSCLE (AK)
NAMVET (AK)
NATIVE (NC)
NAUGTY (KY)
NAUTY (KY)
NCHARG (MS)
NDANGER (ID)
NDULGNT (WA)
NERVOUS (IN)
NEVERL8 (WA)
NITEOWL (WA)
NITOWL (AK)
NJOYN (IA)
NLUV (VA)
NMOTION (WA)
NOCTRNL (ID)
NO HOPE (ID)

NO KIDS (TX)
NOS JOB (TX)
NO SLAK (MS)
NOT DUI (MS)
NOT FAT (MI)
NOTGLTY (WA)
NOTWED (KY)
NO WIFE (IL)
NRRVUS (MI)
NRVOUS (ID, KY)
NSHAPE (WA)
NSTYLE (WA)
NTENSE (KY)
NT GLTY (AR)
NUBGNING (NC)
NULUV (IA)
NVIED (MS)
NVR2OLD (IA, WA)
NXTAZ (CO)
N2LECT (AK)
OBNXUS (IA)
ODFEELN (WA)
OKSOFAR (WA)
OLD GOAT (IA)
OLD GUY (ID)
OLD KID (MI)
OLDPRO (IA)
OLDSALT (WA)
OLDVET (IA)
OLEMAN (IA)
OLFASHN (WA)
OLGIRL (IA)
OL GOAT (MI, TX)
OLLADY (IA)
ONAROL (KY)
ONESTUD (WA)
ONE UP (MS)
ONLY 30 (VA)
ONTHGO (AK)
ONTHWGN (WA)
ONTOUR (IA)
ONTRAK (IA)
ON Z GO (IA, OH)
ON2ER (WA)
OPTMSM (TX)
OPTMST (KY)
OVER 30 (CT, MS, OR)
OVER 40 (MS)
OVER 60 (MS)
OWEYES (IA)
O2BNLUV (ID)
PACRAT (AK, WA)
PAKRAT (IA)
PARTIER (CA)
PARTYR (CA)
PARTYRR (CA)
PARVENU (CA)
PASNBY (AK)
PAST 40 (IA)
PAYN4IT (WA)
PD NFUL (VA)
PHD (KY)
PLABOY (AK, DE, MS, WA)
PLAMATE (WA)
PLAYBOY (ID)
PLMLOCO (WA)
POBOY (WA)
POFOLK (IA)
POOBAH (ID)
POORBOY (IA, ID)
PORGIRL (WA)
PUNK (WY)
PUZLED (VA)
RAPTURE (ID)
RDMAN (AK)

READY (IA, MS)
REBEL (TX)
REDHEAD (IA, ID)
REDHED (IA, ID,KY, TX)
REDNECK (ID)
REFORMD (WA)
RELAXT (MS)
REL WMN (VA)
RISQUE (IA, ID)
ROCKIN (KY)
ROMNTC (TX)
ROOKIE (IA, MS, WA)
RTISTIC (WA)
RTQL8 (NC)
RUNAWY (AK, ID)
SAD BOY (CA)
SADLRSO (WA)
SAINT (AK)
SAMEAGE (WA)
SBURBAN (WA)
SCHATZ (WA)
SCHATZE (WA)
SCHATZI (WA)
SCHAYZY (WA)
SCRAWNY (IN)
SEXEGRL (CA)
SHECUDA (WA)
SHEDEVL (WA)
SHEWOLF (WA)
SHIBOY (WA)
SHLEEK (WA)
SHONOFF (WA)
SHPWRKD (CA)
SHREWD (KY, WA)
SHYGUY (ID)
SINCERE (WA)
SINGLE (AK, ID, MI)
SINGUL (ID)
SIZE 5 (VA)
SKINNY (ID)
SLEEEK (IA)
SLEEK (IA, MS)
SLEEPY (KY, MS, TX)
SLIM (KY)
SLIMED (IA)
SLIMM (IA)
SLOPACE (WA)
SLOPOK (AK, MI, TX)
SLY (WY)
SMIL'N (NC)
SMITTEN (WA)
SNEAK-N (VA)
SNGL (WY)
SOBER (IA, KY, TX)
SO COLD (IN)
SOINLUV (WA)
SOK2BME (WA)
SOLO (MI)
SOPAW (MI)
SOPRANO (WA)
SOTHPAW (WA)
SOUL MAN (IN)
SOUTHPAW (ID, WA)
SPAZZD (VA)
SPOILD 1 (VA)
SPOKEN 4 (IN)
SPOKN 4 (IL)
STARVIN (WA)
STARVN (WA)
STDFST (TX)
STHPAW (KY, WA)
STRCRZY (WA)
STRNGR (AK)
STRSD (MI)
STUCKUP (VA)
STUD (AK, WY)

STUDLY (AK, TX)
SUAVER (TX)
SUBTLE (MI)
SUCCES (AK, ID)
SUKCES (MS)
SUM BUM (TX)
SUPRJU (KY)
SUPRSTR (IN)
SUSPKT (KY)
SVELT (WA)
TAKEN (DE, TX)
TALBOY (ID)
TALLBOY (IN)
TALLGAL (WA)
TALMAN (IA, TX)
TANGUY (WA)
TAN MAN (KY, MS)
TAN 4EVR (VA)
TATOO (WA)
TATOOSH (WA)
TEEDOFF (IN)
TEMPTED (CA)
TEMPTER (CA)
TENASHS (CA)
TENDER (CA)
TENOR (CA)
TENR (CA)
TENRPWR (CA)
TENRSAX (CA)
THE BOD (MS)
THE BOSS (IA)
THE WAG (MS)
THINER (IA)
THIRTY (IA)
THIRTY9 (WA)
THKFUL (TX)
TICKLED (ID)
TIKLISH (VA)
TOMBOY (IA, ID)
TOPCAT (SC)
TO-TAL (KY)
TOURIST (ID)
TRBLAGN (WA)
TRUELUV (WA)
TUFNIT (ID)
TWIN (IA, KY, WY)
TXPAYR (MI, WA)
TX-STUD (TX)
UNCLE (AK)
UNCOMN (IA)
UNDERDOG (NC)
UNEEK (IA)
UNOWHO (IA)
UNIQUE (IA)
UNTAMD (TX)
UNWED (KY)
UP & COMING (NC)
UPNOVR (WA)
U.S. MALE (TX)
U4EAH (ID)
VAMP (IN)
VAMPYR (IN)
VIETVET (IN)
VIP (DE, ID)
VIRGIN (KY, WA)
VIXEN (IA)
VLYGRL (VA, WA)
VRGIN (CA)
VRTIGO (CA)
VRTUOSO (CA)
VRTUOUS (CA)
VRYBLUE (CA)
VRYBROK (CA)
VRYLCKY (CA)
VRYLOST (CA)
VRYLOUD (CA)

VRYPIKY (CA)
VRYPKY (CA)
VRYRICH (CA)
WANTED (MI)
WARHAWK (WA)
WARLOC (MI)
WARLOCK (IN)
WARLOK (MI)
WEBAD (MI)
WEBADD (MI)
WE CARE (ID)
WELLRED (SC)
WEROCK (ID)
WHIMSCL (WA)
WHIMSIE (WA)
WHIZKID (IN)
WIDOWED (WA)
WIFELES (ID)
WILD UTH (VA)
WINNER (IL)
WIZKID (IA)
WKAHOLC (ID)
WLDTHG (IA)
WNDBLWN (WA)
WOMAN (IA, ID, IN, MI)
WOMYN (IN)
WPLASH (DE)
WREKLES (ID)
WYNNER (AK)
XCALGAL (ID)
X CITIN (MS)
XCNTRIC (WA)
XPERT (WA)
X-TA-C (KY)
XTRCASH (WA)
XTRALG (VA)
YESICAN (IN)
YUPPY (MS)
ZANY (IN)
ZBLONDE (WA)
1HR MAN (MS)
1 YUPPY (VA)
10KGUY (IA)
1 STUD (TX)
1 TWIN (TX)
1 2MANY (MS)
19 4EVER (AL)
2 B PHD (MS)
2HIP (WY)
2L8 2W8 (MS)
2RLE 4ME (VA)
2SASSY (AK)
2SHY 4U (MS)
2SOBER (IA)
2SWEET (AK)
2TAL4U (VA)
2WILDE (AK)
29 ISH (VA)
4 EVR L8 (TX)
4 EVR 21 (TX)
4 EVR 30 (TX)
4H MOM (IN)
4TUNATE (ID)
49 ISH (TX)
#1ISME (NC)

CHAPTER 5

That's What I Like

Our hobbies and interests, from AMORI to XRSIZE.

Ask what interests are the most basic to all people, and the answer is food and drink. Food plates (no pun intended) include everything from plain old **HAM & EGG** (VA) to highfalutin' **BELUGA** (AK) **CAVIAR** (AK) and **ESCARGO** (WA). (A particularly involved pun is the California plate on a Ferrari: **FCARGOT**.) **BAGL 1** (AK), **BIGMAC** (IA), **CHOCLIT** (IN), **CORNFLK** (WA), **FUDGE** (IN), **GARLIC** (MI, WA), **GUMBO** (AK, IA), **HMBRGR** (TX), **ICCREM** (IA), **LUV BBQ** (TX), **PRTZEL** (TX), and **RIBEYE** (IA, ND) are others, and for the **EPICURE** (WA), **SCARGO** (WA) and **TRTL SUP** (VA — a rolling testament to our abiding interest in things yummy to the tummy.

Even more prevalent are plates about drinks, especially the alcoholic kind. **BACCHUS** (IA) is clearly a wine fancier; **BEER** (WI) and **BUD LT** (ND) prefer the kiss of the hops. **BURBON** (ID, KY), **CHIVAS** (AK, WA), and **VODKA** (AK) go straight for the hard stuff.

CHIANTI (WA), **CLARET** (ID), **COLDUK** (ID), **COGNAC** (WA), **MOET** (WA), **MR WINE** (TX), **REDWINE** (IN), **VINO** (AK, IA), and **VNROUGE** (WA) realize that in vino there is veritas. The owners of **BUD4ME** (IA), **BUD4U** (IA), **COORS** (DE), **DAQIRI** (AK), **HAPY HR** (MS), **HIBALL** (IA), **HOMBRU** (IA), **HOTTODY** (WA), **HRDLKR** (WA), **JIM BEAM** (IN), **LT BEER** (VA), **PABST** (DE), **SIXPAK** (DE, IA), **TEKILA** (AK), **TODDY** (WA), and **WHISKY** (ID) find their veritas elsewhere.

Those favoring non-alcoholic drinks have chosen **CAWFEE** (VA), **COCOLA** (WA), **COKE** (AK, WI), **ICETEA** (IA), **ICEH2O** (MI), **MTDEW** (IA, WI), **PEPSEE** (VA), **PEPCFAN** (WA), **RTBEER** (IA), **SHASTA** (AK, WA), and the **UN-COLA** (MS). **RC COLA** (MI, TX, WA) has quite a number of admirers, too, as in **ARE CEE** (MS) and **ME-MY-RC** (TX). That's nice, but, gee, they could've had a **V8 JUICE** (VA).

Among our next most basic needs, hence interests, is love, which accounts for such plates as **AMORI** (MI), **AMOUR** (CT), **FRELUV** (AK), quite possibly **HAYRIDE** (IN), **IFLIRT** (MS), **ILUV DR** (VA), **IN2HUGS** (WA), **LAMORE** (ID), **LAMOUR** (IA), **LIBIDO** (MI), **LOVER** (MI), **LV-TEN-S** (TX) and **LUV10S** (OR), **LU-2-HUG** (TX), **PASHUN** (CA), **ROMANCE** (ID), and — get this — **TNTLUVR** (WA). Hubba hubba. **IM44PLA** (WA) is certainly direct enough, and one hopes that **I MOUNT-M** (VA) is a taxidermist.

Right up there with love is a deep interest in **MONEY** (KY, MI, VA). Not that nasty old **CASH** (MS) is really that big a deal, unless, of course, you don't have enough of it when you need it. Still, **DINERO** (MI), **MOOLA** (WA), **WAMPUM** (WA), and **WEALTH** (IA) are never all that far from our minds.

Also, we should never underestimate the hold music has on us, which shows up on a legion of licenses. Some drivers celebrate their favorite instruments: **ALPHORN** (ID); **BAGPIPE** (WA); **BANGO** (MS); **BASSOON** (ID); **CALIOPE** (IN, WA); **CHANTER** (WA), which you must master before taking up the bagpipes; **DRUMMR** (VA); **FIDDLE** (AK); **HARP** (IN); **HNDBELS** (IN); **HPSCHD** (VA); **I PLUNK** (WA), probably a guitar player; **KLAVIER** (WA);

MR GUITAR (WA); **MR PIANO** (VA); **MR TUBA** (MI); **OBOE** (IA); several versions of **OOM PAH** (TX); **PICCOLO** (ID, WA); **PLA SAX** (VA); **SAX-MAN** (AK, IN, MI, WA); **SQZBOX** (IA); **TOOBAH** (MI); **UKULELE** (WA); and **VIOLIN** (MI).

Singers have their plates, too, such as **ACAPELA** (WA), **A TENOR** (ID), **BARITON** (WA), **DOREMI** (WA), **I SING** (MI), **MEZZO** (MS), **SCAT-MAN** (IA), **SINATRA** (WA), **SOPRNO** (TX), even **LIPSYNC** (WA).

A few music plates feature favorite composers, such as **BACH** (OR), **JP SOUSA** (IN), **J.S. BACH** (TX), or **LISZT** (OR); still others stress various kinds of music: **A TRAIN** (IA, MI — no doubt Duke Ellington-oriented jazz buffs), **B BOP** (MS, NC), **BOOGIE** (AK), **BOSNOVA** (WA), **D BLUES** (MS), **FUGUE** (AK), **HMETAL** (IA), **I ROCK** (MI), **JAZMAN** (IA, MI), **LUVJAZZ** (WA), **MIKADO** (TX), **MSJAZZ** (MI), **NEW AGE** (MS), **N2KNTRY** (NC) — possibly before it was cool, **OFFBDWY** (IA), **OPERA (WA)**, **RKN ROL** (IN, MS), **ROC4EVR** (WA), **SONATA** (IA), and **WOTAN** (WA), who must be a devoted Wagnerian. **TAKE 5** (AK) must surely be a Dave Brubeck fan.

Also seen on an occasional plate are musical terms: **ADAGIO** (IA), **BFLAT** (IA), **EFLAT** (AK), **VIR2OSO** (PA), and **VIVACE** (ID, IN, VA).

With music goes dance in its many forms: **BALLET** (AK, ID), **BRN2DNC** (VA), **BUGALOO** (WA), **CANCAN** (AK, MS), **CHACHA** (IN), **CLOGGER** (WA), **DANCER** (IA, IN, MI), **DISCO** (AK), **DOSIDO** (AK, IA, TX), **DOUSHAG** (SC, of course), **FX TROT** (TX — in Texas they use a real fox), **IBBOPIN** (WA), **I BOGEY** (MI), **DANZ** (IA), the delighted **IKNDANC** (AL), **I POLKA** (MI), **RCKNRLR** (WA), **SQDANCR** (WA), **TANGO** (AK, MI, MS), **TUTU** (AK, MS), and **2 STEPR** (VA).

Art and antiques appear, too, as in **ABSTRAC** (WA), **ACRYLIC** (WA), **I CARVE** (IA — though this one might be a surgeon instead), **I DO ART** (ID, VA), **I DRAW** (IA), **PICASSO** (ID), **UPART**, and **VAN-GOH** (TX), which may, of course, merely be on a van.

Somewhat more scarce are references to reading and writing: **A POET** (MS), **BOOKWRM** (WA), **COMIXMAN** (NC), **MSPOEM** (IA), **READER** (AK), and **TH POET** (MS).

Some plates show their owner's interest in travel and in interesting destinations, as in **BEACHIN** (AK), **BYTHESEA** (NC), **CANCUN** (IA), **EUROPE** (IA), **ILOVENY** (WA), **IM4MTNS** (WA), **L TAHOE** (WA), **OAHU** (WA), **OCEANUT** (WA), **RLRD-FAN** (VA), **TRAVLR** (AK), and **TRIPN** (AK). Also **TUSCANY** (WA), **VIENNA** (WA), and **WE4TRVL** (VA).

Plate owners who are physically active display their favorite pastimes in: **A CAVER** (TX); **BOATER** (KY, MI) — here you have to be physically active to get the boat in and out of the water; **BULL RDR** (VA); **BYSCLE** (VA); **CAMPER** (AK, IA); **CAVEMAN** (WA), no doubt a spelunker; **CHERPA** (WA), likely a mountainclimber; **CLFJUMPR** (WA), whatever that is; **CLIMBER** (ID, WA); **CYCLIST** (ID); **FOX HNT** (MS); **HANGTEN** (IN), clearly a surfer, though the surf is very seldom up in Indiana; **HIKER** (VA); **H2O SKE** (MI); **ICEAX** (WA), a climber; **I KAYAK2** (VA); **I SCUBA** (IA, ID, MI); **I SHOOT** (MS); **JETSKI** (IA, ID, MI, VA); **JOGGER** (IA); **MTNBIK** (IA); **N2DMUD** (GA); **N2HRSES** (IA); **RK CLYMR** (VA); **RUNNER** (ID, MI, MS); **SAILING** (CO, WA); **SCOOBA** (ID, MI, VA); **SKYDVR** (TX); **SPELUNK** (IN, WA); **SURFER** (AK, CT); **WHYT WTR** (VA); **WIPEOUT** (IN), another inland surfer; and **WTRSKI** (MI).

Other active sports who like **AHK SHN** (TX) are into **AROWBX** (PA), **CARATE** (IN), **DGSLED** (AK, of course), **DRESAGE** (WA), **FLEXN** (MI), **FROGIN** (AK), **JUDO** (ID, IN), **KUNGFU** (AK, IN, MI, WA), **W8LIFTN** (WA), or just plain **XRSIZE** (AK, IA, ID).

An Idaho resident is a **BULRIDR**, an Indiana skater chose **FIGURE8**, an Alaskan fond of shooting picked **GUNMAN**. **FSTDRAW** gets the drop on you in Indiana and Washington; maybe they should get together with **HAVGUN** in Iowa. They could travel.

I'm a **NINJA**, say drivers in Iowa, Michigan, and Texas; **I PUMPNUP**, says a North Carolina **MRMUSSL** (WA) who's always **FLEX-IN** (MI). **OUI RUN**, declare a Wisconsin couple in a fine Gallic manner. One can only conclude from all this that we Americans must have a lot of time for play, except for one Washington resident whose plate tells us she's just into **HARDWRK**.

Somewhat less physical sounding folks go in for games: **ABINGO** (WA), **BILRDS** (MS), **CHEKERS** (WA), **DARTS** (IN), **MAHJONG** (WA), and **PAWN** (AK), probably a chess player. Also in this category are **PACMAN** (IA, OH), **PINBAL** (MI), **RACM UP** (MS), and **YO YO** (MS).

Those are the biggest categories, but other interests are as scattered as seeds in a windstorm. A Michigan man likes a good **CIGAR**, an Iowan loves the **CIRCUS**. A proper Virginian speaks for **DECORUM**, a Michigan driver for **ETIKIT**. A Washingtonian wants to make a **FASBUC**, and a Texas plate proclaims **GREED**. **HOEHOE** (WA) is likely a gardener, **GUFFAWS** (VA) and **GR8YAKS** (VA) standup comics. The plate **ICLOWN** (IA) can probably be seen at lots of children's birthday parties. Is **HOUDINI** (IN) a magician, like **MRMAGIC** in Washington?

Computer buffs have chosen **HACKR** (NH) and **PC GURU** (MS), and those with a taste for modern-day mythology display **BIG FT** (MS), **SASQTCH** (WA), and **SAW UFO** (IN).

Here and there are people who sound decidedly self-interested: **MEFIRST** (IN), **MEME** (TX), and **ME4ME** (MI), for instance. At least they are honest, like **LV2SPND** (WA) and **YUPE2B** (UT). Heck, there are even people into personalized plates: **EGO TAG** (MS), **LSNZ PL8** (VA), and **TAGNUT** (MI), though this last one might just as well belong to a person who likes garage sales.

A FLYBOY (NC)
ACTION (AK)
ACTR (WY)
A DAWZER (TX)
AEROBIC (IA)
AEROFAN (IN)
AIROBX (NH)
AIRSHO (ID)
AL RUNS (VA)
ANTIQR (WA)
ANTQR (VA)
ARESEE (WA)
A ROBIC (MS)
AROBIK (MS)
AROBIX (AK, MS)
ARTNIK (WA)
ARUNNR (VA)
ASUNBUM (WA)
ATOBAHN (WA)
AV8TRX (OR)
BACHUS (ID)
BANSAI (WA)
BASSON (WA)
B BOOP (KY)
BCHBUM (KY)
BEBOP (IA, IN, KY, WA)
BEBOPN (ID)
BEEBOP (IN)
BEER (WY)
BIG FUT (MS)

BIKER (MI)
BINGO (MI)
BIRDING (VA)
BLKTUX (MI)
BLUES (KY)
BLUGRS (KY)
BOATIN (DE)
BONSAI (MS, TX)
BOOMBOX (WA)
BOXWOOD (VA)
BRBADOS (CA)
BRDCRZE (CA)
BRDCRAZI (CA)
BRDCRZY (CA)
BRDKRZY (CA)
BRDGLDY (CA)
BRDGLVR (CA)
BRDGNUT (CA)
BRDGPLR (CA)
BRDLADY (CA)
BRDNUT (CA)
BRDWALK (CA)
BRDWLK (CA)
BSKTMKR (WA)
BUDS4ME (ID)
BUDWZER (WA)
CAMPIN (AK)
CANOE (IA)
CATLDY (KY)
CATNUT (MI)
CAVER (MI)
CAVING (ID)
CAVMAN (IA)
CBREEZE (WA)
CHINUP (IA)
CHNSAW (WA)
CHOCLT (AK)
CIGARS (IA, VA)
CINEMA (AK)
CKMATE (CO, IA)
CLBMED (VA)
CLOG N (MS)
CLOG R (MS)
CLUBMUD (WA)
COMEDY (MS, WA)
COMICS (MS, WA)
COW GRL (ND)
CRS LITE (VA)
CUEBALL (WA)
CURLIT (KY)
DA BLUS (MS)
DA BLUZ (MS)
DAIQIRI (CA)
DAIQURI (CA)
DANANG (KY)
DANSK (WA)
DESERT (CO)
DOG LVR (TX)
DOGSLD (AK)
DODADO (AK)
DOSEDO (IA)
DRGRCN (ID)
DSNYLND (WA)
ECOLOGY (IN)
ENCORE (TX)
EPICUR (CA)
EPICURE (CA)
EPIKURE (CA)
EPPICUR (CA)
EQESTRN (CA)
ERMINE (WA)
ESCRGO (AK)
EXTASKI (VA)
EYEFLY (MI)
EYESPY (WA)
EZCHAIR (WA)

EZ MONY (MS)
FIDDLER (IN)
FIDDLR (IA)
FILMBUF (WA)
FISHRMN (IN, WA)
FLEMKT (IA)
FLESH (MS)
FLEX (AK)
FLEXIN (AK)
FLEX EM (MS)
FLICKS (MS)
FLUTST (AK)
FLYBOY (VA)
FLY GRL (MS)
FLYGUY (IA, MS)
FLY4FN (VA)
FOTO (WY)
FOXHNTR (WA)
FOXHTR (KY)
FOXHUNT (WA)
FRCOAT (IA)
FREELUV (IN)
FREFAL (AK, MI)
FRISBE (MI, TX, WA)
FRISBEE (IA, ID, WA)
FRISBY (TX)
FRIZBE (WA)
FRIZBEE (WA)
FSHOOK (IA)
F STOP (ID)
FUN FONE (NC)
FUNTAN (VA)
GAMBLER (WA)
GIRLS (KY, MS)
GO CAVE (VA)
GUITAR (IA, ID, IN, MI, MS, TX)
GUNNER (AK)
GUN NUT (MS)
GUNPRO (KY)
GUNS (KY, WY)
GYM (NH)
GYMRAT (OR)
GZPACHO (CA)
HACKER (IA, ID, MI, NH)
HACQUER (WA)
HAIKU (WA)
HANG 10 (TX)
HARMONY (IA)
HARPIST (ID)
HATRICK (WA)
HDBANGR (IN)
HECKLER (WA)
HEVYMTL (ID)
HICNTRY (WA)
HINOTE (KY)
HĹYWOOD (WA)
HOFBRAU (WA)
HOOFER (ID, VA)
HOT TUB (MI, OH)
H-TUB (NH)
HVYMETL (AK, IN)
HVYMTL (IA, ID, IN, KY)
HYRISE (AK)
H2OBED (MI, OH, WA)
H2OBUG (IN)
H2OSKIS (IN)
H2O SKYN (VA)
IAPOET (IA)
I AV8 (KY)
IB JAMR (VA)
ICBRDS (WA)
ICE ACE (MS)
ICESK8 (KY)
ICLOG (KY)
I CUTUP (MS)

IDANCE (IA, IN, KY)
IDEAL (AK)
IDIVE (AK)
I DRAG (KY)
I DRAW (KY)
IDREAM (IA)
IELVIS (IA, WA)
I FLOSS (VA)
I FLY (KY)
IH2OSKI (IN)
I JETSKI (ID, IN)
I KNIT (MI)
I'LL PLAY (VA)
ILOVEHP (WA)
ILUV CATS (IN)
ILUV10S (IN)
I LUV2CUE (NC)
ILVHTHR (VA)
I LV2 SEW (VA)
IMJOGN (VA)
IMUSIC (KY)
IM4FLYN (VA)
INDY (WY)
INDY FAN (IN)
INTOART (WA)
INTO MUD (MI)
INVSTR (ID)
IN2JAZZ (WA)
IN2LIFE (WA)
I PARTY (MI)
IPRTY (VA)
IQUILT (KY, WA)
IRONMAN (IN)
IRUN (DE)
ISAIL (MI, OR)
I SEW (IA)
I SHOP (IA, MS)
I-SING (KY)
ISKATE (IN, MI, OR)
ISKI (ID, IN, KY, MI)
I SMOK (KY)
ISNACK (WA)
ISPEAK (IA)
I SPEED (MS)
IWALK (VA)
IWAN2NO (WA)
JACKPOT (WA)
JACUZZI (WA)
JAWGIN (VA)
JAZZMAN (IN)
JETSKE (IA)
JETSKIR (ID)
JOGN JJ (VA)
JOINT (WA)
JOINTS (WA)
JUDO (WY)
JUJUBN (MI)
JUKEBX (AK)
KAAVR (VA)
KARATE (IN, KY)
KARMA (AK)
KARFONE (WA)
KARNUT (IN)
KARNUTT (IN)
KAYAK (AK)
KAZOO (WA)
KLOG (WA)
KLOMPEN (WA)
KNITTER (WA)
KNITWIT (WA)
KNIVES (WV)
KWIKDRW (CA)
KYAK (WY)
K9SHOW (TX)
LAPLAYA (WA)
LARIAT (AK)

LEGO (IA)
LIONEL (MS)
LIV2SKI (VA)
LOGHOME (WA)
LOTTO (IA)
LOVE K9 (VA)
LOVE60S (WA)
LOV2PLA (ID)
LSTCALL (WA)
LUCIFER (MI)
LUDE (WA)
LUV BOTN (WA)
LUV COCO (VA)
LUV-ERTH (VA)
LUV JUGS (WA)
LUV LFE (TX)
LUVRENO (WA)
LUV R&B (VA)
LUV2ACT (WA)
LUV2BAK (WA)
LUV2BET (WA)
LUV2FLY (IA)
LVCLOGN (WA)
LVEGAS (WA)
LVTREES (WA)
LVTRVL (WA)
LVTSING (WA)
LV2BIK (AK)
LV2CLMB (ID)
LV2FLY (AK, IA, KY)
LV2GLF (ID)
LV-2-PUN (TX)
LV2ROCK (ID)
LV2RUN (AK, ID)
LV2SMYL (VA)
LV2TALK (WA)
LV2TRVL (WA)
LYRICS (DE)
MAGIC (WA)
MA-JONG (TX)
MASSAGE (WA)
MATH (WY)
MATH & ME (VA)
MEFRST (WA)
MEJAZZ (CA)
MEJAZZZ (CA)
MIME (NC)
MOET (KY)
MOPED (WA)
MOPARTY (VA)
MOTOWN (KY)
MOVIES (TX)
MOZART (ID, IN, KY)
MRBUILD (WA)
MRIZOD (IA)
MRMAIDS (WA)
MRMUSIC (WA)
MRQPONS (WA)
MR TUBA (MI)
MRTUX (IA)
MSCHUF (OR)
MTCLIMR (WA)
MTCLMBR (WA)
MTLHEAD (WA)
MTN-DEW (TX)
MTNEER (WA)
MUFDVR (KY)
MUSCLE (KY)
MUSIC (TX)
MUSICMAN (IA)
NASCAR (KY)
N CNCRT (MS)
NC QULTR (VA)
NDLPNT (MI)
NEW LIF (MS)
NEW WAVE (NC)

NFLNUT (MI)
NGHTLFE (WA)
NIBBLER (VA)
NINJA 1 (AK, ID)
NINTNDO (WA)
NOOYAWK (WA)
NUDIST (WA)
NUWAVE (IA)
N2HORSES (IA)
N2HORSN (IA)
N2-SURF (TX)
OFFROAD (WA)
OFFSHOR (WA)
OHRNRY (WA)
OLMPCS (AK)
OOMPA (ID)
OOM PAPA (IN)
OUI SKI (ID, TX)
OUT2EAT (IA)
OZU (VA)
O2BACOP (IN)
O2BBAD (MI)
PACKMAN (WA)
PARFUM (IA, TX)
PAR GOF (TX)
PARTKNG (CA)
PARTY (IA)
PAR3ACE (WA)
PASHON (CA, IA)
PASWRD (TX)
PAY DA (KY)
PBS YES (VA)
PEPSI (WA, WI)
PERL 1 (ND)
PESCADO (WA)
PETROC (AK, WA)
PETROCK (WA)
PIANIST (ID)
PINBALL (WA)
PLA LOUD (VA)
PLANEGAL (NC)
POET (TX, WA)
POETIC (AK)
POLKA (IA)
PORCLN (IA)
PRETZEL (WA)
PRTY (WY)
PRTYLDY (WA)
PRETYMN (KY)
PRTYWMN (WA)
PUTPUT (KY, OR)
QTRHRSE (WA)
QUICHE (AK)
QUILTER (IN)
QUILTR (MS)
QUILTS (KY)
RACEFAN (IN)
RACFAN (VA)
RAP (MI)
RCKNROL (WA)
RIVERAT (IA)
RKNROLL (TX, WA)
ROCKER (MI)
ROC ROL (CA)
RODEO (TX)
ROKHOPR (WA)
ROKNRL (MS)
ROKROL (MI, MS, OR)
ROLX (WY)
ROPING (TX)
ROW SUM (TX)
RUNNAH (MI)
RUNNER (KY)
RUNR (WY)
RVRRAT (IA)
SAIL (WY)

SAILGRL (NC)
SANIBEL (WA)
SANJUAN (WA)
SASQASH (WA)
SAXJAZ (ID)
S*CARGO (TX)
SCARGOE (WA)
SCIFI (AK, WA)
SCUBA (AK, KY, MI, VA)
SEASHO (ID)
SEESHEL (WA)
SEWSEW (WA)
SHOPER (KY)
SHOPIN (AK, IA)
SHOPUP (KY)
SHOTGUN (WA)
SHTGUN (TX)
SHTRBUG (WA)
SINGER (IA)
SINGIN (IA)
SIXGUN (KY)
SIXPACK (IA)
SKATER (AK, KY)
SKEE-BUM (VA)
SKI-BUM (ID, IL, KY, TX)
SKIBUNY (ID)
SKIER (KY)
SKIERS (ID)
SKIFOOL (ID)
SKIH2O (KY)
SKI KRZY (VA)
SKINUT (CO, ID, MI, MS)
SKISNO (KY)
SKYDIV (MI, TX)
SKYDVE (MI)
SKY DYVN (VA)
SK8ER (WA)
SK8TER (KY)

SLPKNT (WA)
SNARF (IA)
SONG4U (IA)
SO PAW (TX)
SPINAKR (WA)
SQDANCE (WA)
SQDANSR (WA)
SQRDNCR (WA)
SRFRGRL (WA)
SSCARGO (WA)
SSPNDRS (WA)
STAMPS (MS)
STEREO (TX)
STRFRY (KY)
SUESHE (WA)
SUESHI (WA)
SUDS (IA, WY)
SUNBUF (KY)
SUN BUM (IL, MI, TX)
SUNFUN (AK)
SUNGOD (WA)
SUNMAN (DE)
SUNSHIN (WA)
SUNTAN (DE, KY)
SUN4ME (ID)
SURFER (KY)
SURFIN (AK)
SYNTAX (AK)
TACLBOX (WA)
TACO (IA)
TAHITI (WA)
TAILGTN (WA)
TAKOFF (IA)
TATTOO (IA, WA)
TATTWO (WA)
TEEVEE (WA)
TEEWEE (WA)
TEKEELA (WA)

TENOR (IN, MI, MS)
TEXTEA (WA)
THE60'S (NC)
THIMBLE (VA)
THRBRED (WA)
TOO-BA (KY)
TOO-TU (KY)
TOUCHE (TX)
TOURIST (IA, WA)
TQELA (WA)
TQUELA (AK)
TRAVL (IA)
TRAVLER (IA)
TRAVLIN (AK, IA)
TRMPET (KY)
TRUMP (ID, MI, WA)
TSAURUS (WA)
TSHIRT (IA)
TSUNAMI (WA)
TTRAIN (ID)
TUBA (WY)
TUUTUU (WA)
TWOTWO (ID)
TX SKI R (TX)
UFO (WA)
UKE (AK)
UMM-PA (KY)
UMPAPA (WA)
US POLO (TX)
VA CAVER (VA)
VARIETY (NC)
VEGAS (KY)
VIBR8R (WA)
VIDEO (IA)
VODO (IA)
VOO-DO (TX)
VOODOO (MI, TX, WA)
VOLCANO (WA)
VOYAGER (IA)
V8 JUCE (MI)
WARGAMR (VA)
WDSTOC (WA)
WDSTOK (WA)
WEE3 SKI (VA)
WEFLY (IA)
WELOVENY (NC)
WEPOLKA (IA, WA)
WE QUILT (IN)
WEROCK (IA)
WEROME (IA)
WERUN (IA)
WESAIL (IA, IN, KY, WA)
WEWALK (IA)
WILD SX (ND)
WINSRF (MS)
WITCH (KY)
WKEND (WA)
WKNDS (TX)
WLDTKY (WA)
WLDWEST (WA)
WLDTHANG (WA)
WNDSRFR (WA)
WNDSURF (IA)
WNSURF (AK)
WUDSTK (WA)
WUDSTOK (WA)
WYPOUT (KY)
W8LIFT (KY)
W8LIFTG (WA)
W8LIFTR (ID, VA, WA)
W8N2SKI (WA)
W8N4SUN (WA)
W8N4WND (WA)
XCARGO (MS)
XERCIZ (KY)
XPOSURE (WA)

XPRESO (WA)
XRCISE (IA)
XRCIZE (IA)
XRSIZR (IA)
XRSYZE (VA)
ZBLUES (WA)
ZNFNDEL (WA)
1 JOGGER (CA)
1 JUGLER (CA)
1 JUGLUR (CA)
1 NINJA (IA)
2BACCO (VA)
2DA BCHS (VA)
2SKI (WY)
2 STEPR (KY)
2ZA BCH (VA)
6 PACK (AK)
6 PAK (AK)
7UP (WY)
8 BALL (CT, ID)

CHAPTER 6

E Pluribus Me

FAT BOB, AQARIUS, seeks F, 18-30. Must like HUNTIN.

If any non-religious activity has achieved the status of a religion in contemporary America, it is sports. Whether as a fan or as a participant, the average American takes sports seriously, and in large doses. Little wonder that our beloved sports find their way onto so many of our license plates.

Some plates describe outdoor sports, such as **BO HNTR** (MS), **BOWHNTR** (ID), **GOHUNT** (IA), **HUNTER** (IN, KY), **HUNTIN** (ID), **I HUNT** (IA, MI), **KILLDUX** (WA), **LV2 HUNT** (ID), **N2HUNTN** (WA), and the like.

Other gun enthusiasts go for **I SHOOT** (AK), **I SKEET** (WA), **SKEET** (AK, ID, MI, MS, TX), **TRAP** (WA), and **TRAPGUN** (WA). Latter day Robin Hoods choose **ARCHER** (AK, ID) or **ARCHERY** (ID).

Those who fish cast about and come up with such plates as **DRYFLY** (AK, ID), **FISHIN** (AK, MI), **FLYROD** (AK, ID, MI, TX), **GNFSHN** (AK), **IMFISHN** (VA), **LV2FSH** (AK, IA), **NIMROD** (IA, KY), and **N2FISHN** (WA). An overall outdoorsman in Washington State chose **HNTNFSH**.

Our nation also teems with teams. Those belonging to fans of a particular team appear later in this chapter, but those that identify a certain sport include, of course, football: **BEST QB** (AK), **BOOT IT** (VA), **ENDZONE** (WA), **FTBALL** (ID), **GO LONG** (MI), **HAFBAK** (NH), **QB SACK** (TX), and **SACKEM** (CO).

Basketball drives into view in **FSTBRK** (WA), **HOOPSTER** (WA), **SKYHOOK** (WA), **SLM DNK** (ND), and **1 ON 1** (NC, ND). No doubt the owner of **ELBOZ** (MI) is a big man whose job is to assert himself under the basket.

Americans who favor "the nation's pastime" display **BASBAL** (IA), **CATCHR** (MI), **FSTPICH** (WA), **HOMERUN** (WA), **IKATCHR**

(WA), **I PITCH** (IN, MI), **LINEDR** (IA), **SLUGER** (MI), and **SQEZPLA** (WA).

Other team sports show up in **GOALIE** (KY, MI), **HKEYPUK** (WA), **HOCKEY** (AK, IA, WI), **H2O POLO** (IN), **ICEHCKY** (IN), **ILVSOCR** (WA), **IN2POLO** (WA), **KRIKET** (WA), **LACROSS** (WA), **N2POLO** (WA), **POLO FAN** (IN), **POLOGAL** (ID), **RUGB NE1** (NC, VA), **RUGGER** (AK), **SCCRNUT** (WA), **SLPSHOT** (WA), **SOCCER** (AK, IN, KY, TX, WI), **SOF BAL** (MS), **SPIKER** (MI), **SQUASH** (ND), **VLYBAL** (IA, IN), and **WTRPOLO** (WA).

More frequent still are plates related to sports that are played individually. Of these the top two are tennis and golf. Tennis enthusiasts identify themselves with **ADD IN** (VA), **DBLES** (MI), **LOV 10 S** (ND), **NETPLAY** (WA), **TEN-IS** (TX), **TENSBUM** (CA, WA), **TENS4ME** (WA), **10SBUF** (ID), **10SNUT** (IA, ID, MI, MS), **15 LOVE** (IA, MS), **4HAND** (IN), **4T LOVE** (IA, ID, MI), **40 LOVE** (CT, IA, KY, MS), and most popular of all, **10S NE1** (AL, CO, ID, LA, MI, OH, SC, UT, WI).

AHGOLF sighs an Idaho tag. Other golfers have chosen **BIRDEE** (MI), **DIVOT** (ID, WA), **DUFFER** (ID), **FAREWAY** (IA), **GOLFNG** (AK), **GOLPHR** (ID), **HOLE N 1** (KY, TX), **I GOLF** (CT, IA, ID, MI, MS), **LV21PUT** (WA), **ONINTWO** (WA), **PAR NO 1** (TX), **TEEITUP** (IA, ID, IN,

WA), **TEEOFF** (IA, ID, MI, MS, WA), **TEE 1 UP** (ID, MS, OH, TX, WA), even **TEE4TWO** (ID). **THKGOLF**, suggests an Idaho plate; **1PUTT**, command plates in Idaho and Michigan. **TITUP2** (VA) is unusual in that it is intended to be read left to right, then right to left: "Tee it up to putt it."

So don't be like **HACKER** (AK), **IH8GOLF** (WA), **ISHANK** (WA), or **I3PUTT** (MI). Get up a **4SUM** (NC), hit the **LINKS** (IN), and **T ITUP** (CO, IN, KY). Maybe one fine day, like a certain Virginian, you will be able to boast of **3HOLSN 1**. So come on, **MRGOLF** (MI) and **MSGOLF** (MI).

After tennis and golf, the next most popular individual sport (according to personalized plates) is skiing. Examples are **SKBUNY** (IA), **SKI BUF** (MI), and the frequently encountered **SKIBUM** (AK, CT, IA, MI, MS, TX). One even finds **SKIMOM** (AK), **SKIGOD** (IA), and **WEE3 SKI** (VA). Other winter sports make occasional appearances in plates such as **ISKATE** (AK, MS, ND), **LUGE** (DE), and **SKATER** (IN).

The more pugilistic sports weigh in with **BLK BLT** (IA), **BOXER** (IA, ID, IN, MI, MS), **KARATE** (AK), **KWIK KO** (ND), **MATMAN** (MI), **PAWS UP** (IN), **RASSLE** (TX), **UPR KUT** (MS), and **WRSTLN** (IA).

Track and field contribute **ARUNR** (IA), **GYMNST** (AK, ID, NH), **HIJMPR** (IA), **HURDLR** (IA), **LV 2 RUN** (IA), **RUN10K** (ID), **SHOTPUT** (IN, WA), and **SPRINTR** (ID).

Aquatic sports enthusiasts offer **ADVR** (IA), **BK SWIMR** (ID), **I DIVE** (KY, MS), **SKI WET** (ID), and **W-SURFR** (TX), and still other sports appear in **HANDBAL** (ID), **I KAYAK** (MS, WA), **RQTBAL** (IN), **SKYDIVE** (IA, ID), **8 BALLL** (ND), and **300 BOLR** (VA).

ABIKER (IA)
ABOWLER (IA)
AJOGER (IA)
A JYMNST (VA)
ARCHRY (AK, ID)
BASEBAL (IN)
B-BALL (KY)
BIRDIE (ID)
BOHUNT (MI)
BOWHNT (MI)
BOWHTR (KY)
BOWHUNT (IN)
BOW PRO (VA)
BOWLER (MS)
BOWLIN (KY)
BOXING (KY)
BOXN (WY)
BRDHNTN (CA)
BRDHNTR (CA)
BRDHUNT (CA)
BRDSHOT (CA)
BSKTBAL (ID)
BUCFVR (KY)
CATCHER (IN)
COACH (IA)
CRO-K (KY)
DBLS (MI)
DIVOTS (ID)
DRAG (WY)
DR GOLF (ID, MS)
DUNK (WY)
DUNKIT (KY)
FAIRWAY (WA)
FENCIN (ID)
FENCING (ID)
FISHING (ID)
FUSBALL (WA)
FUTBAL 1 (VA)
FUTBAW (KY)
FUTBOL (KY)
GLFBUM (MI)
GLFNUT (MI)
GN2 GOLF (ID)
GOALEE (ID)
GOF NUT (ID, MS)
GOLF (KY, WY)
GOLFBUM (LA)
GOLFER (ID, MI, MS, TX)

GOLFIN (MI, MS)
GOLF N (ID, MS)
GOLFNUT (ID, IN)
GONFISH (ID)
GR8 SAVE (WA)
GYMNAST (ID)
HAFBAC (AK)
HKEFFAN (WA)
HUNTING (ID)
H2OPOLO (KY)
H2OSKI (AK, OH, WI)
IBGOLFN (ID)
I BOWL (ID, MS)
ICICLE (AK)
ICYCLE (IA)
IFISH (IA, KY)
IJUMP (IA)
I PUTT (MI)
IRACE (AK)
ISKI (AK, MS, WY)
LCROSS (IA)
LUV2FSH (ID)
LUV2GOLF (AL, ID)
LUV2SKI (IA)
LUV2SWM (IA)
LVGOLF (IA)
LV2FISH (IA)
LV2 SKI (AK, IA)
LV4SOCR (WA)
MIS HITS (VA)
MRPOOL (IA)
N2GOLF (KY)
ONEPUTT (ID, IN)
O2GOLF (KY)
O21PUTT (ID)
PARCAR (KY)
PARGOLF (IN)
PARPUTT (CA)
POLO (IA, IN)
POOL (KY)
PROBALL (WA)
PUTTNUT (IN)
QTRMILE (WA)
RACBAL (AK)
RAQTBL (AK, WI)
RASLER (AK)
RESLER (IN)
ROW4IT (VA)
RUGBY (AK, MI, WI)
SHOTPT (WA)
SHTPUT (WA)
SKI (WY)
SKIER (IA, TX)
SKI HOT (IA)
SKIING (IA)
SKINUT (IA)
SKYDIVR (IA)
SKYDVR (IA)
SKYHOUCK (NC)
SLALOM (KY)
SLMDUNK (WA)
SOFTBAL (ID)
SOKRNUT (WA)
SWIM (IA)
SWIMMER (IA, IN)
SWIMMIN (IA)
TEAITUP (IN)
TEEMEUP (WA)
TEEMUP (KY)
TEEUP (ID, MI)
TEITUP (IN)
TENCBOY (CA)
TENESS (CA)
TENIS (CA)
TENNIS (AK, CA, IA, ID, IN, KY, VA, WA)

TENNISS (CA)
TENNIST (CA)
TENNSBM (CA)
TENNYSS (CA)
TENSBUF (CA)
TENSDOC (CA)
TENSFAN (CA)
TENSFVR (CA)
TENSGAL (CA)
TENSPLR (CA)
TENSPRO (CA)
TENSRQT (CA)
TENSTAR (CA)
TIN PIN (KY)
TNSPLYR (WA)
UP2PAR (KY)
V-BALL (KY)
VOLEBAL (IN)
VOLYBAL (WA)
WEBOWL (TX, WA)
WEFISH (IA, KY)
WEGOLF (AK, IA, ID)
WEHUNT (ID, TX)
WESKI2 (UT)
W8LFTR (PA)
1 GOLF NUT (NC)
1 ON 1 (KY)
10ACFAN (ID)
10KRUN (MI)
10K 42K (VA)
10-NIS (KY)
10S BUM (IA, ID)
10SGAL (WI)
10S FAN (IA)
10S MAN (MI)
10S4FUN (IA)
2 PUTT (IN)
3 PUTT (KY, MI)
4-PUTT (KY)
40 LOVE (KY)
40LUV (IA, MS)
5 KRUN (MI)
5 LOVE (MI)
7 IRON (ID, KY)
9-BALL (KY)

I wouldn't want to be a member . . .

A lot of us are big joiners — we like to know we're part of a group, including the ones into which we were born.

Some of our proclaimed affiliations are signs of the zodiac: **AQARIUS** (WA), **ARIES** (AK, MI), **GEMINI** (AK, ND), **LIBRA** (AK, IA,

IN, MS), **PISCES** (AK, KY), **SCORPIO** (ID), **VIRGO** (IN), and so on.

Others are designations of national origin, such as **A BRIT** (TX), **AUSSIES** (ID), **BASQUE** (ID), **DE TURK** (CA), **DUTCH** (ID, IN, MI), **FRENCH** (MI), **GREEK** (IN), **IM SWIS** (WA), **IRISH** (IN, TX, WA) or **SHMROK** (ID), **ITALIAN** (ID, TX, WA) or **PAISANO** (ID) or **GOOMBA** (WA), **SVEEDE** (WA) or **SVENSK** (ID). A few of these tags use terms not usually considered polite: **IM A JAP** (TX), **JAPJEEP** (WA), **PART WOP** (CA), and **TOP WOP** (MS).

Other tags draw our attention to regional birthrights — **CAJUN** (ID, IN, KY), **SUTHRN** (MI, MS), **YANKEE** (AK, TX), or **YANKY** (VA). What? A Yanky in Virginia, suh? Quick, Miss Becky, fetch me mah gun!

Actually, those last two could just as easily signify affiliation with a professional sports team, as do plenty of other plates: **A KNICK** (VA), **BOSOX** (DE), **CELTIC** (CO, ID), **CUBNUT** (AK), **HWKFAN** (IA), **I METFAN** (NY), **OILERS** (TX), **ORIOLS** (VA), **PACERS** (IN), **PACKERS** (IN), **RAIDERS** (IN, WA), **RAMSFAN** (WA), **VIKINGS** (ID), and others.

Likewise, many plates show state affiliations: **ATEXAN** (VA), **BUCKEYE** (MI), **CALO4YIN** (NC), **CRACKR** (MI), **CT YNKY** (VA), **HOOSIER**

(WA), **N8TV TXN** (VA), **NUYAWKA** (WA), or **OIO** (OH). Far more often, though, plates tied to states will identify the old school ties of a sports fan, as in **AUGGIE** (MI), **GO LSU** (MI), **HOOOOOS** (VA), **IMA HOKE** (VA), **JAHAWK** (TX), **MIZZOO** (TX), **TAA HEEL** (WA), **UGA DOG** (TX), **UOF10EC** (NC), **N DAME** (TX), **RZRBAK** (TX), **WOOFPAK** (SC), **WV HLBLI** (VA), and the very proper **HARVARD** (WA). (Remember the old Tom Lehrer song, "Fight fiercely, Harvard, fight fight fight, impress them with our prowess, do . . .")

A few identify racial origin. **IBBLACK** (WA), meet **IMWHITE** from your own state. Or **INJUN** (TX), or **REDMAN** (MI), who may, of course, just be a chewing tobacco user. Some of the Native American plates are tribe-specific: **CHOCTAW** (WA), **NAVAJO** (IN, TX), **NEZPERC** (WA), and **SHAWNEE** (WA). It's anyone's guess whether **5 NDNS** (NC) should be taken literally.

Civic clubs — **CIVTAN** (MI), **KIWANIS** (WA), **OPTMST** (MI), **2OPTIMIST** (NC), and **ROTARY** (IA, KY, MI) — are on lots of plates, as are the names of many other clubs: **DMOLAY** (AK, ID), **HADASAH** (WA), **LEGION** (WA), **NAACP** (TX), and **PAGAN** (AK, WA). Is there really an **NAAWP** (TX)? Some who see **48 NUTS** (WI) might not immediately recognize that it refers to the 4-H Club, and **INMATE** (DE) isn't in prison — he's a member of a rock band called The Inmates.

The military is saluted on: **AFROTC** (MS), **NAM VET** (MS), **SEMP FI** (MI, MS), **USNAVY** (IA), **USNRET** (WA), and **VET PWR** (MS). Finally, company tags — probably on company cars — are occasionally seen: **ADIDAS** (KY), **ARBYS** (KY), **EXXON** (WA), **MABELL** (WA), **MARRIOT** (VA), and **SHERATON** (NC).

ABUCKEYE (NC)
A DAGO 2 (CA)
AD PIE (MS)
AFL CIO (KY)
A GREEK (TX)
AMA TXN (TX)
AMNESTY (VA)
AMWAY (MI)
A TEXUN (VA)
AUSSIE (MI)
BADGRS (WI)
BAMA NO1 (VA)
BIG RED (WI)
B IRISH (IN)
BRITISH (ID, IN)
BRRTISH (WA)
BUKEYE (WA)
BUKIVAN (CA)
BYU MBA (OR)
CARDS (IL)
CELTIC (CO, ID)
CELTS (IN)
CHARGRS (ID)
CHCUBS (IN)
CHICUB (MI)
CHICUBS (ID, IN)
CIVITAN (WA)
COLTS (KY)
COLTFAN (IN)
CUBBIES (IN)
CUBFAN (AK, ID, IN, WA, WI)
CZECH (IN)
DABRONX (WA)
DEMCRAT (IN)
DN UNDR (MS)
DOLFNS (MI)
EAGLES (ID)
FLA ST8 (MS)
GA DOG (KY)
GAELIC (WA)
GAPEACH (ID)
GIANTS (NC)
GOBAMA (KY)
GO BUCS (ID)
GO CUBS (IL, MI)

GO LSU (TX)
GO PHILS (PA)
GO SOX (IL)
GREEKBOY (NC)
GYANTS (NH)
HAWKFAN (ID)
HIATT (KY)
HINDU (KY, MI)
HOOSIER (ID)
HOOSIERR (NC)
HOOSYER (VA)
HOOZIER (IN)
HUSKERS (ID)
I DRUID (ID)
IIRISH (IN)
ILLINI (WI)
I LUV ILL (IL)
IMA AGI (TX)
IM A LEO (TX)
IMATXN (WA)
IM4LSU (LA, MS)
IM4MSU (KY)
IM4UL (KY)
JAYHAWK (ID)
JETSET (MI)
KENAIR (AK)
KRAUT (WA)
KWANIS (AK, WA)
KYLADY (IN, MI)
KYWOMN (KY)
LAKERS (ID, IN)
LNGHRN (TX)
LN STAR (TX)
LOV UNC (NC)
LSU FAN (MI, TX)
LUV UK (KY)
MABELLE (WA)
MAFIA (MS)
MAYTAG (KY)
MEITAL (CA)
MEITALY (CA)
MEJICAN (CA)
METFAN (MI)
METS (IN)
METS GO (VA)
MIZZO (KY, TX)
NAVY (MI)
NFL MOM (TX)
NOTRE D (MS)
NO.1 TXN (VA)
NYFEMME (VA)
NY YANKS (IN)
O EYE O (NC)
OHIGHO (VA)
OIO ST8 (CA)
OLMISS (TX)
ON WISC (WI)
OSU ONE (FL)
PAESANO (WA)
PAIZANO (WA)
PI KAPPS (IN)
PIKES (IN)
POLAK (IN)
PSTN FAN (VA)
RA TECH (VA)
RAZRBK (MS)
REDSKN (TX)
REDSOX (IN)
ROTC (AK)
RREBEL (ID)
RZRBCK (TX)
RZRBKR (TX)
RZRBKS (TX)
R8R FAN (NC)
SECESH (ID)
SF49ERS (ID)

SIGMA X (MS)
SKINS (KY)
SLAVIC (KY)
SOONERS (IN)
SOXFAN (MI)
ST8FRM (KY)
SUTHNR (MS)
SVENSKI (WA)
SWEDE (KY)
TAHEEL (WA)
TARHEEL (ID, WA)
TAR HEL (TX)
TAURES (ID)
TEAMSTR (WA)
TENASEA (CA)
TENASEE (CA)
TENEZEE (CA)
TENISEE (CA)
TEX-SON (TX)
TEXXUN (TX)
THEJAZ (AK)
THE ROCK (WA)
TRHEEL (WA)
TX-SON (TX)
UKYFAN (KY)
U OF MI (TX)
U OF MO (TX)
U-OF-TEX (TX)
USMC (KY)
UT FAN (TX)
UW BAND (WA)
UW4EVER (WA)
VASSAR (MS)
VFW (MS)
VRGNIA (CA)
VRGNIAN (CA)
VRMONT (CA)
VRMONTR (CA)
WHOZURE (WA)
WUFPCK (AK)
XROTARY (WA)
XTEXAN (WA)
YANKFAN (WA)
YLW*RSE (TX)
1 JRZGRL (CA)
1 KAJUN (CA)
4 CELTS (VA)
4-H (KY)
4 ILLINI (IN)
4 LAKERS (IN)

You can call me Ray . . .

Some car owners share their nicknames; some plates are simply plays on the owner's real name: **HOJO** is an Iowan named Howard Johnson, **HUFFY** (KY) a Mr. Huff, **JAYBIRD** (IA) a man named Jay, **JELLO** (IA) an owner named Jellison, **JELLY** another Iowan named Joeleen. **KINGTUT** (IA) belongs to a Mr. Tutt, **RAIN** (DE) is a woman named Lorraine, **SWAMI** (IA) to a Mr. Swaim, **SWIFTY** (IA) to a Mr. Swift, **TANGO** (IA) to a Mr. Tangeman, **UFIE** (KY) to a driver whose first name is Eufelia, **WITTY** (IA) to Mr. Wittenburg, **ZIGGY** (KY) to a Mr. Zeigler.

One variety of nickname sounds rather flattering: **BIG AL** (TX), **CHAMP** (MS), **CUDDLES** (VA, WA), **DOLFACE** (WA), **DR LUV** (NJ, TX), **FLUFFY** (IA, MS, TX, VA, WA), **FOXY ROXE** (ID), **HUNEBUN** (IN), **JO COOL** (IA), **LEGS** (ND), **MR COOL** (MI), **PUNKIN** (KY, MI, VA), **SWEETP** (AK), **SWT SUE** (MS), and **SWT THG** (MS).

Others are decidedly less flattering: **ANIMAL** (IA), **BOOGER** (IA, ID, KY), **DR. NAS-T** (TX), **FAT-FRED** (NC), **FATSO** (MI), **FLTHED** (IA), **MADDOG** (AK, DE, ID), **PIG LEG** (VA), **PUFFER** (IN), **STINKY** (ID, MI), **STUMPY** (IN, WA), **TODZILA** (ID), **TUBBY** (AK), **2TH PIK** (MS, TX), or **4 EYES** (ID).

There are a goodly number of preppies: **BUFFIE** (IN), **BUNKY** (IN, KY), **BUNKIE** (AK, ID, IN), and **MISSY** (ND); a few that sound like movie characters from the '40s: **SPIKE** (VA), **SUSYQ** (AK, KY), **TOOTS** (AK, MS, ND), and **SNUKUM** (VA).

Some nicknames are cutsie diminutives such as **POOKINS** (WA) and **POOPSIE** (ID). What's the most popular? **BUBBA** (AK, IA, IN, KY, MI, MS, SC, TX). And why is it that **TEX** (IA, ID, IN) is always out-of-state? Finally, it should be "perfectly clear" that **TRKYDCK** in Idaho is "not a crook."

ABDUL (WA)
ACE (TX)
ACE MAN (TX)
ALFIE (ID)
BABBS (VA)
BABOO (WA)
BABSIE (MS)
BABU (KY)
BAD JOHN (IN)
BALDY (WA)
BG DADY (MS)
BG JAKE (ID)
BIG ED (ID)
BIG JOHN (ID)
BIG JON (MI)
BIG TERR (VA)
BINKY (KY)
BLU EYZ (IL)
BOCEFUS (IN)
BOCPHUS (IN)
BOGER (MS)
BUBA (AK)
BUBBLES (AK, IA, IN, MI, MS, SC, TX)
COOTER (KY)
CUPCAKE (IA)
CURLEY (MI)
CUTEY (MI)
DAISYO (CA)
DA KID (CA, IL)
DA KIDD (CA)
DA KIDDD (CA)
DA KILLA (CA)
DI DI (KY)
DIRTY (DE)
DRDOOM (WA)
DRFLGD (MI)
DRFUN (MI)
DRJAZZ (MI, VA)
DRLOVE (DE)
DR ROCK (MI)
DR ZOOM (MI)
DUCKIE (MI)
EASY ED (KY, MS)
FAT BOB (ID, NC)
FATZO (IN)
FLOOSY (MS)
FLUFY (AK)
FOXYROXI (WA)
FRITZY (KY)
GOOBER (AK, MS)
GOOFUS (TX)
HAWKEYE (ID)
HLF PNT (TX)

HLF PT (TX)
HNYBUN (IA)
HNY POT (TX)
HOSS (IA, ID)
IGGY (DE)
JAYBRD (IA)
JIM BEAU (VA)
JOECOOL (IA)
JO KOOL (MI)
JONJON (AK)
JONSEY (KY)
KEEKEE (AK)
LILBIT (AK)
LIL JOHN (VA)
LIL PUMKN (VA)
LITLBIT (IN)
LIZIPOO (CA)
LIZYPOO (CA)
LIZZIE (MI)
LTLBIT (AK)
LUMPY (IA, MI)
LUVDOG (VA)
MADAM-X (TX)
MADDAWG (ID)
MADMAX (IA)
MISPRS (VA)
MOPSIE (TX)
MRLUCKY (WA)
MR OX (VA)
MSPRIS (WA)
MSPRISS (WA)
MUGSY (MI)
MURF (KY)
MZ NAS-T (TX)
NOPAY (NJ)
PEE WEE (ID, MS)
PEPR (ND)
PEWEE (KY)
PMPKIN (VA)
POOHBR (VA)
POOKEY (IN)
POOKIE (IN)
POOKY (MI)
PUDDIN (KY, TX)
PUNKIE (KY, NC)
PUNKN (KY)
PWEE (MI)
SAMBO (KY)
SHORTEY (WA)
SHORTI (AK)
SHORTIE (ID)
SHORTY (IN)
SLUGGO (MS)
SLYM (ND)
SMITTY (MI)
SNOOKM (KY)
SNOOKS (KY)
STEWIE (AK)
STUMP (AK)
SUEZQ (IA, KY)
SUSIEQ (MI)
SUSIQ (MI)
SUZIEQ (KY)
SUZIQ (KY, MS, WA)
SUZEY Q (OR)
SWAMPI (AK)
SWEET PS (VA)
SWTPE (VA)
TBONE (IA)
TEACH (MI)
THE DUKE (ID)
TOOTSI (IA, MS)
TOOTSIE (AK, IA, ID)
TOOTSY (AK)
TROLL (MI, OR, WA)
TUFFY (KY)
WEEZIE (MI)
WLDBILL (ID, WA)

CHAPTER 7

There's No Business Like Show Business

ELVIS lives, and other surprises

Possibly the deepest, the most complex of the plates taken from the world of show business is one from North Carolina: **IYQYQR**. The meaning of this one will not likely be immediately clear. Hint: Say it softly a couple of times, pronouncing each letter separately and avoiding placing stress on any one letter. Got it? No? Try again. For readers who still haven't deciphered this excellent plate, it is an obscure reference to Fred Rogers of *Mr. Rogers' Neighborhood* and the way he smiles sweetly at the kiddies via the tv lens and coos, "I like you just the way you are." This plate is a sort of babytalk version of the same: I wike-ko-way-oo-are. Great stuff! The originator of this plate is to be applauded.

The never-never land of television is also responsible for **A TEAM** (MS, TX, WA), **AWAWEGO** (PA, WA, a line used with explosive grandeur by the late Jackie Gleason), **BO DUKE** and **BOSS HOG** from *The Dukes of Hazzard,* both on Iowa plates; and from *Star Trek,* **BEAMEUP** (AL, IN), **BEEMEUP** (IN), **BEMEUP** (IA, ID, KY, TX), and **BEMUSUP** (ID).

BIONIC (AK) probably refers to *The Bionic Man*, **BEAVE** (AK) and **THE BEAV** (VA) to *Leave It To Beaver,* **BIPPY** (AK) to *Laugh-In* (You bet your bippy!), **BKWEAT** (ID) to Eddie Murphy's popular character on *Saturday Night Live,* or the original Buckwheat on *Little Rascals*. Murphy's Buckwheat is the likely inspiration of **IM OTAY** (MS), **IT OTAY** (MS), and just plain **OH TAY** (AK, IA, KY, MS).

BOBALU has got to be in memory of Desi Arnaz on the old *I Love Lucy* show. One wonders if **BUBALU** (AK) is a country and western counterpart — Bubba Arnaz? The mind boggles.

Around the nation there are variations of **BWYCHD** (MS). In Washington State is a plate that reads **DONAHUE**. There are **KOJAK** (IA, KY), **DRAGNET** (WA), **DYNASTY** (IN, WA), **EYE SPY** (IA), **FIVE 0** (MS), and **JOHN BOY** (TX, WA).

Another Eddie Murphy take-off, this on the green cartoon character, is **GUMBI** (IA).

HOTLIPS (WA) doubtless refers to Margaret O'Houlihan of *M.A.S.H.*; **HULK** (AK, ID) is probably of the "Incredible" variety.

LN RNGR (WA), **TONTO 2** (IL, MI), **HIO SLVR** (IA), **KMOSAB** (TX), and **KMOSABE** (WA) — everybody remembers them. Another Washington motorist tied this one in to the make of his foreign car with the plate **KMOSAAB**. Not bad, masked man.

MZ KITY (TX) must be an old *Gunsmoke* fan, and **PALADIN** (IN, WA) harkens back to a truly distinctive adult western that was light on plot but heavy on two-fisted action.

ROSANNE has a fan in Idaho; **OPRA** has one in Washington; and Richard Chamberlain's best tv miniseries, and the novel on which it was based, have many who remember it on their plates: **SHOGUN** (AK, DE, IA, ID, IN, KY, MI, MS, TX).

Vanna White hasn't turned all those letters for nothing. She's driven about daily on **O VANNA** (ND), **VANAWHT** (TX), and **VANNA** (IA, IN).

From Hollywood and the movie industry comes **AMADEUS** (WA); **BAMBI** (MS); **BATMAN** (AK, IA, IN, MI, ND, WA) and related plates **BATCAR** (KY, MI, WA), **BATGRL** (VA), **BATMBL** (KY, MI), and **BAT MOBL** (ID). On other plates are **BONZO** (VA), **CNDRLLA** (WA) and **CNDRLA** (MI); **DAS BOOT** (ID, IN); **DUMBO** (IA, WA); **ET** (DE); **EZ RIDR** (AK, ID, MS); **GATSBY** (ID); **GIPPER** (MI); **GDZILA** (WA); **GIDGET** (AK); **GLDFNGR** (WA); **GODFTHR** (WA); **LOSTARK** (WA); **MAKMYDA** (WA); **PSYCHO** (ID, KY, WA); **RAMBO** (ID, KY, LA, MI, MS, WA); **ROBOCOP** (IA); **THE JERK** (WA); and **007** (MI, MS, TX).

Star Wars accounts for **DRKSIDE** (WA), **DROID** (MI), **OBIWAN** (AK, IA, WA), **STRSHP** (MI), and **YODA** (ID). Orson Welles's sled in the great film "Citizen Kane" must have inspired **RHOZBUD** (WA), **ROSEBD** (MI, TX), **ROSEBUD** (ID, TX, WA), **ROZBUD** (MI, WA), and **ROZEBUD** (IN).

Other plates have their origins in rock music. Of these, by far the most popular is — you guessed it — **ELVIS** (AK, DE, IA, ID, IN, KY, MI, MS, OH, WA). The long-term loyalty inspired by **THE KING** (WA) is truly amazing. Legions of aging boppers would still do anything **4 ELVIS** (MS), were he alive to accept their favors.

Rock and roll nostalgia also lives on in the likes of **BEATLS** (DE), **RINGO** (DE, IN, MI), **LET IT B** (TX), **AY JUDE** (WA), **HEY JUDE** (IN), and **SGT PEPR** (NC, WA) — not to mention **BIGBOPR** (WA) we knew what he liked — and **BOWZER** (MS), the basso profundo of the group Sha-Na-Na.

DOO WOP (IA, TX) is a generic rock refrain, and some say, a variety of rock music. Individual songs are immortalized on plates such as **CCRYDR** (MI), Chuck Berry's **JNNYBGD** (ID), Little Richard's **2DFRUTY** (VA), **LABAMBA** (WA), **MR EARL** (IA), **MLOYELO** (WA), and **RAVEON** (TX, WA).

The more recent rock scene is celebrated in **AC-DC** (TX), **BEASTY** (IA), **BN JOVI** (IA, IN), **B2B WILD** (VA), **DEF LEP** (MS), **LED HED** (MS), **LED ZEP** (MS, OR), **LE WHO** (WA), **MADONNA** (IN), **RLN STNS** (VA), **STING** (AK, IA, MI, WA), **SKYNYRD** (WA), **STONES** (MI, WA), **U2FAN**

(MI), **U2 LIVE** (MI), **VAN HALEN** (IN), and **ZEPLYN** (MS). Fans of The Grateful Dead weigh in with **DED HEAD** (ID, IN) **DEDHED** (KY), **GF DEAD** (AK), and **RU DED 2** (VA).

Though the majority of pop music plates are devoted to rock, one occasionally sees references to other musical forms. Country tunes show up in **ELVIRA** (ID, MI, WA), and **HANK JR** (MS, TX), jazz in **TAKE 5** (AK, IA, MS, TX), Dixieland in **SACHMO** (MS). Old standards appear in **BLU MOON** (IA), **EBTIDE** (AK, MI), **MOONGLO** (ID), and **TEA4 TWO** (ID). **DOO DAH** (IA) sounds like a real oldie, and a sprinkling of other varieties of pop music show up in **DJAVU** (IA), **SHBOOM** (IA, MI, WA), **MANILOW** (ID), **UPTN GRL** (WA), and **XANADU** (IA, ID, MI, TX).

At least a modest number of motorists devote their tags to the denizens of comic books, cartoons, and the funnies. Disney is represented by **DON DUCK** (WA), **ELMRFUD** (WA), **GOOFY** (AK), **KWZWABT** (WA), **LUNYTUN** (WA) and **MKY MSE** (MI). Other plate owners are responsible for **JUGHEAD** (IN) from the Archie comics, **MR MAGOO** (WA), **MTY MSE** (WA), **POGO** (IA, KY, MI, MS), and **I GO POGO** (WA), **PUDYTAT** (ID), **ARCHIE** (NY — the plate of the CEO of the comic book company), Al

Capp's **SCHMOO** (AK, IA, ID, KY), and one of the more obscure plates, **MOLENE** (TX), from the old Dick Tracy funnies. One of Tracy's arch-enemies was The Mole, whose daughter was Molene.

Of more recent vintage are **FARSIDE** (ID), **GARFLD** (AK), **HE MAN** (IL), **KUDZU** (MS), **SCUBADO** (WA), and **SMRF** (AK, ID, MI, MS, TX, WA).

Others of intermediate longevity are **HAGAR** (AK, WA), **KRYPTON**, the stuff that makes Superman droop (IN), **RD RNNR** (MI), and **SNOOPY** (TX).

Finally, there are the plates of show-biz personalities themselves. Comedian Flip Wilson's plate reads **KILLER** (CA), television tough guy Mr. T has **A TEAM III**, and Willie Mays — an entertainer of the athletic kind — has **SAY HEY** (CA).

EHHH . . . b-d-b-d-b-d-b-d, that's all, folks, except for:

AIRWLF (NH)
AIRWOLF (VA, WA)
AIRWUF (AK)
A OTAY (MS)
A SMURF (MI)
AYEJUDE (WA)
BARBDOL (IN)
BBBBBAD (KY)
BEN HUR (IA, WA)
BIGBIRD (IN, KY, WA)
BIG BYRD (IN)
BIGFOOT (IN, WA)
BIGFUT (IA)
BLONDIE (ID)
BLKBUTY (IA)
BMEUPP (VA)

BMMEUP (ID)
BN JOVI (MS)
BOGART (KY)
BONJOV (DE)
BONJVI (IA, ID, KY)
BOPPER (MS)
BOS HOG (AK, MS)
BRANDO (MI)
BRN FREE (IN)
BTYBOOP (WA)
BUCKWHT (WA)
BUCWEAT (WA)
BUKWEAT (WA)
BUKWEET (WA)
BUKWHT (WA)
BULITT (KY)
BULWKL (KY)
CATCH 22 (IN)
CATCH 23 (IN)
CHEERS (KY, MS)
CHER (MS, WY)
CNDRELA (VA)
CPT KIRK (WA)
CUDZU (KY)
DAGMAR (ID)
DAJUDG (CA)
DAJUDGE (CA)
DAJUICE (CA)
DAKULA (CA)
DAKTARE (CA)
DAKTARI (CA)
DALEIGH (CA)
DARTH (MI)
DAZYMAE (WA)
DEDHEAD (ID, IN)
DESILOU (CA)
EPRESLY (CA)
EQALISR (CA)
EQALIZR (CA)
EQALZER (CA)
EQELIZR (CA)
EQILIZR (CA)
EQLIZER (CA)
EQUALZR (CA)
EQULISR (CA)
EQULIZR (CA)
EQWLIZR (CA)
EVITA (MI)
EX-QS-ME (TX)
EXQZME (TX)
EYEGOR (A)
EZ LUVR (MS)
EZ RIDER (ID, IN)
EZ RYDR (MI, MS)
FALGUY (IA, MS, TX)
FALL GUY (IN)
FALL GY (MS)
FANTOM (ID)
FARRAH (AK)
FERGIE (AK, ID)
FLY ME (AK)
FONZ (MS, WA)
FONZIE (IA, MI, WA)
F TROOP (MS)
G DEAD (TX)
GDZILLA (TX)
GIDGIT (MI)
GODZILA (ID)
GODZLA (MI)
GONZO (IA)
GRINCH (AK, ID, IN, MI)
GUMBY (AK, KY)
GUSTO (TX)
GYPPER (CA)
GZILLA (AK)
HAWKEYE (IN)

HEEHAW (AK, IA)
HLLTWD (MS)
HLLYUD (VA)
HWY2HVN (WA)
HYNOON (WA)
HYOSLVR (WA)
JAWS (DE, IA, ID, WY)
JAWS 2 (IA)
JAWZ 2 (OR)
JEDIBUG (CA)
JEDICAR (CA)
JEDINUT (CA)
JEDITOY (CA)
JONBOY (KY, MS)
JOU DEE (MS)
KAMELOT (WA)
KATWOMN (WA)
KERMIT (AK, ND)
KINGTUT (VA)
KING KUT (VA)
KINKS (DE)
KISS (TX)
KNGFSH (KY)
KOJACK (TX)
KOJAK (TX)
KONG (VA)
KONG JR (VA)
LABOMBA (OR, WA)
LADEDI (WA)
LADY DI (KY, MS)
LA LAW (ID, KY, MS, ND)
LBAMBA (KY)
LDYDI (IL, WA)
LEDZEP (AK, WA)
LEDZEPP (WA)
LEDZPLN (WA)
LENNON (DE)
LOLITA (WA)
LUVBOAT (WA)
LUVRLY (WA)
LZORRO (MI, WA)
L8NGHT (TX)
L8NITE (KY)
MAAVLUS (WA)
MAEWEST (IN, WA)
MAGNUM (AK, IA, MI, VA)
MAGOO (ID, MI)
MAKMIDA (WA)
MAKEMYDA (SC)
MAKMYDY (WA)
ME JANE (CA, IA, ID, IN, KY)
ME JEDI (CA)
MGYVER (MS)
MISTER T (IL)
MK MY DAY (ID, IN)
MYK MOUZ (VA)
MLOYLO (WA)
MMGOOO (VA)
MOONDG (KY)
MPYTHON (IN)
MR BILL (ID)
MR LUCKY (IN)
MRS ET (KY)
MR 007 (MS)
MSPIGGY (WA)
MS SCRLT (VA)
MUPPET (MS)
MY WAY (AK)
MY3SNS (KY)
MY3SON (CO, IN, MI)
MY3SONS (WA)
MY3SONZ (WA)
NANOOK (WA)
NFORCR (TX)

NOID (MS)
NUDNIK (WA)
NUGMAN (VA)
OBWAN (WA)
ODIE (WY)
OL YELER (ID)
OL YLR (OR)
ONLY U (IA, MS, TX)
ON N ON (MS)
OOOTAY (IA, ID, IN, MS)
OPIE (ID, KY)
OPUS (ID, MI, MS)
O TAY (MS, WY)
OUR GNG (MS)
PRNTHSE (WA)
PHANTOM (IN)
PLUTO (KY)
POGO (WY)
POPEYE (IA, ID, KY, MI, TX)
POSEIDN (WA)
POSYDON (WA)
PRINCE (AK)
PS ILOVU (WA)
PS ILVU (WA)
PTR PAN (IL)
PUDYTAT (ID)
RAGMOP (WA)
RAMBO 1 (ID, IN, TX)
RAMBO 2 (AK)
RAMBRO (WA)
RDRNER (KY)
RDRUNR (KY, MI)
RERUN (IA, ND)
ROCKY (ID, KY, MI, MS)
ROOTS (WA)
RTSTUF (KY)
SAD SAK (TX)
SCHMOO (KY)
SCUBDO (WA)
SERPICO (WA)
SHAZAM (IA, ID, KY, MI)
SHAZAMM (ID)
SHBOOM (IA, MI, WA)
SHMOO (IA, MI)
SCHMOOO (IA)
SHUBOP (IA)
SKYKING (WA)
SLIMED (KY)
SLOHAND (WA)
SMERF (IN)
SMERSH (WA)
SMURF (KY)
SNOWITE (IN)
SNO WTE (MS)
SNO WYT (MS)
SPOCK (MS, TX)
STARDST (ID)
STARTRK (WA)
ST TREK (TX)
STRYKER (WA)
SUPERMN (WA)
TARZAN (AK, IA, MI, TX, WA)
TD BEAR (AK)
THE DEAD (ID, IN)
THE DUKE (IN)
THE HULK (WA)
THE WHO (AK, ID, IN, TX)
THE WIZ (AK)
THMPER (AK)
TIN MAN (TX)
TOM MIX (MS)
TONTO (KY)
TOPGUN (AK, ID, IN, MI, MS, TX, WA)

TOTO (MS)
TPGUN (KY)
TREKIE (MI, MS)
TREKKI (MS)
TREKKIE (WA)
TRIGGER (IN, WA)
TRMN8R (MS)
TRUGRIT (WA)
TWIGGY (IA)
TYSON (AK)
UPTNGRL (WA)
U-TARZN (TX)
VAMPIRA (WA)
VAMPYRE (WA)
VANAWYT (WA)
VICEFAN (WA)
WABBIT (VA)
WASCALY (WA)
WEEZY (AK)
WERWOLF (WA)
WILDTHG (WA)
WISEGUY (ID, IN, VA)
WIZEGUY (IN)
WIZ OF OZ (IN)
WLDTHNG (WA)
WLD TNG (MS)
WOLFMAN (WA)
ZEPLEN (MS)
ZEPLIN (MS)
ZEPPLN (MS)
ZERO (WA)
Z HULK (MI)
ZORBA (KY)
ZORO (WY)
ZORRO (ID, MI)
1 GRCHO (VA)

CHAPTER 8

Do As I Say

ENGARDE!

Some personalized plates are couched in the form of suggestions, which vary from the polite or the supportive to challenges and warnings. **AFTA-U** (NH) is polite; **AFTRME** (NH, WA) and **BEFOR U** (MS) is less so. The same gulf separates **BKIND** (AK) or **BHAPPI** (ID) from **BOWDOWN** (WA) or **BNASTY** (IA). By the same token, the supportive message **GOFORIT** (IA, IL, OH) differs markedly from plates like **EAT MUD** (ID, MI, MS) or **GO2HALE** (CA), or the direct warning **BUGOFF** (DE, IA, MI, MS).

Among the outpouring of car tag suggestions are others that issue invitations or offer good advice, some that are self-centered, and still others that are commercially motivated. Of the invitation plates, **AMUZ ME** (MS) is one thing, but **ABUZME** (AK)? Perhaps **ADOPTME** (ID) is on a car whose owner wants to sell it. **BESE ME** (MS) appears to hanker for kisses. Mucho.

Goodness knows what **BITE ME** (MS) wants, or what lies behind the real thrust of **CACH ME** (IL) or **BUST ME** (MS).

Texas has **HELP ME** and **HOLD ME**; Mississippi has **HIT ME** (maybe a card player) and **LIE2ME** (possibly a policeman or a polygraph operator). **TEASEME**, says an Idaho driver; **TEMP ME** invites a Texan; **PICMEUP**, offers a Washingtonian; **TAKE ME**, say plates in Mississippi and Texas. **U SAY NO**, cautions a Texas driver; **TRUST ME** (IA, IN) is the response. There could be a soap opera plot in this stuff. Maybe we could work in **PLAYRUF** (WA) and **TIEMEUP** (WA) and really make it racy.

Good, sensible advice is offered by plates like **AIM-HI** (NH), **BELT-UP** (VA) or **BKLUP** (IA), **BEYOSLF** (AL), **DREAMBIG** (NC), **EAT RITE** (IN), **NODRGS** (AK) or **JSAYNO** (ID), **RECYCLE** (IA, ID), **REDUCE** (TX), **SAVGAS** (KY), or **SAVE UP** (MI, MS). **BUY LOW** (IA, MI, MS, WA) should get together with **SELL HI** in Texas.

Of all the plates in this chapter, in fact, in the entire book, one of my favorites is of this ilk. It must belong to a motorist who has small children. This excellent plate? **PB4UGO** (VA). Parents, can you relate?

BEEFUP (TX) and **PUMPUP** (WA) sound like advice from *Saturday Night Live*'s Hans and Franz, who don't like to see guys who look like "little girlie men." **PUKRUP** (WA) sounds like more fun to me.

Some of these pieces of advice are harder to follow than others. **BEARLY** (IA) or **BGENTLE** (WA) would be a lot easier to live up to than **BE SUAVE** (VA). Either you are or you aren't. **BE YOUNG** (ID, IN) is even harder for many of us. **THKTHN** (WA) is a good deal easier to accomplish than **BE THIN** (MS).

DINE OUT (ID), **EAT-OUT** (TX), or **ESGOEAT** (WA) are far more convenient and seemly than **GONUDE** (WA) or, worse, **SKI NUDE** (VA), and a lot more pleasant than being told by a passing license plate to **SHOVIT** (IA), which, to set the record straight, belongs to a Mr. Shove, who is probably a nice fellow.

A few of these advice plates are quite general and wide open to varying interpretations: **CMUNIC8** (WA), **DECIDE** (ID), **ESCAPE** (ID), **FLEE** (MS), **LOOK** (IA), **STRIVE** (MI), **THINK**

(IA, TX), and **TRY** (MS). A modest number of others at least sound self-centered: **ASK ME** (AK, IA, OH), **COOK4ME** (WA), **DIG ME** (ID), **EN V ME** (MS), **INDULGE** (WA), **ME FRST** (NJ), and **SPOILME** (LA).

Commercial motivation is behind another grouping of these suggestion plates, such as **BI CANDI** (ID), **BIPORK** (IA), **BUY A TUX** (IN), **BUY INS** (MS), **BUY LND** (MS), **BUY MINK** (WA), **BYAHOM** (CO), **BY MY HNY** (IN), **INSURE** (DE), **INVEST** (DE), **LES SUE** (IN), **RENOV8** (ID), and **USEGAS** (IA).

A fairly large group of these plates have harsher undertones. Who knows what fascinating, dire story lies behind **BEGME** (MI). Could **DESTROY** (CA) be in the demolition business, or is there a more sinister explanation? **CMYDUST** (WA) seems to thumb its nose at other cars, as do **EAT DIRT** and **EAT DUST** (WA). **DAREME** (MI) has a rash ring to it; **DROP HER** (VA) sounds negative. **RETCH** (ID) and **GOOSU** (IN) sound less than pleasant. **LUMP IT** (MS) is a rough suggestion, **RAMMIT** (WA) even moreso. **SO SUE ME** (IN) does not immediately put you in a cheery frame of mind. **UBUGME** (ID), **UR UGLY** (TX), and **UR2SLO** (IA, IN, MI, OH, SC) have the same effect.

At the far end of the pleasantness spectrum are plates that issue warnings: **BACKOFF** (IA, IN), **BEWARE** (AK, IA, ID, MI), **BUZZ OFF** (OH), the somewhat more polite **DESIST** (CA), **ENGARDE** (ID), **GET OUT** (AK, MI, WA), **GETOVER** (WA), **IDAREU** (IA, IN, WA), **IFUDARE** (WA), **JST TRY** (MS, TX), **MOVE IT** (ID, IN, KY, MI, TX), **MOVOVR** (CT, MI), **OUT MWY** (VA), and **VAMOOSE** (WA).

AH AH (IL) carries with it an unseen but implied wagging finger. **IHRDAT** (AK) also seems to imply that someone is just **ASKN4IT** (IA). **UDLOOZ** (ID), challenges an Idaho plate; **NOWIMPS**, warns a macho Washingtonian. **GETMUP**, demands a tough Texan. Why so rough, you ask? **DONTASK** (IA, IN). It might be **RISKY-4U** (VA).

ACTTOO (WA)
ADD H20 (MS)
AFTERU (AK, IA, OH, NH)
ARISE (MI)
ASK ME (KY)
ASK 4ME (MS)
AXME (WA)
BABYME (ID, MI)
BAKOFF (IN)
BBQ14ME (ID)
B CALM (ID)
B CAREFL (IL)
B CASUAL (IN)
B CIVIL (ID)
BCOOL (AK, DE, IA, IN, MI)
BCRE8IV (KS)
BCWEAT (AK)
BCWEET (AK)
BEASY (IA)
BEBACK (IA)
BE CALM (MS)
BECIVIL (VA)
BECOOL (IA, MI, MS, VA)
B CREATV (ID)
BE FIT (MS)

BEGONE (WA)
BETCHA (AK, IA)
B FIRM (ID)
BEFREE (AK)
BE FUN (IA)
B FREEE (VA)
B GENTLE (WA)
BE GLAD (TX)
BEGOOD (IA, MI)
BE HAPE (MS)
BE HAPI (MS, TX)
BE HAP E (TX)
BE HAPPY (ID)
BEHAPY (AK, IA, ID, MS, TX)
BEHAVE (IA, MI, TX)
BEHOLD (AK, MS)
BE KIND (ID, MI, MS, TX)
BEKOOL (IA, MI, TX)
BE LOVD (ID)
BEMORE (IA)
BENICE (IA, IN, MI, MS)
BEPHYSCL (VA)
BEQUICK (IN)
BEREAL (VA)
BE SAFE (MI, MS)
BEZACT (OR)
BEXLNT (ID)
BFIT (IA)
BFURST (VA)
BGOOD (IA, IN, MS)
BGOOD4U (SC)
BGROSS (ID)
BHAPPY (AK, IA, ID, IN)
B HAPY (ID)
BIKALOT (IN)
BILLME (MI)
B JOLLY (MS)
B KOOL (MS)
BLEAN (OR)
B LOGICL (KY)
BMINE (AK)
B NICE (MS)
BN STYL (MS)
BOGGIE (MA)
BOGGY (VA)
BREAL (CA)
BREEFME (CA)
BRING IT (VA)
BSHARP (IA, KY, NC)
BSTRONG (WA)
BSUNY (AK)
B SURE (MS)
B SWEET (OR)
BSWIFT (IA)
B TWINS (MS)
BUCKLUP (AK, IA, ID, IL, IN, TX)
BUCLMUP (ID)
BUDS 4 U (OH)
BUGOF (ID)
BUG OUT (IA, MS)
BUKL UP (MS)
B UNEAK (VA)
BUNIQUE (IN)
B URSEF (MS)
BUUGLY (IA)
BUYAPIE (IN)
BUY ART (IN)
BUY BEEF (ID, IN)
BUY BUD (MI)
BUYBUY (IA)
BUY COKE (IN)
BUYCRAB (WA)
BUYGAS (WA)
BUY NOW (IN, MS)

BUY PORK (IN)
BUYSELL (WA)
BUY SOD (IN)
BUY STOX (IN)
BUY TERM (IN)
BUY 1 (ND)
BUZOFF (ID, IN, MI)
BWARE (IA, ID)
BWILD (IA, ID, MI)
BWISE (MI)
BYBEEF (IA, MI)
BY GOLD (MS)
BYLAND (IA, MS)
BYOUNG (MI)
BYPORK (IA, MI)
BZZOFF (MI)
B4ART (MI)
B4REAL (AK, MI)
CACHME (DE)
CA GIRL (IA)
CALL ME (ID)
CALL SOS (ID)
CAN IT (WA)
C ART (NC)
CAUTION (LA)
CEE ME (KY)
CELEBR8 (ID)
CHERE (AK)
CHILL (DE)
CHILOUT (WA)
CHILLOUT (WA)
CLEANUP (ID)
CLIMBHI (WA)
CLMDOWN (WA)
CMEFLY (MI)
CRYWOLF (WA)
CRY4ME (WA)
CUDDLE (MS)
CURLUP (WA)
DEALEM (KE)
DESRVIT (CA)
DNTGVUP (IN)
DO IT (MI)
DOITNOW (WA)
DOLUNCH (WA)
DORITE (SC)
DO XLR 8 (OH)
DREAM BIG (NC)
DREM-ON (AL, LA)
DROOL (IA)
DT WORY (MS)
DUCK ME (OR)
EASEUP (IA)
EAT BBQ (TX)
EAT BEEF (ID)
EATFISH (AK)
EAT FIT (ID)
EAT HOG (SC)
EAT MEX (TX)
EATMUP (MI)
EAT OUT (TX, WI)
EATOWL (OR)
EATPIE (VA)
EAT VEAL (IN)
EDUCATE (WA)
ENJOY (AK, IA, IN, KY, MI, MS)
ENJOYIT (IA, IN)
ENLITEN (WA)
ENVYME (IA, ID, MS, WI)
EXCEL (KY, MI)
EXCUSME (IN)
EXELR8 (TX)
EXHALE (WA)
EXQZME (AK)
EZ DOZ IT (ID)

EZDUZIT (AK, IA, IN)
EZ NOW (ID)
FACEIT (IN)
FADAWAY (IN)
FALO ME (IL)
FASN8ME (NC)
FASTER (ID, MI)
FASTUH (MI)
FAX IT (KY)
FLEX (MS)
FLOR IT (MS)
FLOSM (WA)
FLOSS (IA, WA)
FLOSSEM (WA)
FLOSSM (WA)
FLY HI (MS)
FLY LOW (MI)
FLY ME (TX)
FLYMOR (IA)
FLYRITE (WA)
FLYRT (WA)
FLY TWA (MS)
FLY W ME (IA, VA)
FLY4FUN (IA)
FLX4ME (WA)
FOLO ME (MS)
FOX EM (TX(
FRGITIT (WA)
GDEUPGO (ID)
GETAJOB (ID)
GET BAC (MS)
GET BACK (ID, IN)
GET BAK (MS)
GET BUSY (IA, ID, LA)
GET DOWN (IN)
GETEMUP (WA)
GET FIT (AK, ID, IN, KY, MI)
GETHOT (AK)
GET IN (TX)
GETIT (AK, ID)
GETITON (WA)
GETOFF (AK, KY, TX)
GET ON (ID)
GET ONE (MS)
GETREAL (ID, WA)
GETSOM (WA)
GETSUM (WA)
GETTAN (IA, IN, MI)
GETUMUP (WA)
GET U1 (MS, TX)
GETWELL (WA)
GETWET (AK, IA, IN, MI, VA)
GET WILD (IN)
GET YLD (MS)
GIDYUP (ID)
GIDYYUP (ID)
GIG EM (MS)
GIT BAK (MS)
GIT FIT (KY, MS)
GIT GON (MS)
GIT WET (ID)
GITY UP (MS)
GIV BLD (TX)
GIVHUGS (WA)
GIVEUP (IA, TX)
GO (MI)
GO ACURA (VA)
GOAHEAD (ID, WA)
GO ARMY (ID)
GOAWAY (IA, MI, WA)
GOBAD (IA)
GO BIKIN (VA)
GOBYBY (AK, IA)
GO EAST (VA)

GO EASY (MI, MS)
GO EZY (MS)
GOFAST (AK, ID, IN, KY, MI, MS)
GO FISH (AK, MI, ND)
GO GETM (ID)
GO GETR (IL)
GOHOME (IA)
GO HOSS (TX)
GOLOCO (KY)
GO-ON-BY (TX)
GO SLOW (ID)
GO TOIT (MS)
GOWEST (DE, IA, KY, MI)
GOWILD (IA, ID, MI, TX)
GOW4IT (MI)
GO2FARR (CA)
GO2FAST (CA)
GO2GUAM (CA)
GO2HAL (CA)
GO2 IT (MS)
GO2JAIL (CA)
GO2MARS (CA)
GO4BRK (AK)
GO4BROC (CA)
GO4BROQ (CA)
GO4BUST (CA)
GO4BUX (CA, TX)
GO4CASH (CA)
GO4FUN (CA)
GO4GSTO (CA)
GO4IT (AK, IA, IN, MI, NC, WI)
GO4LOVE (CA)
GO4 ME (TX)
GO4MORE (CA)
GO4PHD (TX)
GO 4TH (TX)
GROWUP (MI, WA)
GUESS (IN, KY)
GVFOOD (IA)
GYMMEE (NH)
GYTAJOB (CA)
GYTITON (CA)
G2BKING (CA)
HANG ON (MS, TX)
HAVE FUN (IN)
HAVFUN (AK, IA, MI, MS)
HAVMRCY (IN)
HEDEMUP (WA)
HOLD IT (TX)
HOLDOUT (IN)
HONYDO (IA)
HONYDU (IA)
HOPE (KY)
HOPE 4 US (VA)
HOP2IT (KY, MI)
HUGAKID (WA)
HUGALOT (WA)
HUG ME (ID, MI,OH)
HUGMEDO (ID)
HUGME2 (MI)
HUMOR ME (ID)
HUNI DO (TX)
HUNYDO (AK)
HURTME (KY)
HURY UP (MS)
HUSH (IA, ID)
HUSTLE (WA)
IDAREM (IA)
IDAREU (MS, VA)
IDAREU2 (IA)
IDAREYA (WA)
IHRDAT (AK)
IM ON 2U (ND)

IMPROV (WA)
INDULG (KY)
INHALE (WA)
INNOV8 (WI)
IN V ME (MS)
IOKUOK (KY)
ITL B OK (CA)
JOINUP (WA)
JOINUS (WA)
JSTASK (IA)
JSTDOIT (IA)
JUSDOIT (IN)
JUST ASK (ID)
JUSTRIME (IN)
JUZ DO IT (VA)
KACH ME (CT, TX)
KECH ME (TX)
KEEP BAC (VA)
KEEPUP (IA, MS)
KIDS 1ST (NC)
KISHME (WA)
KISME (WA)
KISNTEL (WA)
KISSME (KY, TX, WA)
KOOLIT (WA)
KTCHME (WA)
KUDLME (WA)
LAFALOT (WA)
LAFNLUV (WA)
LAYLOW (MI, MS, WA)
LEASEIT (IN)
LESCRAM (WA)
LESGO (AK, MS)
LETGO (IA, MI)
LETITBE (WA)
LETMEB (TX)
LETMEBY (WA)
LETRGO (AK)
LETSBOP (WA)
LETSGO (AK, IA, MI, MS, TX)
LETSGOO (VA)
LETSPET (WA)
LETSROC (WA)
LETSROK (WA)
LETSWIM (IN)
LETUBU (IA, MS)
LETZGO (IA)
LEZDOIT (WA)
LEZGO (TX, VA)
LINEMUP (IA, IN)
LINE UP (MS)
LISTEN (KY)
LITNUP (CT, IA, WA)
LIVITUP (IN)
LI 10 UP (FL)
LIVFAST (WA)
LIV FRE (GT)
LIVHARD (WA)
LIVVVVV (WA)
LIV2TEL (WA)
LOOKB4U (WA)
LOOKIE (IA, MS)
LOOKOUT (WA)
LOOKUP (IA, MI)
LOSE WT (MS)
LOVEME (IN, MI, TX)
LQQK (KY)
LQQKE (IA)
LQQKEE (IA, IN)
LQQKIE (IA, ID, IN, KY, MI)
LQQKY (AK, IA)
LRN2FLY (WA)
LRN2SKI (ID)
LSN2ME (KY)

LTMEBY (WA)
LTSCRUZ (WA)
LTS GO (MS)
LTSPLAY (WA)
LTSPRTY (WA)
LTSROCK (WA)
LUKOUT (IA, TX(
LUSEN-UP (VA)
LUSNUP (MS)
LUV KIDS (VA)
LUVME (IA, TX)
LUVMOR (IA)
LYTENUP (WA)
MAKE ME (MS)
MAKE UP (MS)
MARYME (IA, ID)
MIX ME1 (VA)
MOTIV8 (WI)
MUSH (DE)
NIXLUV (ID)
NJOYIT (IA)
NO SWET (MS)
NOTNOW (DE)
NOT 4 U (ND)
NUKE IT (MS)
NUTS 2U (IA, OH)
NVEST (MS, WA)
NVRQIT (WI)
NVME (NC)
OBEGUD (WA)
OBYONE (IA)
OBYTWO (IA)
OGO ONN (MS)
ORELAX (WA)
ONWARD (IA)
ORGNIZE (WA)
PARTDWN (CA)
PARTYHI (CA)
PARTYON (CA)
PARTYUP (CA)
PASSME (AK, MS, TX)
PAY ME (MS, TX)
PAY NOW (MI)
PAY UP (IA, MS, TX)
PCUR UP (TX)
PEELME (WA)
PEELOUT (WA)
PHONEME (WA)
PICMUP (WA)
PIGOUT (MS, WA)
PLAY ME (ID, TX)
PLAMOR (IA)
PLA2WIN (WA)
PLA2WN (AK, WA)
PLA2WYN (WA)
PLEASME (WA)
PRA4SNO (ID)
PRTYNKD (WA)
PUBLISH (VA)
QUIT (VA)
QUITIT (IA)
RACEME (CT, IN, MI, WA)
RACEON (IA)
RACKEM (MI, WA)
RACM (WA)
RACKMUP (WA)
READ (IA)
READON (IA)
RECYKL (TX)
REELAAX (IA)
RELAX (IA, ID, MS)
RELAXX (MS)
RENTIT (ID)
RESQME (IN, WA)
RETRACT (WA)
REUSEIT (ID)

REVEL (AK)
RIDE EM (TX)
RIDE M (TX)
RIP (KY)
ROCK ME (ID)
ROC ME (ND)
ROCK ON (TX)
ROLLON (AK, IA, MI)
ROW4FUN (WA)
R.S.V.P. (KY, MI, TX)
RUNAMUK (ID, WA)
RUN SAFE (ID)
SADDLUP (AK, IA)
SADL-UP (ID, TX)
SAILON (VA)
SALUTE (IA)
SAVE (TX)
SAVE ME (MS)
SAVE H2O (ID)
SAVGAS (SC)
SAYBY (WA)
SAYBYBY (WA)
SAYBYE (WA)
SAYCBON (WA)
SAYCHZ (WA)
SAYCHZZ (WA)
SAYNO (AK, IA, IN, KY, MI, MS)
SAYYESS (AK, MI, MS)
SCAT (IA)
SCOOT (KY)
SEDUCE (MI)
SEE-US (KY)
SEE-3D (KY)
SEND4US (ID)
SHAKEIT (WA)
SHAKEME (IA, ID)
SHAP-UP (OR)
SHHH (IA, TX)
SHHHH (IA, TX)
SHINEON (WA)
SHOUT (IA)
SHOWME (AK, IA, ID, MS)
SHUSH (IA)
SICKEM (ID)
SING (IA, MI)
SKIFREQ (WA)
SKI H2O (TX)
SKINAKD (WA)
SKISAF (IA)
SKI SNO (TX)
SKI USA (TX)
SKI2DI (AK, IA)
SKI2DY (AK)
SKI2ME (AK)
SKI4FN (AK)
SKI4IT (AK)
SK84FN (WA)
SK84FUN (WA)
SLAP ME (TX)
SLEEP (KY)
SLIMUP (IA)
SLPWELL (ID)
SMILE (AK, IA, KY, MI, VA)
SMIRK (IA)
SMKGSUX (WA)
SMOOCH (MI)
SMYLE (AK)
SNEEZE (IA)
SNIF (IA)
SNIFLE (IA)
SNIVEL (ID)
SNO4ME (AK)
SNO 4 US (VA)
SOSUME (KY)

SPEND (KY)
SQEZME (DE)
SQZE ME (MS)
SQZ ME (MS)
SRFNAKD (WA)
STAYFIT (WA)
STEPHI (AK)
STOP (DE, KY)
STOPIT (AK)
SUCEED (TX)
SUEME (TX, WA)
SUFFER (IA)
SURFNOT (WA)
SWIM (MI)
TAKITEZ (WA)
TAKME (WA)
TALK (IA)
TALK2ME (IA)
TEAS ME (MS)
TEEZME (MI)
TELL ME (MS)
TEND2IT (CA)
THGUY4U (VA)
THK BIG (TX)
THK SNOW (VA)
TIP ME (MS)
TKOFF (WA)
TLKALOT (WA)
TNK SNO (NJ)
TONEUP (WA)
TRNMEON (WA)
TRUS ME (MI)
TRUST (IA, MI)
TRYBUD (WA)
TRYLAMB (WA)
TRYME (AK, IA, ID, MI, MS, WA)
TRYME2 (MS, WA)
TRYRCRY (WA)
TRY TO (IA)
TUFFIT (ID)
TY1 ON (KY)
UBCOOL (IA)
UBFAT (ID)
UBNICE (WA)
UBUIBI (KY)
UBUKLUP (WA)
UBU (AK, IA, ID)
UCAN W8 (MS)
U CANT (MS)
UDLOOZ (ID)
UDLOSE (ID, KY)
UDLOZE (ID)
U-FLOSS (TX)
UGUESS (IA)
UKNDUIT (WA)
UMOVE (WA)
UNAYGO (WA)
UNDOIT (AK)
U NUTS (TX)
UO ME (TX)
UPAYME (ID)
UNWIND (IA, MI, TX)
URELAX (MS, WA)
URENTIT (WA)
URN4IT (KY)
U R SLO (TX)
U-R-SUM 1 (TX)
URTOSLO (SC)
UR2NEAR (WA)
UR2NVS (WA)
UR2SLO (IA, IN, MI, OH, SC)
UR2SLOW (IA, ID, WA)
UR2UGLY (WA)
USEZIP (WI)

U SMILE (MS)
UUGLY (WA)
UWISH (IA)
U2CLOS (WA)
U2SLO (MI)
U2SLOW (WA)
WACHIT (AK)
WAKEUP (MI, MS, TX, WA)
WALKON (WA)
WASHIT (ID, MI, WA)
WASHME (TX, WA)
WATCHIT (ID)
WAVWBY (KY)
WHOA (IA, IN)
WIN BIG (TX)
WINGIT (AK, IA, KY)
WISEUP (WA)
WNARACE (WA)
WORKOUT (WA)
WRITE (IA, TX)
WRK4IT (AK)
W8FORME (WA)
W8LIFT (WA)
W84ME (WA)
W84MEE (WA)
W8UP4ME (VA)
XCAPE (AK)
XCELR8 (IN, MI, MS)
XCITME (MI)
XCUZME (MI)
X*PRESS (TX)
XQSME (IN)
XQSSME (IN)
X QZ ME (MI, OH)
XQUZME (IN, MI)
XQZME (IN)
XRCISE (MI)
XXRADON (IN)
YURSLO (ID)
100K (ID)
123HOP (IA)
4 GET IT (ID, MI, OH)
4GMENOT (ID)
4GTNOT (AK)
4 PLAY 2 (OH)

CHAPTER 9

Shout It Out

Exclamations, greetings, and ALOHA.

Among the most curious of personalized plates are those that appear as exclamations, or exclamation-like noises. When you see one of these roll past, you can only guess at its exact meaning, though some have more discernible explanations than others. **AHHH** (KY, NH) is clearly an expression of satisfaction, probably in the car itself. But what of **AHSO** (IA, NH, TX)? Sounds Japanese, but why? Is the driver of Japanese descent, or was the car made there? Or, like the popular **BANZAI** (AK, IA, ID, MI, MS, TX, WA), is it just an expression of satisfaction in the car's looks or speed?

Is **AA CHOO** (TX) an allergist or someone suffering from allergy? What is **AHAHA** (NH) laughing at, and with what is the Yankee-accented **AH-YUP** (NH) agreeing? Is **AHWOMEN** (WA) an avid appreciator of the fair sex, or is this a feminist reprise to the usual end of prayer — amen? Is **ALLYOOP** (ID) a trapeze artist or acrobat? Is **AKPHHT** (IA) mimicking the all-purpose sound made by Bill the Cat of funnies fame? Are the originators of **HI YO** (MS) and **AWAAAAY** (WA) imitating the Lone Ranger's customary exit line?

Sure and **BEGORA** (AK), there are some strange plates in this category, **BGORGE** (AK). **AW YEAH** (MS). **ANHOW** (ID)! **EXQZME** (MS) if I'm not sure what all of 'em mean, but **GDGRIEF** (WA). **DANG-ME** (TX) if I know what or who a Texas driver is trying to scare with **BOOO**, or just what **BOYOBOY** (WA) is so happy about, or why **BUTBUT** (AK) seems to be stammering. **EARS2U** if you can figure it out and shout **EUREKA** (AK, MI). Speaking of that cliched expression, someone once said Eureka! in front of Chico Marx. That quick-witted comic replied, "You don-a smell-a so good-a youself." **BIGADD** (WA) he was clever. **FERSURE** (WA), **FURSURE** (WA).

The exclamations on some plates sound old fashioned: **GADZOOK** (WA), which I have never seen used in the singular; **EGADS** (MI), which sounds stuffily British; the proper Virginian **DEA DEA**; **FIDL DD** (TX); **GR8SCOT** (IN); **HANGIT** (WA); **HIP HIP** (MS); **INDEED** (IA); **JEEPERS** (ID, WA); **MYMY** (AK, MI); **OKYDOKY** (WA); **O MERCI** (ID); **PSHAW** (IA, WA); **TSK** (ID); **TUT TUT** (IN, MS); or **ZOUNDS** (AK).

Others sound more current: **BAAAD** (MS), **UNREAL** (MS), **WO DUDE** (MS), and **WUTEVR** (ID), or street-smart, as in **CHOMAMA** (WA), **JOMAMA** (AK, IA, ID, MS), **SAY HEY** (MS), **SAY MAN** (MS), **UMAMA** (IA, MS), and **YOMAMA** (AK, IA, IN, MI, MS, TX).

A fair number of these plates are high in connotative meaning. **DOWAHH** (WA) puts one in mind of yesteryear's singing group Tony Orlando and Dawn. It was Dawn who got to sing the do-wah part, plus an occasional **DOO WOP** (ID, IN, MI) for variety. But never a **DOO DAH** (ID, KY) or a **DODADAY** (WA). That was the way they doo-dah'd in a much earlier day.

Is **MM GOOD** (MS) a steady Campbell Soup customer? What is **LAND-HO** (MS, WA) — sailor or realtor? **TOBADD** (VA) we don't know if **WEDOGGY** (ID) is someone who watches

Beverly Hillbillies reruns, or if **WHOOPIE** (WA) is a Goldberg fan, or what the story is behind **2THERSQ** (NC).

Speaking with a foreign accent are such plates as **AH-RIBA** (TX), reminiscent of the song "La Bamba"; **C BOHN**, which must come from the French part of North Dakota; **BLIMEY** (MI); **DENADA** (TX, WA); **HOOTMON** (WA); **KEBELLA** (WA); **MAMA MIA** (VA); **OLAY** (IA); **OMERDE** (WA), which wouldn't have made it past the censors in most states; **OUIOUI** (ID, MS, WA); **PROSIT** (TX); **SAY MOI** (TX, WA); **SCUZI** (WA); **TALEHO** (AK, MS, WA); and **VOILA** (IA, MI, WA).

ATABOY and **ATAGAL** belong to a Texas husband and wife; **AW NUTS** goes with a bolt and screw company in that same state; **KABOOM** is the plate of a Mr. Boom in Iowa, as well as fellow boomers in Texas and Washington. **HOHO** is the plate of a Mr. Hoholick in Texas; **MERCEME** is on a Virginia Mercedes.

Quite a lot of these exclamation plates sound positive: **AHH YES** (TX) sounds oh so satisfied, as do **HAPIDA** (TX), **HM-BOY** (TX), **HEL-YEA** (TX), **NOPRBLM** (ID, IN, WA), **OBOY** (TX, WA), **OHWOW** (AK, IN, KY, MS, WA), **OK BABE** (CT), **OOWEE** (MS), **OOHLALA** (AK, IA, ID, IN), and **RAHRAH** (WA). **TADAAH** (MI) sounds triumphant, **HEEHEE** (WA) and **TEEHEE** (ID, IL, MI, WA) delighted, **WAAHOO** (MS) and **YIPPEE** (IN, MI, MS, TX) jubilant. If it's good news, then **MZLTOV** (AK).

Apparently less pleased with things are **AARGH** (TX), **AHDANG** (WA), **DOGGONE** (IA), **HO HUM** (ID, IN, KY, MS), **HUMBUG** (AK, ID, KY, MS), **MAYDAY** (MI), **NOTNOW** (AK, IN, MS), **NOWAY** (AK, IN, MS), **OH DARN** (IN), **OH HECK** (ID, VA), **OH HALE** (MS), and **OPOOP** (WA). **OMYGOD** (IA) sounds downright alarmed, **PHOOEY** (IA, TX) disgusted, **SIGHHH** (WA) and **SOBEIT** (IN) resigned.

Still less positive are **FOOE 2U** (OH), **GOLDAM** (WA), **NUTS 2 U** (MI, OH), **U JERK** (MS), **ULOSER** (IA), and **UTURKY** (WA). **OI VAI** (VA).

WHEW (MS), there are so many of these plates that could be included here. **OOHWELL** (TX), it's a good thing I **LUV TO** (TX) do this stuff. **PSSSST** (ID). Don't tell anyone I said so, but writing about these plates is a **PSACAKE** (IN).

AAAAHH (ID, MI)
AAARGH (TX)
AAH (DE)
AAHHH (MI)
ACHOO (TX, WA)
AFTA-U (TX)
AH (TX)
AH-AH (TX)
AHCHOO (IN, KY, MI, TX, WA)

AH HA (IN, TX)
AH HECK (IN)
AHHHHHH (IN)
AHH LIFE (IN)
AHH YES (TX)
AHLIFE (ID, MI)
AH YEAH (MS)
AH2FLY (ID)
ALIOOP (ID)
ALRITE (KY)
AND HOW (MI)
ANYTYM (MI)
ARRRGH (ID, KY)
AT-A-GRL (TX)
AT EASE (MS)
AT LAST (ID, MI)
AU DAD (MS)
AU MOM (MS)
AWRITE (ID)
AYUH (AK)
BAAD (MS)
BA HAHA (MS)
BANZII (ID)
BBANZAI (VA)
B-BEEP (KY)
BEABEEP (IN)
BE BEEP (ID, MI, MS)
BEEBEEP (IN)
BEEEEP (TX)
BEEP (KY, MI)
BGOSH (VA)
BINGO (MS)
BLASTIT (ID)
BONZAI (ID, IN, KY, MS)
BONZI (MS)
BOOM (MI)
BOOWHO (ID)
BOUTIME (ID)
BRAZZZ (CA)
BRAZZZZ (CA)
BRAVO (WA)
BRRR (ID)
BRRRR (AK)
BRRRRR (ID)
BRRRRRR (VA)
BUT-MA (KY)
CANDO (WA)
CAN-DU (OR)
CDNT W8 (MS)
CERIOLY (PA)
C HEAR (KY)
DADGUM (IA, WA)
DA HE GO (TX)
DATSME (WA)
DFN8LY (KY)
DIDNOT (WA)
DIGGITY (WA)
DITTO (MI)
DODAH (WA)
DODAHH (WA)
DOODAH (KY)
DOGONIT (IN)
EAT DUST (IN)
EEEE (MI)
EEEEE (MS)
EEEEK (WA)
EEEK (MS)
EEE HA (TX)
EEEHAA (WA)
EEK (IN, KY, MI)
EEK EEK (MS)
EEEYOWW (WA)
EENUFF (MI)
EEYAHOO (WA)
EGADD (AK)
ENUF (MI)

EXQSME (DE, MS)
EZ NOW (MS)
FAIRNUF (WA)
FORSURE (IN)
FUGITIT (MS)
GDGOLLY (WA)
GDYUP (MI)
GEEHAW (AK, MI)
GEE-KIDD (VA)
GEEWHIZ (IN)
GEE WIZ (MI, MS)
GETDOWN (IA)
GETEUP (AK, IA)
GETIUP (MS)
GET T UP (TX)
GEWHIZ (ID)
GETYUP (TX)
GIDEUP (IA, MI)
GIDIUP (IA)
GIDY-EP (TX)
GIDYUP (AK, IA, ID, KY, TX)
GILOVIT (LA)
GIMME (MS)
GIT E UP (ND)
GITIUP (MS)
GITY UP (TX)
GLORYB (AK)
GOBABE (IA)
GOGOGO (MS, OR)
GOLLY-G (TX)
GOSH (AK)
GOTCHA (AK, IA, ID, MI)
GOTIT (IA)
GRR (IN, MS)
GROWL (TX)
GRRR (ID, MI, MS, TX)
GRRRR (IN, KY, MI, TX)
GRRRRR (ID, IN, MI, MS, TX)
GRRRRRR (ID)
GWHIZ (IA, NH)
GWHIZZ (IA, NH)
GWIZZZ (VA)
GYTEUP (CA)
GYTIUP (CA)
GYTREAL (CA)
GYTTEUP (CA)
GYTTUP (CA)
HA (NH)
HA HA (IN)
HAHAHA (AK, IN, MI)
HAIL NO (MS)
HARES2U (IA)
HAR HAR (MS)
HAWHAW (WA)
HECK (IN, KY, MI, WA)
HEEHEE (KY)
HEIDIHO (IN)
HELP (AK, ID, MS, TX)
HELP ME (MS)
HERENOW (WA)
HEY HEY (MI)
HEYNOW (IA)
HICCUP (TX)
HITIME (MI)
HIYOH (WA)
HLYCOW (IA, VA)
HMMM (AK, MS)
HMMMM (IN)
HMMMMM (MI, MS)
HO HO (KY)
HOLYCOW (IA, ID, IN)
HOHOHO (AK, ID, MI)
HOO HOO (TX)
HOTDAWG (WA)

HOW NICE (ID)
HRUMPH TX)
HUMMBUG (ID)
HUSH (MS)
HUSH UP (MS)
HYDEEHO (WA)
HYDHO (WA)
IGOTCHA (IA)
IHEEYA (MS)
IIBAD (MI)
IIMUCH (MI)
IKNOW (MI)
ILOVE U (MS)
ILOVU2 (MS)
INEWIT (WA)
IOSILVR (WA)
IOSLVR (WA)
I TOLDU (MI)
JEEPRS (KY)
JEEWHIZ (CA)
JEEWIZ (CA)
JEEZ (CA)
JOMAMA (AK, IA, ID, MS)
KABOOM (KY)
KERBOOM (WA)
KOOOOEE (WA)
KRRUNCH (VA)
LOVE II (MS)
LUV YA (TX)
MAAYBE (WA)
MAYBE (MS)
MAY-DA (KY)
MEE MEE (MS)
ME TOO (ID, MI, MS)
MMBABY (AK)
MMMMMM (MI)
MYMY (AK, MI)
MY MY MY (AK, MI, OH)
MYOHMY (ID)
MYWORD (KY)
MZL TOF (TX)
NEXTIME (WA)
NIC TRY (MS)
NJOKE (NJ)
NOBIGEE (ID)
NOBULL (IA, MI, WA)
NODEAL (WA)
NO DOUBT (MS)
NO KIDN (MS)
NO MO (KY, MS)
NO MORE (MS)
NO PROB (MS, VA)
NOSWET (AK, ID)
NOTBAD (MI)
NO TELN (MS)
NO WAY (AK, IN, MS)
NOT ME (MS)
NOT SO (MS, TX)
NOT YET (MS)
NUTTS (ID)
NVR AGN (MS)
NVRMIND (WA)
NVRMND (AK)
NYAAAH (KY)
OBINGO (WA)
O BULL (MS)
OCRUD (IA)
ODEARIE (WA)
OFFUD (WA)
OFFWEGO (WA)
OGLORY (ID)
OGWHIZ (IA)
OHANGEL (VA)
OH BABE (MS)
OHBABY (AK, IA, ID, IN, KY, MS, ND, WA)

OHBOY (IA, MS)
OH BUNK (IN)
OH DEER (MS)
OHECK (IN)
OHGOSH (WA)
OHHEC (DE)
OHHNOOO (ID)
OHHUH (VA)
OHHMY (IA)
OH JJ (VA)
OHKAY (ID, WA)
OHMAN (AK)
OH MY (KY, MS)
OHMYMY (MI)
OHNO (ID, MI)
OH NUTS (MS)
OH OH (MS)
OH RATS (MI)
OHWELL (KY)
OHYAY (AK)
OHYEA (AK, ID, MS)
OH YEAA (MS)
OH YEAH (IN)
OH YES (ID, MS)
O JOY (ID)
OK (ID)
OKDOKE (ID, MS)
OKFINE (ID, MI)
OKOKOK (WA)
O ME (MS)
OMERCY (IA, WA)
OMGOSH (AK)
O MY (MI, MS)
OMYGAWD (WA)
OMYGOD (WA)
OMYGOSH (TX, WA)
O MY WORD (VA)
O NOOOO (MS)
OOBABY (IA, MS, TX)
OO BULL (TX)
OOEE (MS)
OOHBOY (IA, TX)
OOH NOO (MS)
OOH-WEE (LA, MS, TX)
OOH YEH (IN)
OO LALA (ID, MS, TX)
OOOAHH (IA)
OOOAHHH (VA)
OOO EEE (MS)
OOOO AH (VA)
OOOOPS (OR)
OOOO WEE (IN)
OOPS (IA, KY, TX, VA, WY)
OOPSIE (TX)
OOW WEE (MS)
OOWEEE (MS)
OPOOH (MI, TX, WA)
ORATS (TX, WA)
OSHESH (WA)
OSHOOT (DE)
O SHUX (MS)
OSURE (IA)
OUCH (MS)
OUI (MS, WY)
OUCHHH (MS)
OVCORSE (IN)
O WELL (MS, TX)
O WOW (TX)
O YEA (MS)
OYEAH (IA, ID, MS)
O2CARE (ID)
O4SURE (AK)
PARTYHO (CA)
PARTYTYM (CA)
PEKEBU (WA)

PHINALY (WA)
PKABOO (WA)
PLEASE (TX)
PRESTO (AK, IA, TX)
PROST (WA)
PTYTYM (VA)
PUFPUF (WA)
RATS (ID, VA)
REALLY (MS)
SAAY (WY)
SAME2U (CO, ID, KY)
SAY (IA)
SAYHEY (KY)
SCUZEME (ID)
SCUZME (WA)
SEZ ME (MS)
SHAZAM (WA)
SHAZZAM (WA)
SHEESH (TX)
SHE-SH (KY)
SHZAM (WA)
SICEM (KY, WA)
SILLY U (CT)
SKDOO (IA)
SOITGOZ (WA)
SPLAT (ID, IN, MS)
SQUEAK (ID)
SRPRIZ (AK)
SURE (MS)
SUREDO (IA)
SUREIDO (WA)
SURELY (AK, IA)
SURE UR (MS)
SURFSUP (ID)
TA DA (MS)
TA DAA (MS)
TADAH (MI)
TAHDAH (ID, WA)
TALEEHO (WA)
TALEYHO (WA)
TALIHO (AK, MS)
TALLEHO (WA)
TALLEYO (WA)
TALLYHO (IA)
TALY HO (MS)
THANKS (AK, IA, IN, MS)
THANKU (IA, ID, IN, MI, MS)
THANX (AK, IA, MS)
THNK U (MS)
TIMMBR (ID)
TOBADD (VA)
TOO BAD (MI)
TOUCHE (IA, ID, MI, MS)
TUFLUCK (IA)
TUFLUK (IA, MI)
TUSH (ID)
UANIMAL (WA)
UBECHA (ID, WA)
UBET (AK, ID, KY)
UBETCHA (AK, IA, WA)
UBETT (IA)
UBETU (WA)
UBETYA (IA, WA)
UDAWG (WA)
UDEVIL (WA)
UDEVILU (IN, WA)
UGH (WA)
UHHUH (IA, ID, IN, KY, MI, MS)
U IDIOT (MS)
U LOOZ (MS)
U LOSE (MS)
ULOSER (IA)
U LOSE2 (MS)
UMMGOOD (WA)

UMMHUM (WA)
UMOMA (IA)
UNOIT (DE, KY)
UREKA (TX)
UTURKE (WA)
UUBET (WA)
U UGLY (MS)
UULALA (IN)
U WIN (MS)
U WISH (IN, KY, MS)
U2BUDY (KY)
WAAAAAH (WA)
WAGONHO (WA)
WAHOO (AK, IA,MS)
WAM-BAM (TX)
WATEVER (IN)
WAY OUT (MS)
WEGOTYA (CA)
WHATEVR (AK, IA, SC)
WHEE (AK, WY)
WHEEE (AK)
WHEEEE (AK, MI)
WHEEEEE (SC)
WHOA (ID, MI, TX, WY)
WHOA LUV (VA)
WHOOOP (TX)
WHOOP (IN)
WHOOPEE (WA)
WHOOPIE (WA)
WHOPIE (WA)
WHYNOT (KY)
WOBABY (VA)
WOO (ID)
WOO ME (KY)
WOOOO (ID)
WOOF (ID)
WOOMAN (AK)
WOOPEE (AK, MS)
WOO WOO (MS)
WOPARTY (VA)
WOTFUN (IA)
WOOOW (MI)
WOW (IA, MI, SC, WY)
WOWEE (ID)
WOWMAN (IA)
WTAGUY (CT)
WUPDEDO (WA)
X-CUS-ME (TX)
XCUZ ME (TX)
XQQZME (KY)
XQSE ME (MS, TX)
XQSME (AK)
XQSMEE (VA)
XQUS ME (MS)
XQZME (TX, UT)
YAH HAA (TX)
YAHOO (AK, IN, MI, TX)
YAHU (WY)
YAKYAK (KY)
YARIGHT (ID)
YEA BOY (TX)
YEAHBOY (WA)
YEAHHHH (WA)
YEAHOO (IA)
YEA 4 ME (TX)
YEEEES (IA)
YEEEEHA (WA)
YEEEHA (KY, MS, WA)
YEEEHAA (ID, MS, TX)
YEEHAAA (WA)
YEEHAAW (WA)
YEE HAH (MS, TX, WA)
YEEHAW (KY, TX, WA)
YEOW (MS)
YEP (MS)
YEP YEP (MS)

YES (AK)
YESDEAR (WA)
YESDEER (WA)
YES MAM (MS)
YESSAM (TX)
YES SIR (MS)
YES YES (MS)
YIKES (AK, IA, IN, TX, WA)
YIP PEA (TX)
YIPEE (AK, WA)
YIPEEE (AK)
YIPES (WA)
YOUBET (KY)
YOUWISH (WA)
YOW (MS)
YOWSER (OR)
YOWZA (MS)
YUMYUM (AK, MI, MS)
ZIPZAP (KY)
2 YOU 2 (MS)
4GETIT (AK)
4GETU (VA)
4 SOOTH (KY)

An offshoot of these exclamation plates are those that are greetings or farewells, from the homey **HI YAWL** (MS) or **HOWDY** (AK, IA, IN, KY, MS) to the more exotic **ALOHA** (AK, DE, IA, ID, IN, KY, MS), **BONJOUR** (IN, WA), **BONSOIR** (VA), **GUTNTAG** (WA), **SALAAM** (MI), and **SHALOM** (KY, MI, WA).

If memory serves, **ONGAWA** (TX) was the way the locals greeted each other in old Tarzan movies, and many of us first heard **ADIOS** (AK, DE, IA, ID, IN, TX) in westerns, adult or otherwise, before we studied Spanish in school. We picked up **AVAST** (MI) from swashbuckling pirate films, and the first **CIAO** (AK, IA, ID, KY, MI) to reach these ears was from Italian movies.

HEYVERN actually belongs to an Iowan named Vernon but reminds you of a certain inmate of tv and the movies — you know, the one with bug eyes and a mouth the size of Rhode Island. **GIDDAY** (ID) got an enormous boost in popularity from the movie *Crocodile Dundee,* and **HEY HAE** (TX) sounds like Fat Albert from the old Cosby cartoon show.

HEY LUV (MI, TX) likely refers to the opening music from Garrison Keillor's radio show; **BYBYLV** (AK) probably is in honor of the Everly Brothers. From out of the deepest '60s comes **L8RG8R** (AK, KY, PA).

Sounding more like current teen-talk are **HEYDUDE** (ID, WA), **CUDUDE** (VA), **HIFIVE** (WA), **LTR DUDE** (WA), **SAYHAY** (WA), and **YO BABY** (AK, IA, ID, IN, MI, MS, SC). Filled with youthful affection are **HEY QT** (IA, TX, VA), **HIBABE** (AK, ID, MI, MS, TX), **HI BABY** (TX), **HI DOLL** (ID), and **HI FOX** (AK).

Written in the language of older folks are **FARWELL** (WA), **HEIDIHO** (ID), **HEIDI HI** (VA), **HOW-D** (TX), **TAHTAH** (CO), and **YOO HOO** (MS). Those of us who are just the right age will recall that **UPNAWAY** (WA) was Superman's way of saying **BYEBYE** (AK, KY, MI, VA). **ODAD** (MS) also sounds familiar. That's the way my children always greet me when they need cash.

Well, **SAYHEY** (IA, WA), that's about enough on this subject. **ILLBCNU** (KY, OR, WA) — possibly in all the old familiar places.

AADIOS (MI)
AALOHA (TX)
AAY YOO (TX)
ADIEU (ID, MI, TX)
AH-DIOS (TX)
AH-LO-HA (TX)
AHOY (AK, IA, ID)
ALOHA 90 (VA)
AWAIGO (MI)
BCNU (CO, IN, KY)
BCNUL8R (ID)
BCNU2 (ID)
BCNYA (MI)
BCNYA2 (MS)
BCN YOU (WI)
BE CNU (MI, MS)
BI-YAL (KY)
BI YALL (MS)
BI YAWL (VA)
BONJOR (IA)
BY (IA)
BYBY (AK, WY)
BYBYE (IN)
BYBY 2U (MS)
BYE (AK, WY)
BYEBY (IA)
BYE BYE (ID, IL)
BYEGUY (IA, MS)
BYENOW (AK, WA)
BYE YAL (MS)
BYE 2 U (MS)
BY2YOU (KY)
BY4NOW (AK, WA)
CEE YA (KY)
CIAO (WY)
C U (VA)
CU BYBY (UT)
C U BYE (MI, MS)
CU L8R (VA)
CUL8TR (KY)
CYA (AK, IA, IN, MS)
CYAA (IA)
CYABYE (AK, IA, IN)
CYALATR (AL, WA)
CYAL8ER (WA)
CYAL8R (WA)
C YALL (MS)
C YAWL (VA)
EHDUDE (ID)
GATA GO (TX)
GBYE (IA)
GDAY (AK, IA, WA)
GOODBY (AK, MI, MS)
GOTA GO (MS)
GOT2GO (IA, MS)
GOT 11GO (VA)
GTTARUN (WA)
HA-DO (NH)
HAYDUDE (WA)
HA-Y-E (NH)

HAYMAN (MS)
HAYOU (VA)
HAYU (IA)
HELLO (AK, ID, IN, KY)
HELO2U (TX)
HEY (ID, MS)
HEYBOY (IA)
HEY BUB (MI)
HEY BUD (IN, MI)
HEYDOC (ID)
HEYFOX (AK, IL, TX)
HEYHEY (AK, IN)
HEYHO (AK)
HEY MA (ND)
HEYMAN (ID, MS, VA)
HEYMOM (KY)
HEYMON (IA, KY, MI, MS, TX, WA)
HEY NOW (AK, ID, IN, MI, MS)
HEY PAL (TX)
HEYTHR (VA)
HEY U (KY, MI, MS, WY)
HEYVRN (IA)
HEY YAL (MS)
HEYYALL (IN)
HEY YO (MS)
HEYYOU (IA, MI, MS, OH, SC)
HI (AK, IA)
HIBOY (IA)
HIBUD (IA)
HI BY (MS)
HI D (MS, TX)
HI-D-DO (TX)
HI DEE (MS)
HI DERE (TX)
HI DI (TX, VA)
HI DUDE (IA, MS, VA)
HIGH5 (IA)
HIGOD (AK)
HIGUY (IA)
HI GUYS (ID)
HIHO (AK, IN)
HIITSME (IN)
HI KID (TX)
HILADY (AK)
HI LOVE (TX)
HI MOM (IN, KY)
HIQTPI (VA)
HIQUTY (VA)
HITHERE (ID)
HI U ALL (OH)
HI U QT (IL)
HIYA (IA, MS)
HI YAL (MS)
HIYALL (AK, IA, ID, IN, KY, MS, OH)
HI YA QT (MS, OH)
HI2UAL (VA)
HOW-DE (TX)
HOWDEE (TX)
HOWDIE (ID, MS, TX)
HOWDYY (TX)
HOW-UAL (KY)
HOWWDY (IA)
HULLO (IA)
HWDY (WY)
HY-YAL (KY)
HY YALL (TX)
IBCINU (AK)
IBCN U (AK, DE, ID, KY, MI, OH, SC)
IBCNU 2 (MS)
IB GONE (MI)
IBZNU (ID)

ICU (AK)
ICUNAYL (NC)
ILBCNU (AK, IN, WA)
ILBCNU2 (WA)
ILBCNYA (WA)
ILLBZNU (WA)
ILL CU (KY)
ILLCU2 (WA)
IM-GON (KY)
LATER (MI)
L8TER (MS)
NICE2CU (IN)
OK BYE (IN, KY)
SEEEYA (MI)
SEE U 2 (MS)
SEE YA (IN, KY, MI, MS)
SEE YAA (IN, MI)
SEEYAH (MI)
SEYAH (IN)
SEE YAL (MS)
SEE YA2 (MS)
SEE YOU (MS)
SHOLOM (AK)
SOLONG (AK, IA, IN, MI)
TAA (MS)
TA TA (MS)
TALLYHO (ID)
TUTALOO (WA)
TUTALU (WA)
UPNAWY (WA)
YO (KY, MS)
YOBABE (IA, MS)
YO BABI (MS)
YOBABIE (VA)
YOBUBBA (ID)
YOCUZ (SC)
YODUDE (IA, ID, KY, MS)
YOHO (IA, MI)
YOO HOO (MS)
ZULATER (IN)
Z UL8R (ND)

CHAPTER 10

Every Act An Animal Act

AARDVRK, ZEBRA, and other BEASTLY plates.

Most of us are crazy about all creatures, great and small. They travel with us wherever we go — on our license plates. Some travel with a lot of us. Of all our animal friends, the most popular on personalized plates are the fearsome **SHARK** (AK, IA, ID, IN, KY, MI, MS, TX, WA) and **TIGER** (AK, IA, ID, IN, KY, MI, MS), plus the wily **TOMCAT** (AK, DE, IA, ID, IL, IN, KY, MI).

Next in popularity are the nutsy **SQUIRL** (AK, IA, ID, KY, MI, MS, TX) and the more menacing **COBRA** (AK, IA, ID, IN, MI, MS, TX), **MOOSE** (AK, IA, ID, IN, KY, MI, MS), **COUGAR** (AK, IA, ID, IN, MI, MS), **EAGLE** (IA, ID, IN, KY, MI, TX), **RHINO** (AK, IA, ID, MI, MS, WA), **SNAKE** (AK, DE, IA, ID, MI, MS), and **WOLF** (AK, IA, IN, MI, MS, TX). Seemingly out of place in such rough company is the **POODLE** (AK, IA, ID, IN, MI, WA). Maybe these are fierce attack poodles.

Whether fierce or snuggly, whether they fly or swim or run, critters from **AARDVRK** (WA) to **ZEBRA** (AK, ID, MS, WA) find their way onto our plates. Why such interest in the animal kingdom? Perhaps because of the names that auto makers have assigned to models of their cars: **BOBCAT** (AK, IA, ID, KY, MI, TX), **COBRA, COUGAR, EAGLE, JAGUAR** (IA, WA), **MUSTANG** (ID).

For the most part, animals that find their way onto license plates via the automotive models are creatures of the fierce, macho sort. Others, such as the **FOX** (IA, MS) or **RABBIT** (AK, IA, KY) may not sound powerful and dominant, but are at least of the swift and maneuverable ilk, and hence suit our sense of "what's fittin' " for our present-day equivalents of the cowboy's horse, the knight's charger.

Still, these "lesser critters" account for only a very few of the animal plates chosen by motorists. It would be hard to imagine a Ford **ALY CAT** (KY, MS, ND), a Buick **BAT** (IA, MI) or **BEDBUG** (AK) or **BTTRFLY** (WA), a Chrysler **CATFISH** (ID, MS, WA), or a Chevy **CLAM** (IA) or **CHICKEN** (IA).

After suffering car trouble, I can envision selecting for my plate **A GOAT** (IA), **CRAPPIE** (IA), **DINOSAR** (WA), **DTYDOG** (WA), **HIPPO** (AK, ID), **MULE** (ID, MI, MS), **RAT** (MI, MS), **SKUNK** (AK, MI, MS), **SLUG** (AK), **TOAD** (DE, IA, ID, MI, WA), or **TURKEY** (ID, IN, ND).

Those who like to be different might find appeal in identifying with the rarer species: **ANACNDA** (WA), **BICHON** (SC) a once rare breed of French dog, **CDLFISH** (WA), **CMONSTR** (WA), **GNU** (WA), **IGUANA** (IA, MS, WA), **LLAMA** (AK, IN, MI, TX), **MALMUTE** (WA), **MANTA** (IN, WA), **PUFFIN** (AK), **RMADILA** (WA), **STARFSH** (WA), **WAPITI** (WA), **WOMBAT** (ID, MS, WA), or **YAK** (VA).

Some drivers go for animal sounds: **ARF-ARF** (IA), **BAAAA** (MS), **GRROWL** (AK), **MEOOOW** (MS), **MOOOOO** (MS), **OYNQUE** (WA), **PURRRR** (AK, KY, TX), **QUAAACK** (WA),

RIBBIT (AK, IA, KY, MI, MS, TX), **WHINNEE** (VA), and **WHOOO** (WA).

Those among us who identify with the cute and cuddly adorn our plates with **A DOVE** (MS), **BAIRCUB** (WA), **BAMBI** (DE), **BUNNY** (AK), **CHPMNK** (CO), **HUGAPUG** (WA), **KITTEN** (CT, ID, KY, MI, WA), **LAMB** (AK, KY) or **LAMCHP** (AK) or **LAMKIN** (KY, WA), **PUDECAT** (WA), or **WHTDOVE** (WA).

The manly motorist can opt instead for **A BEAST** (AK, MS), **APEMAN** (VA), **A WOLF** (IA, ID, MS, OR), **BULLDOG** (IA, ID, LA), **ELTORO** (AK, IA, ID), **GORILLA** (ID, WA), **MR BEAR** (IA), **MR LION** (MS), **MTLION** (WA), **OX** (AK, MS), **PITBUL** (IN, WA), **TMBRWLF** (WA), or **WLDBUL** (IA).

The more placid among us can choose **COW** (MI, MS) or **MOOCOW** (ID, MS, TX). Those who want a more ominous plate to keep strangers at a distance might like **A COBRA** (MS, WA), **BHIVE** (AK, IN), **BLKCAT** (ID, MS), **BLKWDOW** (WA), **DOBRMN** (MI), **MADDOG** (IA, IN, MI), **PIRANHA** (WA), **RATLER** (ID, WA), **REPTILE** (WA), **SSNAKE** (MS), **VIPER** (IN), or **VULTURE** (WA).

Others have come up with plates that incorporate animal-connected figures of speech: **BRHUG** (IA), **CATSMEO** (WA), **CROBAIT** (WA),

KITNISH (WA), **LKYDOG** (IA), **MOOSJAW** (IA), **OL BAT** (MS), **OLD GOAT** (ID), **OL HOSS** (MS), **SHEWOLF** (IA, WA), **TOADIE** (IA), **TOPCAT** (AK), **TOP DOG** (AK), **WOLFMAN** (IA), and **9 LIVES** (AK). And then there are the plays on words: **DANIMAL** (IN), **EWE-TOO** (TX) belonging to a Mrs. Lamb, or **PIG LEG** (VA), probably Mr. and Mrs. G's initials.

One wonders if **FAWN** (MI, MS, WA) belongs to car owners with Bambiesque leanings, or to admirers of Oliver North's secretary. Are the owners of **GATORS** (KY, MS) swamp people or alumni of the University of Florida? Is **GLOWORM** (WA) someone with a fond childhood recollection of catching fireflies in a glass jar, a naturalist, or a fan of the Inkspots?

Might **GRAFOX** (AK, MI) be the nickname for a gentleman with distinguished silver temples? Is **HOUNDOG** (WA) a hard-core, never-say-die (or dead) Elvis fan? Is **QUENBE** (IA) a reference to the buzzing kind, or a take-charge lady? Does **SWNSONG** (WA) belong to a senior citizen who figures he has bought his final auto?

So there you have it—animals of all shapes and sizes, from **ANT** (ID, MS) to **ELPHANT** (VA) and **WHALE** (AK, MS). What can we say?

We love 'em — even those of us who hardly ever so much as see an **ANIMUL** (CT) or a **CRITER** (AK, MS).

A BAER (TX)
A BASS (MS)
A BEAR (AK, ID, MS)
A BISON (WA)
A COON (MS)
A EAGLE (MS)
AFGHAN (WA)
A FROG (IA, MI)
A GATOR (IA)
A GOOSE (TX)
AIRDALE (IN)
ALECAT (KY)
ALI CAT (MI, MS)
ALIKAT (KY)
A LION (MI)
ALY CAT (MS, ND)
A MINK (VA)
ANALOPE (ID)
ANIMAL (AK, ID, IN, MI)
ANIMALI (ID)
ANIMALS (ID)
ANIML (MI)
ANML (WY)
ANUMAL (VA)
A PANDA (IA, MS)
APE (MS)
APLUSA (MS)
A PONY (IA, MI)
A POOCH (WI)
ARDVRK (MI)
ARKHOG (MS)
A ROACH (IA, MS)
A ROBIN (WA)
A SNAKE (IN, KY)
A SNIPE (WA)
ASP 1 (WA)
A TOAD (IA)
A TROUT (MS)
BAAA (TX)
BAAAAA (IA)
BAA BAA (AK, IA, ID, MI, WA)
BAD DAWG (ID)
BAD DOG (ID, MI, TX)
BADGER (IA, ID, MI, MS, ND, TX)
BADGERS (VA)
BAD WOLF (ID)
BASS (ID, KY, MI)
BBULDOG (ID)
BEAGLE (IA, KY, MS)
BEAGLES (IN)
BEAR (ID, KY, MI, MS)
BEARCAT (IN)
BEARCUB (IN)
BEARS (ID, MI)
BEAST (ID, MI, MS)
BEASTE (ID, MS)
BEASTS (ID)
BEASTY (ID)
BEAVER (AK, IA, ID, IN, MI, MS)
BEEAST (AK)
BEETLE (MI)

BGFSH (ID)
BIG BULL (IN)
BIG DOG (ID, IN, KY)
BIG FISH (ID)
BIGHORN (ID)
BIRD (IA, ID, KY, MI)
BIRDDOG (WA)
BIRDOG (ID)
BISON (ID)
BLACKOX (WA)
BLK BEAR (ID)
BLK BIRD (ID)
BLKBRD (KY)
BLK CAT (ID, MS)
BLK DOG (ID)
BLKKAT (WA)
BLKWIDO (ID, WA)
BLUBIRD (ID, WA)
BLUE HEN (KY)
BLUEJAY (IN)
BLUE OX (IN, MS)
BLUOX (MI)
BLU PIG (VA)
BOAR (IA)
BOBKAT (ID, KY)
BOWEVIL (WA)
BOW WOW (ID, IN, TX)
BRDCAGE (CA)
BRD DOG (CA, MS, TX)
BRDNST (CA)
BRDSFLY (CA)
BREBEAR (CA)
BRONCO (CO, IN)
BTRFLY (ID, KY)
BTRFLYS (IN)
BUFALO (IN, MI)
BUFFALO (IA, IN)
BUFFLO (MI)
BUG (IA, IN, MI, MS)
BUGSPIT (ID)
BULDAWG (IA)
BULDOG (MS, TX)
BULL (ID, IN, KY, MI)
BULLDG (MS)
BULLPUP (ID)
BUL-PUP (TX)
BUSY B (CT)
BUTRFLI (VA)
BUZARD (IA, ID)
BUZZARD (ID, IN)
CALF (ID)
CAMEL (MI)
CANARY (DE, ID, KY)
CANINE (MI, WA)
CARDINL (WA)
CARDNAL (IN)
CARIBOU (ID)
CAT (IA, IN, KY, MI)
CATAMNT (WA)
CATBIRD (WA)
CAT BOX (WA)
CATCRZY (WA)
CAT EYE (AK, IA)
CAT EYES (ID)
CAT FAN (WA)
CATFSH (IA)
CATHAIR (ID)
CATLADY (WA)
CATLDOG (WA)
CATLUVR (WA)
CAT MAN (AK, IA)
CATNIP (IA)
CATS (MS, MS)
CATTLE (IA, IN, KY)
CAYOTE (ID)
CGULL (WA)

CHEETAH (ID, IN)
CHICK (KY, MI)
CHICKEN (IA)
CHICKN (MI, MS)
CHIKEN (IA)
CHIKN (DE)
CHINOOK (WA)
CHIPMNK (WA)
CH KEN (VA)
CHNOOK (WA)
CHPMUNK (IN)
COBWEB (WA)
COLLIE (IA, ID, IN, MI)
COLT (MI)
CONCH (WA)
CONDOR (MI, TX)
COON (MS, WA)
COOGAR (MI)
COOTIE (MS)
CORGI (AK)
COW (WY)
COWCALF (ID)
COWPIE (ID)
COYOTE (AK, IA, ID, IN, KY)
COYOTES (ID)
CRAPIE (KY)
CRAWDAD (WA)
CRICKET (ID, IN)
CRIKET (IA, ID, KY, MI, MS, WA)
CRIKIT (IA, MS)
CRIQET (ID)
CRITTER (IN)
CRITTR (ID)
CROC (MS)
CROW (MS)
CRYWOLF (IN)
CTFISH (KY)
CUDA (KY)
DAKSUND (CA)
DAS BUG (IA)
DAWG (ID, MI, WA)
D BEAR (ID)
DBEAST (ID)
DED BRD (ID)
DEFOX (VA)
DER FLEA (WA)
DER HASE (WA)
DER WOLF (WA)
DETOAD (CA)
DMOOSE (WA)
DOE (MI)
DOG (WA, TX)
DOGBONE (WA)
DOG CAT (MI)
DOGMEAT (MS, WA)
DOGPAK (MS, WA)
DOGS (ID, IN, KY)
DOLFIN (AK, MI)
DOLPHIN (IN)
DONKEY (IA, KY)
DOVE (IN, MI)
DOXHUND (ID)
DRAGON (AK, IA, ID, IN, MI)
DRAGUN (ID)
DR FISH (NC)
DSNAIL (CA)
DSNAKE (CA)
DUCK (DE, KY, MI)
DUCK DOG (WA)
DUCKS (ID)
EAGLET (AK, ID)
EELSKIN (WA)
EELSKN (MS)

ELAFANT (WA)
ELEPHT (MI)
ELFUNT (WA)
ELK (IA, ID, KY, MI, WY)
ELK FEVR (WA)
ELKHNT (ID)
EL LOBO (TX)
ELPHNT (WA)
EL PUMA (AK)
EQUINE (CA, ID)
EQUINES (CA)
FAAROG (IA)
FALCON (ID, MI)
FASTCAT (NM)
FAT HOG (VA)
FELINE (MS, WA)
FERRET (ID, TX)
FEZANT (WA)
FIDO (AK)
FILLI (IN)
FILLY (WA)
FIREFLY (WA)
FISH (IA, IN, WY)
FISHAWK (WA)
FLEA (MS)
FLEAS (MS)
FLICKER (IN)
FLMINGO (IN)
FLMNGO (KY, TX)
FOX DEN (IN)
FOXTAIL (WA)
FRAWG (WA)
FROG (DE, IA, IN, KY, MI, MS, WY)
FROGE (MS)
FROGG (MI)
FROGGE (MS, TX)
FROGGI (AK, ID, MS)
FROGGY (IA, ID, MI, MS)
FROGIE (MS)
FROGS (MI, MS)
GATER (ID)
GATOR (ID, IN, KY, MI, MS)
GATOR 1 (VA)
GAZELLE (IN, WA)
GEESE (WA)
GIRAFE (MI)
GIRAFF (MI, WA)
GIRAFFE (WA)
GLOBUG (IL, MS, WA)
GOAT (KY, WA, WY)
GOBBLER (WA)
GOOSE (AK, IA, ID, KY, MS, TX)
GOPHER (KY)
GORILA (MI, WA)
GOZLING (CA)
GRAWALE (WA)
GRAWLF (WA)
GRAWOLF (WA)
GRAYCAT (IN)
GRAYFOX (IN)
GREYFOX (IN)
GREYHND (WA)
GRILLA (MS)
GRIZZLY (IA, ID, IN, MS)
GRNHOG (ID)
GROUSE (ID, KY, MI)
GRRILA (TX)
GRYSEAL (WA)
GR8DANE (WA)
GR8 WHTE (VA)
GT DANE (AK)
GUPPIE (ID)
GYRAFE (CA)

GYRAFFE (CA)
HALIBT (AK)
HALIBUT (WA)
HAWG (KY, WA)
HAWK (IA, ID, MI, MS, WY)
HAWKBIL (IN)
HMIGBRD (WA)
HNYBEAR (WA)
HNY B (MS)
HNY BEE (MS)
HOG (MI, TX)
HOGG (WY)
HOG PEN (TX)
HONEYB (ID)
HONKER (MI)
HOOTOWL (IN, WA)
HORNET (AK, MS)
HORSE (AK, KY, MS)
HORSES (ID, KY)
HORSFLY (WA)
HORSHU (WA)
HORS LVR (VA)
HUSKIE (AK)
H2O DAWG (IN)
H2O DOG (ID)
H2O K9 (ID)
IMA HOG (TX)
IMA SWAN (WA)
INSECT (AK, IA, KY)
JACKAL (ID)
JAYBIRD (IA, ID)
JAYBRD (IA)
JBIRD (WA)
JOONBUG (WA)
JUN BUG (MI, MS)
JUNEBUG (IA, ID, IN, WA)
KANGARU (NC)
KANGROO (WA)
KATFISH (ID, MS, WA)
KEYOTE (WA)
KITCAT (ID)
KITFOX (ID, MI, TX)
KITKAT (IA, WA)
KITTN (MS)
KIT-TN (TX)
KIYOTE (IA)
KIYOTEE (WA)
KIYOTI (WA)
KOALA (KY, MI, TX, WA)
KODIAKS (WA)
KONDOR (TX)
KTDIDS (WA)
KTYKAT (MI)
KYYOTE (MS)
K9 (TX, WA)
K9 FOOL (TX)
K9 HAUS (WA)
K9 HOUSE (WA)
K9 LOVER (WA)
K9 RTIST (WA)
K9 SHO4 (WA)
K9 SKOOL (WA)
K9 STYL (SC)
K9 TAXI (WA)
LABADOR (WA)
LABDOR (VA)
LADYBG (AK)
LADYBUG (ID, IN)
LAMA (WY)
LDY BRD (MS)
LDYBUG (IA, KY, MS, TX)
LEECH (WA)
LE MULE (TX)
LEPARD (MS)

LEPHANT (WA)
LIL BEAR (ID)
LIL FOX (AK)
LIL HAM (NC)
LIL PUP (IA)
LION (IA, MS, TX, WY)
LIONESS (IA)
LIONS (AK)
LIZARD (IA, KY)
LIZRRRD (CA)
LIZURD (CA)
LIZZARD (CA, ID)
LLLAMA (ID)
LLAMAS (MI)
LNGHORN (WA)
LOBO (AK, ID, IN, TX)
LOBSTA (AK)
LOCUST (TX, WA)
LONGHRN (IN)
LONWOLF (ID, IN)
LOON (AK, MI)
LOST DOG (WA)
LTL FAWN (ID)
LTL FOX (AK)
LTL RAT (AK)
LTORO (WA)
LUPINE (MI, WA)
LYNX (AK, MI)
LZY CAT (WA)
MABEAR (AK, TX)
MAGPIE (MI)
MALTESE (WA)
MAMA BEAR (NC)
MASTIF (MI)
MASTIFF (ID)
MEEOOW (TX)
MEEOW (MI, TX)
MEEOWW (KY)
MEOW (AK, ID, IN, KY, MI, TX)
MEOWRR (KY)
ME-OWW (TX)
MEOWWW (TX)
METAFOX (WA)
MEYOW (TX)
MIAU (VA)
MINK (KY, MI, WY)
MMMOOOO (ID)
MO B DIK (TX)
MOBI DK (TX)
MOLE (IN, MS, TX)
MOLHOL (IN)
MO. MULE (TX)
MONGRL (WA)
MONKEE (TX)
MONKEY (AK, ID, KY, MI, TX, WA)
MOO (TX)
MOOER (VA)
MOOO (KY)
MOOOOO (MS)
MOTHS (KY)
MOUSE (AK, ID, IN, KY, MI, MS)
MOUSER (ID, IN, MS)
MOUZER (AK)
MR ANT (MS)
MR BASS (MS)
MR BEAR (IA)
MR CAT (KY)
MR DUCK (MS)
MR FISH (AK, MS)
MR GOAT (IA, MS)
MR HAWK (MS)
MR HOG (AK, IA, MS)
MR MULE (IA)

MR PUP (MS)
MR RAT (AK)
MR SKUNK (WA)
MR TOAD (IA)
MR WORM (MS, TX)
MRS RAT (MS)
MS ANT (MS)
MS CAT (MS)
MS COON (MS)
MS DAWG (MS)
MS DUCK (MS)
MS FROG (AK)
MS HAWK (MS)
MS MULE (ID)
MS PIGGY (IA, TX)
MS WORM (MS)
MS WREN (MS)
MT GOAT (IA, ID, TX, WA)
MTN GOAT (WA)
MUD BUG (MS)
MUDHEN (MI)
MUD MULE (ID)
MUD RAT (ID)
MUDTRTL (VA)
MUEL (AK)
MULE (MS, TX, WY)
MULEMAN (IA)
MUSCRAT (WA)
MUSKIE (WA)
MUSKRAT (WA)
MUS RAT (MS)
MUTT (MI)
MY COW (IA)
MY GOAT (IA)
MY HAWK (IA)
MY HOG (IA)
MY HOSS (TX)
MY MEOW (AK)
MY MINK (TX)
MY PIG (WA)
MY PONY (WA)
MY POOCH (WA)
MY PUMA (WA)
MY PUP (WA)
NOBULL (IA)
NUPUPY (WA)
OCTOPUS (WA)
OINK (KY)
OL-BEAR (LA)
OLD BAT (ID)
OLD DOG (IA, KY)
OLD HEN (ID)
OLDOG (AK)
OLGOAT (AK, ID)
OLMULE (VA)
O MEOW (VA)
OPOSSM (MS)
OSPREY, (AK, ID, WA)
OSTRICH (WA)
OTTER (AK, IN, MI, TX, WA)
OWL (AK, IA, KY, MS, WA)
OWLEKAT (VA)
OWLET (WA)
OWLS (ID, MS)
OX-BUL (NC)
OXKART (TX)
OXYOKE (ID)
OYNK (MI, WA)
OYSTER (AK, MS, TX)
PANDA (IA, ID, IN, MI)
PANDAS (KY)
PANTHR (ID, MI)
PANTHUR (WA)
PARROT (AK, CA, IA, TX)

PARROTT (CA)
PEACOCK (ID, WA)
PELICAN (ID, WA)
PENGWEN (WA)
PENGUIN (IA, ID, IN)
PENGWN (AK, WA)
PENGWUN (WA)
PENGWYN (WA)
PERCH (DE, WA)
PESCE (WA)
PHEZANT (WA)
PIG (MS)
PIGEON (MS, WA)
PIGLET (AK, IN, TX)
PIGPEN (IA, IN, KY, TX, WA)
PIGPENN (WA)
PIGS (IN, MS)
PIGSTY (WA)
PINTO (WA)
PIRAHNA (WA)
PIRANA (WA)
PISCES (WA)
PITBUL (TX, WA)
PLTYPUS (WA)
PNGUIN (TX)
PNTHER (AK)
POLCAT (AK, IA, ID, MS, WA)
POLECAT (WA)
POLYWOG (WA)
PONY (AK, IA, ID, MI, MS, WY)
POOBEAR (IA)
POOCH (AK, IN, MS)
POSSMM (VA, WA)
POSSUM (IN, KY, TX)
PPABEAR (WA)
PUDICAT (WA)
PUFFIN (WA)
PUG (WA)
PUP (AK)
PUPPIE (IN)
PUPPY (AK, MS, TX)
PUPYDG (VA)
PURR (AK)
PURRR (AK, TX)
PUSYCAT (WA)
PUTKAT (KY)
PUURRR (MS)
PUZTCAT (WA)
PYTHON (KY)
QUAIL (MS)
QUAKQAK (WA)
RABBITS (ID)
RABIT (MS)
RACCOON (WA)
RACOON (MI)
RAKOON (VA)
RAM (MI)
RATCAR (AK)
RAT MAN (TX)
RATS (MI)
RATLR (MI)
RATTLR (TX)
RAVEN (AK, IA, ID, KY, MS, ND)
RAW DOG (AK)
RAZORBK (WA)
RBRDUCK (ID)
RDHOG (IA)
RDKILL (MI)
REDBIRD (WA)
REDBRD (WA)
REDBUG (MI)
RED DOG (AK)

RED FOX (AK, ID, MS, VA)
RED HAWK (ID)
RED HEN (AK, ID, IN)
RED PONY (NC)
RED WOLF (IN)
REPTYL (KY)
RHYNO (AK, MI)
RIBBET (AK)
RIBETT (IA)
RIBIT (IA, MS)
RINO (MI)
RMADILO (WA)
ROACH (IA, KY, MS, TX)
ROADKIL (IN)
ROKFISH (WA)
ROOSTER (ID, WA)
ROOSTR (IA, MI)
ROTWILR (IN)
ROTWLER (IN)
RUDEDOG (WA)
RYNO (ID)
SALMON (AK, IA, MI, TX)
SCORPN (AK)
SCOTTIE (WA)
SCOTTY (WA)
SEABIRD (WA)
SEAGUL (AK, CT, IA, MS)
SEAHAWK (IN)
SEAL (MS)
SEALPUP (WA)
SEALS (WA)
SEAHWK (AK)
SEHORSE (AK)
SHAD (AK)
SHARPEE (WA)
SHARPEI (WA)
SHE CAT (TX)
SHEEP (ID, MI, TX)
SHELTEE (WA)
SHELTIE (WA)
SHEWOLF (IA, WA)
SHIHTZU (WA)
SHOWDOG (WA)
SHRIMP (AK, IA, MS, TX, WA)
SLEDAWG (WA)
SLI FOX (MI)
SLUG (AK)
SLV FOX (MS)
SLVRFOX (ID)
SLY DOG (MS)
SLY FOX (IN, LA, MI, MS, TX)
SNAIL (IN, MS)
SNAILS (IA)
SNIPE (MS)
SNOBRD (GA)
SNOWOWL (WA)
SOCKEYE (WA)
SOI PIG (TX)
SOKEYE (AK)
SPIDER (AK, IA)
SSNAKE (MI)
SSSNAKE (WA)
SQUID (TX, WA)
SQUIRRL (ID)
SQURIL (MS)
SQURRL (ID)
STAG (DE)
STARFSH (WA)
STNGRAY (WA)
STNGRY (TX)
STORK (IN, KY, MS, TX, WA)
STUDOG (MI)

STURGON (WA)
SU E PIG (TX)
SUNDOG (WA)
SUN FOX (WA)
SWAN (AK, IA, MI, MS)
SWINE (MS)
TABBIE (MS)
TABBY (AK, WA)
TABYCAT (WA)
TADPOLE (IA, IN)
TADPOL 1 (AK, MS, VA)
TANAGER (WA)
TARPON (ID)
TERMITE (WA)
TERRAPN (VA, WA)
TERTLE (WA)
THBEAR (IA)
THBIRD (IA)
THE BAT (ID)
THE BUG (IA, ID)
THE CAT (AK, ID, KY, MI)
THE CUB (MI)
THE DOG (MI)
THE ELK (MI)
THE FLY (AK, IA)
THE FOX (IA)
THE GOAT (ID)
THE HEN (IA)
THE HOG (IA)
THE PIG (IA)
THE PUP (MS)
THE ROO (MS)
THE RAT (IA)
THE SQRL (ID)
THE WORM (WA)
THOMCAT (IA)
THRUSH (MI, MS)
TIGERR (ID)
TIGGRR (TX)
TIGRES (AK)
TIGRESS (VA)
TIGRRR (AK, IA)
TOADY (IA)
TOMKAT (KY)
TRMITE (WA)
TROUT (IA, ID, IN, KY, MI)
TURBOT (AK, IN, MI, WA)
TURTLE (AK, IA, ID, IN, MI, MS)
UGLY DUK (ID)
UNACORN (WA)
UNACRN (WA)
UNEKORN (WA)
UNICRN (AK, MI, WA)
UNIKORN (WA)
UNYCORN (WA)
UNYKORN (WA)
VARMIT (ID)
VENOM (ID, MI)
VIPER (ID, IN)
VIXEN (ID)
VULPINE (WA)
WAABIT (WA)
WABBIT (IA, ID, IN, MI)
WABBITT (ID)
WABIT (IL, MI)
WALEYE (MI, WA)
WALLEYE (ID, IN)
WALRUS (AK, WA)
WARBLER (WA)
WAR PONY (ID)
WATERAT (WA)
WDTICK (WA)
WEASEL (AK, IA, ID, KY, MS, WA)

WEAZEL (MI)
WEAZLE (OR)
WETDOG (KY)
WHALES (ID, KY, WA)
WHINNY (ID, TX)
WHIPITT (WA)
WHO OWL (MS)
WHTRAT (IA)
WILCAT (MI)
WILDCAT (IN, WA)
WILD HOG (WA)
WILKKAT (WA)
WLDCAT (IA, ID, MI, TX)
WLD GSE (KY, VA)
WLD LFE (TX)
WOLF (WY)
WOLFMN (TX)
WOLVES (ID, IN, KY, MI)
WOM-BAT (OR)
WOMBATT (WA)
WORM (AK, IN, MS)
WORMS (ID, TX)
WTRBUG (WA)
WTRDOG (MI)
WUD DUK (MS)
WUD DUX (MS)
WUFF (OH)
YELO DOG (ID)
YORKIE (ID)
Z FOX (IN)
Z MOUSE (ND)
1JUNBUG (CA)
1MOUSE (KY)
1 RED FOX (VA)
1 WORM (MS)
2 NA*FSH (TX)
4 PAWS (MS)
4 PETS (MS)
4 QUAIL (MS)
9 LIVES (AK)
79 MEOW (NM)

CHAPTER 11

My Car, Right or Wrong

Is ABE LNKN OVRDHIL, or 4ALL2NV?

ABE LNKN (VA); **ACK-ACK** (TX), surely on a Pontiac; **BEAMER** (KY, ND), the yuppie nickname for a **BMW**; **BMW4ME**, on a South Carolina Hyundai; **DADCAD** (OR); **DASBENZ** (NC, WA); **FOXXE** (VA), on an Audi Fox; **HNYBNY** (IA), on a VW Rabbit; **PINTOAD** (VA); **RADILAC** (WA); **SOB STORI** (NC) and **KEMOSAAB** (WA), on Saabs; **TOY YODA** (VA); **U-CAD-U** (TX); **UGOSLAV** (WA); and **WADWABT** (WA) — all these are fanciful plates that describe the car's make.

Other such plates are more straightforward, as in **A DASHA** (TX), **AHANDA** (NH), **AHEALEY** (ID), **AVANTI** (AK, KY), **CADLAC** (IA), **CMYJEEP** (VA), **DESCORT** (CA), **DESOTA** (CA), **DLOREAN** (ID, WA), **FLEETWD** (IN), **IMNMGB** (VA), **MYBMW** (AK), **MYBENZ** (AK, KY), **MYEDSEL** (IN), **MYZUZU** (ID), **PHIAT** (WA), **PONYAK** (TX), **POORSH** (WA), **RABBIT** (AK), **TORNADO** (IA), or **TRYUMPH** (WA).

Volkswagen owners appear to take special delight in this sort of plate, as in: **ABUG** (IA), **AONEBUG** (CA), **BEATLE** (AK), **DEEBUG** (MI), **GROOVW** (CA), **IMABUG** (AK, MI), **ITS A BUG** (IL), **LADEBG** (VA), **MYBUG** (AK), **RAREBUG** (WA), and from Virginia, a VW plate with a fine sense of Civil War history: **VIGSBUG**. **RUGBUG** (AK), one must assume, is snug as a bug in a rug.

It's probably true that convertible owners, like blondes, have more fun, witness: **ALFRSCO** (WA), **ARAGTOP** (WA), **DROPTOP** (ID, WA), **FLIP-LID** (NC), **FLIPTOP** (ID, WA), **NOTOP** (ID), **NOTOP4ME** (NC), **RAG DOL** (TX), **RAGTOP** (AK, IA, ID, IL, IN, MI, WA), **SOFTOP** (AK, ID, KY, MI, MS), **TOPDWN** (IA), and **TOPLES** (AK, IA, ID, MI, MS). Very few car owners brag that their car is a **HARDTOP**, as does one Washington state driver.

Still other motorists use their plate to describe something else about the type of car they own: **DER DSL** (VA), on a VW diesel; **COUPE** (WA); **DUALCAM** (WA); **FITS-2** (TX); **FO BY FO** (TX); **GULWING** (WA); **INJECTD** (WA); **REBUILT** (IA); **ROADSTR** (IN); **TUTONE** (AK); **TWNCAM** (AK), **USEDCAR** (WA); **4NKAR** (IA); and **5 SPEED** (MS). Some others are:

A69RAY (VA)
ABENZ (CA, IA, TX)
ABRAT (AK, TX)
ABUGG (AK)
ACHORD (KY)
AHEALY (AK)
ALANTE (KY)
AREDCAR (IA)
ATHING (KY)
ATUF67 (VA)
AWOODY (MS, WA)
BAD BIRD (ID)
BAD BUG (ID, KY)
BAD CAD (ID, MI)
BAD TRK (ID)
BEAMER (KY)
BEEMER (ID, KY)
BIG TWUK (ID)
BLK BUTY (IL)
BLKJEEP (VA)
BRAT (MI)
BRATT (DE)
BRD2LOV (CA)
BRD2NV (CA)
BRD4DAD (CA)
BRD4MOM (CA)
BRD4POP (CA)
BRD4RNR (CA)
BRD54ME (CA)
BURETA (VA)
COUP (WA)
CRXTASY (IA)
DAIMLER (CA)
DAIMLR (CA)
DASAUTO (WA)
DASBMW (OR, WA)
DAS CAR (MI)
DEEZUL (MI)
DESCORT (CA)
DETRUCK (CA)
DETRUK (CA)
DIESEL (KY, MI)
DUDES-GT (NC)
DZUBARU (NC)
EDSEL (KY)
ELBUICK (ID)
FORD USA (VA)
FUNBUG (MI)
FYRBRD (VA)
GOLD BUG (VA)
GRAFOX (IA)
GTO2GO (ID)

HEP CAT (TX)
HOT 4RD (MS)
IGOYUGO (MS)
IMABRAT (IN)
IMACAD (IA)
IRAGTOP (WA)
IRAJAG (AK)
ITS A BUG (IL)
JAGNIT (KY)
JAGTIME (IN)
JAP BMW (TX)
JAPCAR (TX)
JAXRABT (WA)
JEEEP (CA)
JEEPISH (CA)
JEEPIST (CA)
JEEPZEE (CA)
JEEPZIE (CA)
JEEPZTR (CA)
JEEP4ME (CA)
JEEP4US (CA)
KADETT (WA)
KADOLAK (WA)
KEEN VAN (VA)
LECOUPE (WA)
LE LUDE (TX)
LGGEND (TX)
LIL TWUK (VA)
LILYOTA (WA)
LOTUS (KY)
LTL BIGR (VA)
MAMASMAX (NC)
MA'S BIRD (VA)
MEINIAC (CA)
MEINTOY (CA)
ME&MY GT (VA)
MPULSE (KY)
MRVET (DE)
MSTANG (KY, MI)
MSTNG (VA)
MY CAD (FL)
MYCEDZ (AK)
MYCUGR (AK)
MY JAG (KY)
MY KUGR (TX)
MYLIMO (AK)
MYLASER (WA)
MY MAX (KY)
MYSPYDR (WA)
MYTHING (SC)
MYYODA (ID)
MY4DOOR (WA)
MY57CAM (VA)
NTEGRA (MI)
OLDSRAG (ID)
ON AL4S (TX)
OUTLAW (IA)
PAMARO (WA)
PARTBUG (CA)
POORSH (KY)
POPTOP (KY)
PORSHHH (WA)
PRELEWD (WA)
RAAGDOL (WA)
RADCAD (WA)
RADGHIA (WA)
RAGDOLL (ID, IN)
RAGGTOP (ID, IN)
RAGTIME (WA)
RAGTYM (WA)
RAREJAG (IN)
RDSTER (TX)
REDBUG (KY)
REDJAG (KY)
RED TA (VA)
RITZRAG (WA)

ROLBAR (WA)
RU-B-RED (VA)
SAMURAI (IA)
SAMURI (AK, IA)
SFTTOP (WA)
SHADEUX (WA)
SHOWCAD (CA)
SKIBURU (WA)
SPIDER (IA)
SPTFIRE (IN)
SPYDERR (VA)
SUM BNY (TX)
SUPEROO (WA)
THEBUG (AK)
THING (IA, VA)
THUMPR (KY)
TIN CAT (VA)
TOOTONE (WA)
TOPDOWN (ID)
TOPLESS (ID, WA)
TOPLIS (AK, KY, MI, MS)
TOP LS (MS)
TOPLSS (AK, ID, KY, MI, MS)
TOPLUS (KY)
TOPLZZ (MI)
TRANZAM (WA)
TRIUMF (MI, WA)
TRIUMP (KY)
TRYUMF (WA)
TUTONE (KY)
USED (AK)
VAN GO (KY)
VAN-I-T (VA)
VANTASIA (NC)
VEE SIX (MS)
VRTIBLE (CA)
VRY RED (TX)
VSIX (CA)
VSIXER (CA)
VSIXPWR (CA)
VW4EVER (WA)
V12XKE (MS)
WUZBUS (AK)
YOTAFUN (WA)
ZFORTWO (WA)
ZFOR2 (WA)
1BADV8 (KY)
1 BAD XE (VA)
1JUS4FN (CA)
1 LE CAR (VA)
1 OWNR (KY)
1STANG (KY)
4CARBS (KY)
4N MADE (VA)
4N TOY (ID)
5SPEED (KY)
9TEEN9T (NC)
57HEVN (KY)

Drivers of older cars have special plates all their own. Some come right out and call their auto an **OLDDEE** (VA), **OLDHEEP** (VA),

OLTIMER (WA), **AIRLOOM** (WA), or **ANTEEK** (IA, ID, KY, MI, VA).

And why not? If you own a **RESTORD** (WA) **RELIC** (IA), or even if your car's an **OVR-DHIL** (WA) old **WRECK** (TX), why not have a little fun and use your license tag to tell any and all that **IWUZA 10** (VA). Sound a loud **AHOOGA** (ID, NH, TX) on the **OLD DOLL** (VA)'s horn, and let 'em know it's still **VIABLE** (TX), still **ONDROAD** (WA).

Let 'em know your car might be a **DINOSRR** (KY, VA) from a **BIGONE** (MI) era, but it's not **EXTNCT** (WA) yet. Try to think of your car as a **4 RUNNER** (TX) of less mature automobiles, not a **CNILE** (MI) old **HASBEN** (ID) you keep around **II PUSH** (WA), or **4 SCRAP** (KY).

Yes sir, if the old **FLIVRR** (AK) is **KEPT-UP** (TX) right, it's liable to get its **2ND WIND** (IN) and last until it's a **CLASSIC** (IN). If not, it could at least be **FUN 2FIX** (VA).

ABUSED (MI)
AHOOGA (AK)
ALIZZY (WA)
AMODEL (MS)
ANTEAK (IA)
ANTEK (MI)
ANTIQ (IA)
ANTIQS (IA)
ANTIQ 1 (AK)
ANTIQ 2 (AK)
AOOGA (DE, IA)
AOOGAH (DE, IA, TX)
CRANKIT (ID)
EXTINCT (IN)
HEPCAT (ID)
IMAREC (MI)

ITLL DO (MI)
ITL RUN (MI)
IT SHOT (MI)
JALOPY (KY)
JUNQUE (IN)
KLASIC (KY)
KLUNKER (ID)
KLUNKR (MI)
LVMY67 (VA)
MY HEAP (TX)
MYOLGAL (WA)
MYOL55 (VA)
MY PEST (TX)
NIFTY50 (WA)
NOI Z (VA)
OLDCAR (AK, DE)
OLDIE (WA)
OLDIES (WA)
OLD ONE (MI)
OLDY (WY)
OLENUF (KY)
OLFTHFL (WA)
OL PRO (TX)
OLSTYLE (WA)
OLTIMR (WA)
OL 59 ER (VA)
OOGAH (IA)
OOOGAH (AK, IA)
OSOOLD (WA)
RTFACT (OR)
RSTLSS (WA)
RUST 1 (DE)
TH CAN (VA)
TINLIZ (WA)
TIN LIZZIE (IA)
TINLIZY (WA)
TOO OLD (MI, TX)
USED (KY, TX)
Z JALOPY (WA)
1 OWNER (TX)
2 OLD2 (KY)
4 TIRES (TX)
65 RAGTP (VA)

ACYLUM (IA) says it well: this owner sees his car as **AWAYOUT** (ID), a pleasant **KOKOON** (AK) in which he can banish care and strife and simply **ESCAPE** (AK, IN, TX), or find **RESPIT** (WA) and **FREDM** (IA).

Now, for some people an auto is no more than transportation from here to there — **ACR2DRV** (VA). **ACUR4ME** (WA), however, sees his car as good medicine, as **HIS R&R** (VA), or perhaps even as a **PANACEA** (WA) for what ails him, or as an **OASIS** (AK) from care and woe.

Many drivers good naturedly admit that their car is largely **A TOY** (MI, ND), as in the plates: **ADULTOY** (IN, WA), **AGR8TOY** (ID), **ATOY4ME** (ID), **BIG TOY** (ID), **FASTOY** (TX), **MEGATOY** (WA), **MY1TOY** (ID, WA), **NUTOY** (AK), **OUR TOY** (AK, ID, IL), **PLATOY** (ID, KY), **POWRTOY** (WA), **R NU TOY** (TX), **THETOY** (AK), **TOYCAR** (IA), **TOY4PA** (OR), **TXS TOY** (TX), or **WLD TOY** (ND).

In a similar vein, other drivers admit their car is **ALL4FUN** (ID), **FOR FUN** (ID, MI), a **FUNCAR** (ID), **JUS4FN** (AK), **4FUN** (AK), **4GRINS** (AK, MI), **4KICKS** (AK), **4NJOYN** (ID), or **4PLAY** (AK, SC).

For others, their car is an **EGO CAR** (OH) or **EGOTRP** (AK, KY). It takes courage to admit that something as expensive as a car is mainly **4 MYEGO** (IA, KY, MI, ND, WI) or **4MY KIX** (MS). **MYCRISIS** (NC) appears to bespeak someone of middle age. It reminds me of a favorite uncle who in his fifties, bought a red convertible and called it his "mid-life Chrysler." More utilitarian, and consequently easier to own up to, are: **CHUKWGN** (WA), **COPCAR** (MI, WA), **D TAXI** (VA), **INTWRK** (VA), **KRUBUS** (MI), **LIMO** (IA), **LMBRWGN** (WA),

SHUTTLE (ID), **TAXI** (IA, MI), **TOETRK** (WA), and **2DEMALL** (PA). The California plate **MEATWGN** belongs to a butcher. These, however, pale beside cars used to pick up **CHICKS** (AK), or as a substitute for **MYYUTH** (ID), or as a **SEXTOY** (VA) **4HOT FUN** (VA).

Liking to feel one-up, some drivers regard their car as **12BSEEN** (AL), as a status symbol **4ALL2NV** (ID), or **4U2CIT** (VA), or **4U2NVME** (ID, SC). Those who are attracted to speed prefer such plates as **RACECAR** (IN), **TO FLY** (NC), **WE DRAG** (MS), or **4PASSNU** (ID).

Perhaps it is people who feel like they practically live in their cars who go for plates such as **HOM4US** (VA), **MICASA** (AK), **MYHOME** (AK), or **2ND HOM** (MS).

If you drive **THE ARK** (IA) to **THE ZOO** (IA), you sound like you're planning to load some critters up in case of flood. **EWEHAUL** (WA) must be on the pickup truck of a sheep rancher, **MALETRK** (WA) on the vehicle of a macho postman (one who rings twice). Is **SPYONU** (VA) on the car of a jealous spouse or a private detective? Who knows, but much more open sounding is **UCME ICU** (AL).

More businesslike are the motorists whose cars are a **PERK** (IL), or a **WRITOFF** (WA), or a **TAXTOY** (AK). While these plates are honest enough, they're not nearly so likable as **PASFIER** (CA), which is a charming admission of child-like pleasure, or **5THQTR** (IA). Is that like golf's 19th hole?

ADLTOY (MS)
ALLSHO (MI)
ALL4SHO (ID)
ASFALT 1 (VA)
ASYLUM (ID)
A TOY (ID, IN)
CATVAN (KY)
DAITRPR (CA)
DAKRUZR (CA)
DALEGS (CA)
DATOY (MI)
DATRIPR (WA)
DOGKAR (KY)
DOGVAN (MI)
DUNEBUG (WA)
FNOFIT (TX)
HOBBY (IA)
IM A TOY (TX)
IM4FUN (IN)
JOYTOY (AK)
JUSATOY (IN)
JUS4FUN (ID)
LILTOY (AK, KY)
LOGTRKN (WA)
MA TOY (NC)
MD BUGY (MS)
MISUSE (IA)
MITOY (AK)
MY-FEET (TX)
MY HA B (NC)
MY TAXI (TX)
MYTOY (AK)
NEWTOY (KY)
PACECAR (IA)
PASECAR (CA)
PLATHNG (WA)
PLAYTOY (ID, IN)
R-AN-R (KY)
R-TAXI (KY)
RUFTOY (AK)
SKIBUS (ID)
SKIVAN (AK)
SNOBUG (AK)
SNO BUS (ID)
SNOPLOW (WA)
SUM TOY (MS)
TAXEE (IA)
TAXICAB (IA)
TAXTIP (AK)
THEBUS (IA)
TOW CAR (MI, MS)
TOW TRK (TX)
TOY (KY)
TRUCKN (IA)
TWUCK IN (VA)
TX TAXI (TX)
VEGIVAN (WA)
XSCAPE (KY)
2ABUSE (IA)
2BCOOL (MI)
2BWILD (MI)
2ENJOY (TX)

2ND HME (MS)
2RELAX (IA)
4CRUZIN (ID)
4FISHIN (ID)
4FISHN (KY)
4HUNTIN (ID)
4KRUZN (AK)
4LUVN (AK)
4MI DOGS (VA)
4MYFUN (IA)
4MYLUV (IA)
4MYSELF (IA)
4 PLAYN (MS)
4RACIN (AK, MS)
4SALE (AK, TX, WI)
4SCAPE (OR)
4THESNO (ID)
4TRIPS (IA)
4U2ENVY (IA)

CHAPTER 12

God and Country

You don't BYAMRCN? No? Then you'd better REPENT!

BLESSED (IA, IN) is he (or she) whose license plate celebrates **FAITH** (ID, KY, MI, WA) by shouting **ALELUYA** (WA) or **HOSANA** (IA), or reminds us to **PRAY** (DE, IA, MI, TX, WA) or **REPENT** (AK, IA, KY, MI, TX, WA) or **WITNESS** (VA) or **WORSHIP** (NC).

All across America, people pile into the family **ARK** (MS), **GO2MASS** (CA) or to **CHURCH** (IA, MI, WA), and **ASKGOD** (MI, MS, WA) that **HVNSENT** (WA) **BLES N** (OR) come down to each true **BELIEVR** (WA) who **THXGOD** (IA, WA) and promises to **SINNOT** (WA), but **OBEYGOD** (WA) in all things.

Up front the **PADRE** (IN) or **REVREND** (IN) will **PREACH** (MI) the **GOSPEL** (AK, MS, WA), offer **PRAYER** (IN, MI, TX, WA), and proclaim the **GOOD NUS** (VA) that **HELIVZ** (MS, TX, WA) and that **HELUVSU2** (WA).

Some motorists express their relationship with **GOD** (MS, NJ, WA) in very familiar terms. **GOD AND I**, says a North Carolina driver; **GOD N I** is in Mississippi; **GODNME** appears in both Mississippi and Washington. **IO GOD 1** (MS), says one **PILGRIM** (WA); **IMSAVED** (WA), says another. Yet another identifies himself as an **X HEATHN** (WA). **I TITHE**, says a Virginian. **HALO** is the plate of an Iowan named Mr. Angel.

GETSAVD, suggests a Washington motorist; **DO PRAY**, reminds a Mississippian. **GOD B4U** (MS) reminds us of the proper priorities for those of us who would **BSAVED** (AK). Others couch their messages in the form of questions: **RUSAVED** (MS, WA), **RU4 GOD** (MS), **RU4 JSUS** (WA), and **SAVDRU** (WA).

Presumably most of these plates belong to Baptists, Methodists, Catholics, and Jews — members of mainstream American congregations — but the occasional plate also proclaims **BAGWAN** (AK, IA), **MOONIE** (ID, MS), or **ZEN** (KY, WA).

Before the fall from grace of Jim Bakker and the subsequent lessened influence of cash-crazed cathode Christianity, one saw more plates like **PTL** (IA, WA), **PTLLADY** (WA), and **PTLMAN** (WA).

Wouldn't you like to know the story behind **JUDAS** in Washington and **LUCIFER** in Mississippi? Or maybe you wouldn't. It might be safer to stick with plates that celebrate saints: **ST JOHN** (MI, WA), **ST JUDE** (IN, WA), **ST LUCIA** (WA), or the children's favorite, **ST NICK** (TX). Or plates that feature the drivers' favorite **PSALMS** (IA, ID, IN), as in **PSALM 1** (KY, WA), **PSALM 23** (TX, WA), and also numbers 9, 16, 22, 25, 27, 32, 34, 37, 40, 51, 63, 91, and 96.

A few motorists apply a touch of religion for somewhat less than fully spiritual ends, for example, **PRA4SRF**, **PRA4SUN**, and **PRA4WND**, all from Washington state. But **FEARNOT** (WA). **HEAVEN** (IA, ID, MI, TX) holds a place for all who **LUV GOD** (IN, MS, TX) and seek **NULIFE** (IA) through whichever religion one might choose. Considering the vast number of religious alternatives, **THX2GOD** (WA) for that. **AMEN** (IA, ID, IN, KY, MI, WY), brethren and sistren. **AAAMEN** (TX).

ALELUIA (WA)
ALLELU (WA)
ANGEL (MS)
APOSTLE (WA)
ARCANGL (WA)
ASK HIM (TX)
BAPTIST (IA)
BEHOLY (MI)
BELIEVE (WA)
BIBLE (MI)
BLESED (TX)
BLESSD (IA, MI, MS, TX)
BLESSST (WA)
BLESST (MS, TX)
BLEST (MS, TX)
BLEST 1 (MS)
BLESSU (IA, IN, MI)
BLESSU2 (IL, IN, WA)
BLES U (TX)
BLE55ED (VA)
BORNAGN (IA)
B READY (MS)
BUDDHA (KY)
BYFAITH (WA)
B4GIVEN (WA)
B4JESUS (WA)
CALVARY (IN)
CHERB (WA)
CHRIST (MI, WA)
CHRIUST (DE)
CINNER (MI)
CLERGY (KY)
CYNFUL (MI)
DEVINE (ID, MI)
EASTER (IN, MI, WA)
ELIJAH (IN, MI)
ELOHIM (MI, MS)
FORGIV (IA)
FORGVE (KY)
FORGVN (IA)
GALILEE (IN)
GENESIS (IA, WA)
GLORY (IA)
GOD CAN (IN, KY, MI, MS)
GOD DID (MS)
GODFRST (WA)
GODGAVE (IN, WA)
GOD IS (KY, MS)
GOD IST (MS)
GODIS1ST (NC)
GOD LED (MS)
GOD LUV (MS)
GODLUVU (WA)
GODLVSU (WA)
GODMAN (KY)
GOD NUS (MS)
GOD RULZ (IN)
GOD WIL (MI, MS)
GOD WILL (IN)
GODS KID (IN)
GODS4U (I)
GODWON (MI)
GODZKID (IN)
GOD 1 (KY)
GOD 1ST (MI, MS)
GOD 3N1 (MS)
GOD 4ME (MS, TX)
GOD 4U (MS)
GOD 4US (MS)
GOLIATH (ID)
GOOD NUS (VA)
GOSPEL (MI)
GO2GOD (CA, MS, TX)
GO2GOD2 (CA)
GO2GSUS (CA)
GO2HEVN (CA)

GO2JSUS (CA)
GO 4 GOD (CA, IA, KY, MI, TX, WA)
GO 4 GSUS (CA)
GRACE (ID, MI)
GUD NEWS (VA)
GZSAVES (CA)
GZSLIVS (CA)
GZSLVS (CA)
GZSONLY (CA)
GZSLRD (CA)
GZUSZVS (CA)
GZUSFAN (CA)
GZUSLVZ (CA)
GZUSNME (CA)
GZUSNOS (CA)
GZUSROX (CA)
GZUSWIL (CA)
GZUS1ST (CA)
GZUS4ME (CA)
GZUS4U2 (CA)
GZUSCAN (CA)
GZUZNUS (CA)
HALLUYA (ID)
HEARGOD (WA)
HEAVN (TX)
HELIVES (WA)
HELIVS (WA)
HELOVSU (WA)
HELUVSU (WA)
HE'S REAL (NC)
HOLY 1 (IA, TX)
HOSANAH (WA)
HOSANNA (WA)
HOZANA (WA)
HVNCENT (WA)
IAMLOVE (WA)
I-B-LEVE (TX)
IB 4GIVN (VA)
ILOVGOD (WA)
IM4GOD (MI, WA)
IPRAY (IA)
IPRAY2 (KY)
I RISE (VA)
ISAVED (MS)
ISHARE (IA)
JCSAVES (WA)
JEESUS (CA)
JEESUSS (CA)
JEESUZ (CA)
JEEZIS (CA)
JESUS (FL, ID, KY, MI, MS, NJ, TX)
JESUS C (MI, MS, NC, TX)
JESUS IS (IN)
JESUS 1 (MS)
JEWISH (WA)
JEZYS (MS)
JOYFUL (IA)
JOYOUS (IA, MI)
JOY2U (VA)
JSUSAVS (WA)
KNOWGOD (WA)
KRYST (AK)
KYRIE (WA)
LAMBOGD (WA)
LETGOD (MI, MS, WA)
LIV4GOD (IN)
LOVEGOD (IN)
LOV GOD (MS)
LPRAY4U (IA)
LUCIFER (WA)
LUVGIFT (WA)
LUVGOD (IA, MI, WA)
LVGIFT (TX)
LVHEALS (WA)

LVNGOD (AK)
MBLEST (WA)
MOONIE (ID, WA)
MYLORD (WA)
NEWLIFE (WA)
NJESUS (MS, WA)
OHGOD (WA)
OHMAGOD (WA)
OHMYGOD (WA)
ONE GOD (MI, MS, TX)
ONE JC (MS)
01 LORD (MS)
PRAISE (IN)
PRAY (WY)
PRAYED4 (ID)
PRAYER (DE)
PRAY4US (WA)
PRAZGOD (IN, WA)
PRAZHIM (WA)
PRAZHM (M)
REBIRTH (WA)
REBORN (IA, KY, WA)
REBURTH (WA)
REJOICE (IA, ID, WA)
REJOYC (IA)
REV (MI)
REVERAND (ID)
R*FATHR (TX)
RGHTOUS (VA)
RUSAVD (MS, WA)
RUSAVED (WA)
RU4HIM (WA)
SACRED (IA)
SAINT (NC, TX)
SAVED (AK, MS, NJ, TX, WA)
SAVIOR (MS)
SINFUL (MI)
SONRISE (VA)
ST JAMES (IN)
ST JOAN (MI)
ST MARYS (IN)
TELGOD (MI)
TENKGOD (CA)
TENQGOD (CA)
THE ARC (MI)
THE ARK (MI, MS)
THE WAY (MS, TX)
THK U LD (TX)
THNKGOD (WA)
THXLORD (WA)
TRIGOD (AK)
TRINITY (WA)
TRUST HM (VA)
TRYGOD (AK, IA, KY, MS, TX, WA)
TRYGZUS (WA)
TRY HIM (MS)
UPRAY2 (MS, WA)
UREPENT (WA)
UR4GIVN (WA)
VAN4GOD (WA)
VIAGOD (MI)
WE PRAY (MS)
YAHWEH (AK, IA, KY, MI, TX)
YAWEH (MS)
YES GOD (MI)
YESLORD (WA)
1 FAITH (MS)
1 GOD (MI, MS, TX)
1 JESUS (MI)
1 LORD (IA, MS)
1 SAINT (MS)
2 PRAY (MS)
4 BIBLE (IA)

4 FAITH (MS)
4 GIVEN (ID, KY, MS, SC, TX)
4GIVN (ID, IN, MS)
4 GOD (MS)
4 JESUS (AK, IA, MI, MS, WI)
6 4GSUS (VA)

This land is my land.

Serving God seems to be more on our collective mind than serving Caesar. Only a handful of personalized tags salute the flag. Of those that do, some show pride in one's country: **LUV USA** (MS), **USA BEST** (IN), **USAOK** (IN, WA), **USA A*OK** (TX), **USA NO1** (IN, KY), **USA4EVR** (WA), **USA4ME** (KY, WA), and **YESUSA** (MI).

Others may be the plates of people who fear for their jobs: **BYAMRCN** (WA), **IBUYUSA** (IA, IL), **NOT4N** (IA, IN), **NOT 4UN** (IN), **YBUY4N** (IN).

FLAGWV (WA) and **US FLAG** (TX) certainly don't sound like flag burners, and **C THE US** (TX) and **SEE USA** (CT) also sound proud of their native land. We may not have had much to cheer about in recent scraps with other countries, but in Oregon **WE1WW2** (We won World War II) is still celebrating the big one.

A modest number of plates address political issues: **DETENT** (CA), **END WAR** (MS,

TX, WA), **ERA** (AK, IN, MS), **ERA NOW** (AK), **ERAYES** (WA), **GO4ERA** (VA), **NONUKES** (WA), **PRO LIF** (WI), **JOIN NRA** (WA), **IRSUCKS** (WA), **KO55MPH** (WA), **X55MPH** (WA), and **55Z 2LO** (MS). There are even a few holdovers that express such merry Reagan-era fantasies as **AXTAX** (WI) and **LESSTAX** (WA).

ALL USA (MI)
AMERCAN (IN)
AMERICA (ID, IN, WA)
AMERIKA (WA)
BORNUSA (IN)
BUYNUSA (IN)
BUYUSA (AK, IA, ID, IN, MI, MS, WA)
EQUALITY (CA)
ERA (CA)
ERAVAN (IA)
FLYUSA (MS, WA)
GO VOTE (TX)
LBERTY (MS)
LESTAX (KY)
LIBERTY (WA)
LIBRT (WA)
LIBRTY (WA)
LOVEUSA (IN, WA)
MADE US (OR)
MDNUSA (AK)
MR GOP (IL)
MUGWUMP (WA)
NO NUKE (SC, WI)
NO4NJNK (ID)
ONE USA (MI)
PASBILL (CA)
PATRIOT (IN, WA)
P8TRIOT (WA)
PROLIFE (IN)
PRO LYF (MS)
RPBLCN (TX)
SUS (DE)
USA (AK, IN, KY, MI, WA)
USAMADE (IN, WA)
USAMAID (IN)
USA*MEX (TX)
USA NO1 (IN)
USAONE (KY)
USA 4 ME (OH)
USBILT (IA, MS, ND)
USBUILT (WA)
USFLAG (KY)
USMADE (IA, ID, KY, MI)
US MALE (IL, MI)
VOTE DEM (IL)
VOTE GOP (IL)
X55 (WA)
55 HAHA (MS)
55 IZ2LO (CA)
55S 2LO (MS)

CHAPTER 13

A Mixed Bag

AINT IT nice URA 10?

AINT IT? asks a Mississippi license plate in apparent reply to "Boy, that's some fine lookin' car," or some other such compliment. By contrast **COOLHUH** (NM) seems to be fishing for a compliment, as are **BIG HUH** (MS), **HOWRWE** (AK), **HOWZIT** (MI), **NEAT HUH** (ID), **NICE EH** (MS), **NYCEHUH** (WA), and **WHOS BAD** (IN). One can't be sure, but **NTEDGRT** (VA) seems to be asking, "Isn't Ted great?"

Other plates in the form of questions sound a note of challenge: **ARUREDI** (WA), **IMA10RU** (WA), **IZZATSO** (WA), **OH YEAH** (MI), **ORWHAT** (IA), **RUCRZY** (IA), **RU NEXT** (MS), **RU REDY** (MS), **SEZ WHO** (ID, MI), **SOWHAT** (AK,

IA, ID, IN, MI, MS, TX), **UAGAIN** (WA), or **UHEARME** (WA).

Question plates such as **AM I** (WA), **HOW** (MI), **IAMRYOU** (WA), **IDNIT** (MS), **RU SURE** (IA), **UNOWHAT** (WA), **U WHAT** (MS), **WHATIF** (IA, MI, MS, TX), **WHAT 4** (CT, MI, TX), **WHO** (IA, MI), **WHUT** (MS), **YDIDU** (MS), and **4 WHAT** (MS) are less than clear in meaning.

Tinged with suggestiveness, or so it might seem, are **DO YA** (MS), **IAMRU** (AK, WA), **IDU DU U** (VA), **IMEZRU** (IL, MS, OH, WA), **IMRDRU** (WA), **RU BAD 2** (ID), **RUEASY** (WA), **RUESE2** (WA), **RU1TOO** (TX, WA), and **UWANNA** (IA, WA). **IM HIRU** (MS), **RU BUZN** (MS), **RUHIGH** (WA), and **RU NUMB** (IL) have connotations of, shall we say, real substance.

Many such plates get quite specific, as in **AMIBLUE** (ID, VA), **DO U SKI** (TX), **IHAPYRU** (WA), **RUFIT** (WA), **RUFUZ** (WA), **RU NASTY** (VA), **SINGLRU** (WA), **WHYRENT** (WA), **WHY 55** (AK, MS, WI), **YB FAT** (DE, OH), **YBI4N** (PA), and **YGRO UP** (MS, VA). **YW8-4U** (PA) is probably an impatient driver, or else a husband inexorably headed for divorce.

Good usage is flouted in **HOW U BE** (TX), **HUIB** (WA), **SAYWATT** (IN, WA), **SHONUF** (MS), **WHO B U** (MS), **WHO HE** (TX), and **WUTIT-B** (VA). **WHODAT** (AK, IA, KY, MS)?

WOOZAT (IN) say who dat? Maybe a fan of the New Orleans Saints?

So **YB DULL** (MS)? **RUREADY** (WA) to dream up a question for your own plate — maybe a Telly Savalas-like **WHOLUVSU** (NC), a philosophical **YMIHERE** (ID), or for the literary-minded, something special along the lines of **2 BR NOT** (VA). **WHO KNOS** (VA) what you could come up with if you try?

A WHAT (MS)
DIDWHAT (WA)
DOIOU (MI)
DOIOU2 (MI)
DO U TAN (TX)
DOWHAT (MS, WA)
DO YOU (MI, MS, TX)
FST ENF (MS)
GESSWHO (ID)
GESWHO (IA, TX)
HOWDO (ID, MI)
HOWMUCH (IA, IN)
HOWRU (AK, IN, MS)
HOWRYA (ID, IN)
HOWRYOU (IA)
HOWRYU (TX)
HOW YAL (TX)
HOWYOUB (WA)
HOWZIT (AK)
HUH (IN)
IMEZRU2 (WA)
IML8RU2 (WA)
IMOKRU (DE, MI, WA)
IROKDOU (WA)
ISKIDOU (ID, SC)
KNUPLAY (WA)
NICEHUH (IN, WA)
NO WHAT (MS)
NOWWHAT (WA)
NOW WUT (MS)
OH YEA (KY)
ORRWHAT (WA)
OYEAH (MI)
REALLY (KY)
ROCN RU (VA)
RUA10 (DE)
RU BLU2 (MS)
RUCOOL (IA, KY, WA)
RUCRAZ (IA)
RU CRAZY (WA)
RUFAST (KY)
R UFIT (KY)
RUFIT2 (WA)
RUFREE (WA)
RU GOOD (MS)
RUGTNIT (WA)
RU HAPPY (WA)
RU HIP (WA)

R-U-HP (KY)
RU KYND (VA)
RU KRAZE (VA)
RU LOST (KY, MS)
RUSECUR (WA)
RU SEXY (TX)
RU SNGL (TX)
RUSURE (KY)
RUWILD (KY, TX)
RUXITED (ID)
RU4LSU (MS)
RU4ME (IA)
RU4REAL (IA, WA)
SAYWAT (IA, TX, WA)
SAYWHA (WA)
SO WAT (KY)
SOWHATT (ID)
SO WHUT (MS)
SO WUT (MI, MS)
SUEWHO (IA)
UNOWHO (WA)
UPRDOWN (WA)
UREADY (TX, WA)
UWANNA (KY)
U-WANT-1 (TX)
U-WANT-2 (TX)
U2 HUH (MS)
U4 REAL (MS)
WANT 1 (VA)
WAT NOW (MS)
WATS UP (KY, MS)
WATZAT (IA)
WAWAZAT (IN)
WCH WAY (MS)
WHASSUP (IN)
WHASUP (KY, MI, MS)
WHAT (MI, TX, WY)
WHAT AM I (VA)
WHAT NOW (IN)
WHATNXT (WA)
WHATSUP (ID, WA)
WHAZAT (IA, MS)
WHAZUP (IA)
WHERE2 (MI)
WHOAREU (WA)
WHODAT (AK, IA, MS)
WHOISIT (VA)
WHO ME (ID, MS)
WHO MEE (TX)
WHO NEXT (IN)
WHO R U (MS, TX)
WHO THAT (VA)
WHO U (MS)
WHOZAT (TX)
WHOZIT (MS)
WHOZNXT (WA)
WHUS UP (MS)
WHY (MS)
WHY ASK (MS)
WHY BNML (VA)
WHY-FLY (TX)
WHYME (AK, IA, ID, IL, IN, MI, MS)
WHYME2 (VA)
WHY NOT (CT, IA, ID, IN, MI, MS, TX)
WHYTRY (IA, MS)
WHYUS (IA, TX)
WUTSIT (AK)
WUTS UP (MS)
WUTZUP (MS)
WUZ UP (TX)
Y (KY)
YAWANA (IA, MI)
YBFAT (ID)
YB GOOD (MS)

YBHI (MS)
YB HIGH (MS)
YBNICE (KY)
YBNORM (VA)
YBNORML (IN)
YBNRMAL (IN)
YBNRML (KY)
YB SAD (KY)
YBUY 4N (MS)
Y KNOT (KY)
Y ME (KY)
YME MAC (VA)
YI WORK (MI)
YNOT (ID, MI, WY)
YNOTT (KY, MI)
YRUFAT (CT, IA, IL, MS)
YRUMAD (MI, MS)
YRUSLO (MS, SC)
YRU2LO (MS)
YRU4ME (VA)
YSTARE (VA)
Y WORRY (KY, MI)
YYME (MI)
1FINE RU (VA)

O U QT, URA 1DER.

Very few plates have been used to pass out compliments. Once in a great while I see one and shout **WAY2GO** (MI, SC) to the driver. Or **ATABOY** (IA, MS, OH)! **NICE2CU** (ID), they reply.

The tiniest handful of compliment plates are fairly general, like those above. **I DZRVIT** (IN) seems to be a self-compliment. **ILIKEU** (WA) has a nice, friendly ring, and is answered by **ILIKEU2** (IN, WA). **THKS DR** (TX) gives credit where credit is no doubt due; **URA 1DER** (VA) sounds sincerely pleased; and **WLDONE** (MI) is either a compliment or someone ordering a steak.

More of these plates, however, are of the romantic or flirting kind: **CRAZY4U** (IN), **HIUQTU** (IN), **ICUQT** (AK), **ILOVEU** (KY, MI) and **ILUVU2** (MI), **O U QT** (OH), **UBABE** (AK), **UDARLIN** (WA), **UFOXU** (WA), **UR4ME** (MI), **USENDME** (WA), and **UWLDTHG** (ID).

URA 10 (MS) recalls the movie that introduced Bo Derek as a sex symbol and elicited one of the shortest movie reviews on record. ''Macho Ernie'' Wyatt, a great Georgian, wrote: ''*10* is an absolutely awful movie. I recommend it highly.''

ATTABOY (IN)
ILUVU (IN, MI)
ILUVYA (IN)
NIC 2CU (WI)
QT PIE (MI)
UFOX (WA)
UNICE (MS)
UQDPIE (KY)
UQTPIU (MS)
URFINE (WA)
URGOOD (WA)
U-R-LUVD (TX)
UR OK 2 (OH)
UR2 COOL (ID)
UR2KOOL (ID)
UR 2 MCH (TX)
WA-TA-GO (TX)

KICNBAK
in your rolling PLAPEN.

Especially for the young, cars are **ABLAST** (IA, VA), **AGAS** (MS), **AHOOT** (TX, WA). **A SPORT** (ID) uses his car for **CRUISN** (MS, OR)

— as a **FUNMBLE** (ID) for **PARTYN** (TX) and **HVINFUN** (IA).

A HAPIVAN (WA) can be **MEGAFUN** (WA), a **RAMBLN** (IA) **PLAPEN** (IA) for the guy or gal who's ready to **PRTY DN** (TX). So if you're **RDY4FUN** (IA), climb aboard the **FUNXPRS** (WA) and get set for **KICNBAK** (WA) and doing some serious **PAR T N** (MS). **FA LA LA** (ND) and **TRA LALA** (VA), just call me **MR FUN** (OH). This **EZGOIN** (AK, ID) **JIV TRKY** (VA)'s really **ROLLIN** (AK) now.

Come on! We're going to have a **TONAFUN** (IA). On second thought, never mind. This sounds too much like a Richard Simmons commercial.

ALLNFUN (WA)
AL4FUN (IA)
BCRUZN (ID)
BIG FUN (MI)
BREAZEN (CA)
BREAZIN (CA)
BREAZN (CA)
BREAZNN (CA)
BREEEZN (CA)
BREEZIN (LA)
BREEZN (DE)
BRZWGN (KY)
CHILLN (KY)
COASTN (IA)
CPTFUN (WA)
CROOZN (KY)
CRUISIN (IL)
CRUSER (AK)
CRUSIN (AK, MI)
CRUZIN (AK, KY)
CRUZN (MI)
CRUZN BY (KY)
CRUZZR (VA)
DOINITUP (NC)
DRFTER (AK, IA)
DRIFTER (IA)
EZCOME (WA)
EZGO (WA)
EZLIFE (ID)
FERFUN (ID)
FN2DRIV (ID)
FORKIX (IA)
FTLUSE (MI)
FUNCTY (WA)

FUN TOY (TX)
FUNFOR 2 (IA)
FUNFUN (IA)
FUNLVN (AK)
FUN4ME (KY)
GDTIME (AK)
GROOVY (IA)
GRTFUN (VA)
GR8LIFE (ID)
GYPSY (IA)
HAP IN N (TX)
HAVN FN (MS)
HAVNFUN (IA)
HPY-DAY (TX)
HVNFUN (IA, MI)
IBCRUZN (SC)
ICRUSA (IA)
IRFUN (WA)
ITSFUN (AK)
JSTFUN (VA)
JST4FN (IA, KS)
JST4FUN (IA)
JST4KIX (IN)
JS4FUN (IA, KY)
KICNBAC (WA)
KREWSN (MS)
KREWZN (KY, MS)
KRUSIN (IA, MS)
KUTNUP (KY)
LAYNBAK (VA)
LUVTCRZ (VA)
MORFUN (IA)
N JOYME (VA)
OUT4FUN (LA)
PHUN (MS)
PLAY-N (ND, TX)
PLUMFUN (ID)
RAMBLON (ID)
REALFUN (IA)
RECESS (IA)
ROAMIN (AK)
ROMPIN (KY)
ROVIN (AK)
RUN FRE (ND)
SOMEFUN (ID)
SUM FUN (MS)
TOOLIN (IA)
TRAVLN (AK)
1CRUSIN (VA)
1MRFUN (IA)
14FUN (MI)
4CRUZEN (IA)
4CRUZN (IA)
4KICKS (IA)

DADZILA and MEGAMOM had TRPLETS

California motorists have **AONEDAD** and **AONEMOM**, also **AOKWIFE**. Washington has **ARADDAD**, **DADZGRL**, and even **DADZILA**. In

Idaho is a busy man, **DAD OF 13**, who has quite a lead on Ohio's **DAD OF 4** or Virginia's **MA OF 6**.

It must be a large New Mexico family that chose **FMLYZOO** for its car, and **GEMINI** (IA) is likely on the auto of a family that has **TWINS** (IN, MI). **BIG PAPA** (ID) or **BIG MAMOO** (IA, MI) might have to issue a curfew to get their **SML FRY** (MS) **INBY10** (UT).

Was it a romantic young **NULEWED** (WA) who dreamed up **T4TWO** (OH), or **U-ONLY** (TX), or **U N ME** (OH, TX), or **2UBTRU** (VA)? Or was it a **FXYGRMA** (WA)?

The traditional role of wife and mother has been portrayed on plates in every conceivable variation. **BG MAMA** (MS), **BZYMOM** (VA), **DFRAU** (IA), **MAA MOO** (MS), **MAMA** (AK, MI), **MAMMY** (ID, MI), **MOM** (TX), **MEGAMOM** (WA), **MOMMEY** (VA), **MOTHER** (IA, MS), and **MUDDER** (IN), for example.

DADDY (IA, ID, IN, KY) plates also appear frequently, and often identify dear old **DAD** (IA, IN, KY, MI) as the person who shelled out the long green to buy **SISTER** (MI) or her **BIGBRO** (ID) their car, as in **DAD BUYS** (VA), **FROM DAD** (IA, IN, MI), **IODADDY** (AL), **IOUDAD** (KY, MI), **IOU POP** (MS), **THNXPA** (IA), **THX DAD** (TX), **WASDADS** (ID, WA), and **WOWDAD**

(IA). Perhaps this explains the Idaho plate **POORPOP**.

One wonders which spouse is responsible for **YES DEAR** (IN), and if **WED4EVR** (WA) represents a wish for the future, or if, alas, if speaks more to the past. It's a wonder that the owners of **TRPLETS** (IN, WA) had time to bother with personalized plates at all. What kind of a **MOTHR HN** (AL) is **MT MAMA** (IA)? Also, what happened to explain the plate **DADSMAD** (IN)?

From **ME N YOU** (TX), **HE SHE** (TX) — you know, families with **NO KIDS** (CT) — suddenly come **4 GIRLS** (IA) or **5 BOYS** (IA), or even **12 KIDS** (IA).

WE3KNGS (WA) sounds like a Christmas carol but might just belong to a family named King. The plate **5 BUCHS** (TX) is the property of a Buchanan family, **5 CENTS** (TX) of the Nickel family.

GR8MOM (MS), **GR8DAD** (AK), **9TH KID** (VA) — real family stuff. Gee, Beav, sort of reminds you of the Brady Bunch.

A DADDY (MS)
A FAMIL (MS)
AFBRAT (ID)
ALBOYS (??)
ALLBOYS (ID)
AMIGOS (MI)

ARMY MOM (IN)
A1 MOM (KY)
A1 POP (KY)
A1 WIFE (IN)
BESTMOM (IA)
BESTPA (IA)
BIGDAD (KY)
CMOMGO (ID)
DADCAR (IA)
DADDYO (AK, MI)
DADMOM (IA)
DAFOLKS (ID)
DAPAPA (IA)
ELPAPA (ID)
FAMILY (IA, ID, IN, WA)
FAMLYFN (WA)
FATHER (MS, TX)
FMLY TOY (ID)
FOR US (MS)
FUN4US (AK)
GOMOMGO (WA)
GRAMA (IA)
GRAMAW (IA)
GRAMMA (MS)
GRAMMY (MI, MS)
GRAMP (MS)
GRAMPA (MI)
GRAMPS (MI)
GRANDAD (IA)
GRANDMA (IA, IN)
GRANDPA (IA, IN)
GRANEE (IA)
GRANMA (KY)
GRANNI (IA)
GRANNIE (ID, IN)
GRANNY (IA, ID, IN, MI)
GRANPA (IA, KY)
GRANPOP (IA)
GR8KDS (AK)
HUBBY (IA)
ILOVMOM (WA)
I LUV MOM (IN)
IMHIS (AK)
IMPOP (IA)
I ODAD (KY)
IODADY (MS)
IOMA (WA)
IOMOM1 (MS)
IOMYDAD (WA)
IOMYMA (VA)
IOUDAD (KY)
IOU MA (MS)
ITSOURS (IA)
ITSUS2 (AK)
ITZOURS (WA)
JRSBUG (IA)
JRSHOM (IA)
JST4US (VA)
JUSUS2 (AK)
JUSWE2 (AK)
LOVE DAD (IN)
LOVERS (IA)
LUVKIDS (IN)
LUVUDAD (IN)
MAAMAW (KY)
MAINMOM (IA)
MAMA GO (VA)
MAMA MIA (VA)
MAMAW (KY)
MA N KD (MS)
MAWMAW (AK, IA)
MAMPOP (MI)
MEANDU (MS)
MISUMOM (WA)
MOMBUS (IA)
MOMCAR (IA)

MOMDAD (IA, KY, MI, MS)
MOMMIE (IA)
MOMMY (AK, CT)
MOMNO1 (KY)
MOMOF3 (AK)
MOMOF8 (VA)
MOMPOP (DE)
MOMSCAR (IA)
MOMSVAN (IA)
MOMVAN (AK)
MR MOM (IN, MI)
MRMRS (DE)
MSMOM (AK)
MUMOF4 (VA)
MY TWINS (IN)
MY 3 BOYS (IN)
NEWBORN (WA)
NEWDAD (AK)
NEWKID (MS, VA)
NEWKIDS (VA)
NO1DAD (AK, IA, IN, KY)
NO1MOM (AK, IA, IN, MI)
NO1POP (AK, KY)
NO1SON (IA, ID)
NO1WIFE (IN)
OLDAD (AK, IA)
ON DAD (KY)
OURCAR (IA)
OUR MOM (MS)
OURS (NJ)
OURKAR (VA)
OURMOM (AK)
OURTRK (IA)
OURVAN (IA)
PAPPY (KY)
PAWPAW (AK)
POPOF5 (IA)
PORPOP (ID)
RADADDY (WA)
RAD DAD (TX)
RUGRAT (MI)
SIX 0 US (ND)
SQUAW (MI)
SUMDAD (WA)
TENQMOM (CA)
TGETHR (VA)
THANX MA (IN)
THEPOP (AK)
THXGRPA (ID)
THXMOM (ID)
THWIFE (ID)
TIME4U (IA)
TOPMOM (AK)
TOYFOR2 (IA)
UANDI (WA)
UANDME (WA)
UANI (DE, WA)
UNCLE (MI)
U-ONLY (TX)
USNWIF (VA)
USPLUS2 (VA)
WE THRE (VA)
WIFEY (AK)
WIFIE (TX)
WOWMOM (IA)
YERMOM (AK)
YOUNME (WA)
1MRMOM (VA)
1-PAPA (KY)
2BRATS (AK)
2ZENUF (VA)
3SENUF (IA)
4DAD (IA)
4PADRE (VA)
4UDAD (MI)
4U-MOM (MI, TX)

4 U N ME (TX)
4 US (TX)
4 US 2 (TX)
4 US 4 (TX)
5 GIRLS (IA, MI)
5 KIDS (AK)
5 OFUS (AK)
5ZENUF (IA)
5ZNUF (TX)
6OFUS (AK)
12 OF 13 (VA)

CRUSHER and BUZSAW were MACHO

Far removed from those homey, loving family plates are the **MACHO** (CO), muscle-flexing, hair-covered plates of tough guys: **AMBUSHR** in Idaho, **BRUISER** and **BUZSAW** in Iowa, **CRUSHR** in Alaska, **DBEAST** of Delaware, **DR DOOM** in Illinois, **HITMAN** in Michigan and Kentucky, **L-BRUTE** in Oregon, **PBLC ENMY** in North Carolina, **SLASH-R** and **THE HUN** in Texas, and **TROUBLE** in Louisiana and Indiana.

Whatever the cause of the impulse, some of our fellow drivers want to let us know that if you mess with them, it's going to be **BAD NUZ** (ND) and they'll **KRUSHU** (WA). They'll show you **NOMERCY** (WA) and **NOQWOTR** (VA) 'cause they're on a **RABID** (WA), **SAVAGE** (AK, MI) **RAMPAGE** (WA).

Beware the **DSPRADO** (IN, WA) **HDBANGR** (WA) whose car or truck is a **DEADLY** (IN, MS) **FEARWGN** (WA), a **PRDATR** (MI) of the highways and a **MENACE** (AK, ID, MI) to society.

So unless you want **TRUBLE** (AK, IA, KY), stay away from this **BURLY** (IA), **VENOMUS** (WA) road **WARIOR** (MI, MS), or he'll **WHOMP** (AK) you good. He's **2TUF4U** (AK), and who knows, he might even be a member of **Z MOB** (MI).

BADGUY (IA)
BADMAN (IA)
BAD NEWS (IL)
BANDIT (MI)
BRUTAL (IA)
BRUTE (KY)
BRUZER (MI)
DANGER (AK)
DANGRUS (WA)
EVIL (ID)
HE MAN (MS)
HNGNTUF (IN)
HOODLUM (ID)
IBTUFF (WA)
IMTRBL (AK)
IMTRBLE (WA)
IMTUFF (IA, TX)
IRONMAN (IA)
IRUFF (MI)
KDTRBL (WA)
KILER (MS)
KILLER (ID, KY, MI, MS, NJ, TX)
KRUSHER (WA)
LETHAL (TX)
LETHUL (TX)
MAULER (AK)
MRBAD (IA)
NOMURCY (WA)
OUTLAW (AK, ID)
OWTLAW (MS)
PRDATOR (WA)
PROWLER (IA)
PROWLR (IA)
RAMTUF (WA)
RAMTUFF (WA)
RAWMEAT (WA)
ROWDY (TX)
RUFBOY (ID, KY, TX)
RUFFIAN (WA)
RUFIAN (IA)
RUFNEK (AK, MS)
SLAYER (MI, OR, WA)
SNIPER (MI)
SOTUFF (IA)

STALKER (ID)
STALKR (IA)
SWNGFST (WA)
TEROR (AK)
TERROR (IA)
TOUGH (IA)
TOUGHY (ID)
TROUBL (MI)
TRMNATR (ID)
TRUBL (AK)
TUF BOY (MS)
TUFENF (AK)
TUFF (KY, MI)
TUFFGUY (WA)
TUFFSS (MI)
TUFGUY (IA, IN, MS, WA)
TUFINUF (WA)
TUFMUDR (WA)
TUFFY (AK, MS)
TUFTUF (WA)
TUFUNUF (IN)
TUTUFF (MS, WA)
U-B-TUFF (TX)
VENOM (AK, IA, WA)
VICIOUS (IN)
VIPER (IA)
VISHUS (AK, IA, ID, MS, ND)
WARRIOR (VA)
Z KILLER (VA)
2 TOUGH (AK)
2 TUFF (KY)

CHAPTER 14

Neither Fish Nor Fowl

Have a DULL plate? Could be DULLER.

Some of the most thought-provoking of all personalized plates are those that don't fit neatly into any of the categories in this book. A fair number of these provocative plates are inexplicable unless you know their owners' names. In Oregon, for example, lives a Ms. Vowles whose plate reads, appropriately, **AEIOU**. **BRUNCH** belongs to a Mr. Bruncheen in Iowa, **COUDBE** to a Mr. Mabie, also of Iowa, **CUTBAX** to a Mr. Baxter of Kentucky, and **MONEY** to a Mrs. Money of Delaware. **DEECEE**

(KY) belongs to the Washington Apparel Group Inc.

FUGITT (TX) doesn't refer to what tempus does, but to the car's owner, a Mr. Fugitt. **CURLYQ** (IA) is on a car belonging to a Ms. Cue, **COBWEB** (TX) to a Mr. Cobb, **BOOZER** (TX) to a Mr. Boozer, **HUFNPUF** (IA) to a Mr. Huff, **MRCLEAN** (IA) to a Mr. McClean. Similarly, **MRLOVE** (IA) adorns the auto of a real Mr. Love; **FOXXXX** (TX) belongs to a Mr. Fox; and **MRSOB** (IA) isn't what first meets the eye, but belongs to a Mrs. O'Brian. **WEDGIE** (IA) doesn't mean what you might suppose; instead it is owned by a pizza business. The plate **RAZOR** is the property of a Mr. Razor of Kentucky.

Also in Iowa, a state whose residents seem to specialize in this sort of plate, a car with **DULL** on its license plate belongs to a Mrs. Dull. Mr. Dull's plate? Did you guess it? That's right: **DULLER**.

Highly favored among people named McDonald is the plate **EIEIO** (AK, CO, MI, NJ, OH, UT, WA, WI). Wisconsin also has **EIEIOH**.

JUNGMAN might sound like the plate of a Jungian psychologist, but merely belongs to a Mr. and Mrs. Jungman of Iowa. **PUTOFF**

(IA) sounds like what we wait until tomorrow to do rather than taking care of today, but is actually the property of a Mr. Pottorff. **LARNCE** (VA) is a plate with a southern accent that belongs to someone named Lawrence; **LUMPEE** belongs to a Mr. Lumpee of Texas, **PIFFLE** to a Mr. Pfile of that same state, and **NEW-1** (KY) to a Mr. New.

RAUNCH (IA) is the tag of a Ms. Raunch, who is probably just as sick and tired of being kidded as is a Ms. Waddle, whose plate reads **WADDLE** (IA). **A-SALOM** (TX) isn't a Muslim greeting, but the plate of a Mr. Salom. **A CENT** (TX) belongs to a motorist whose name is Penny.

SINNER (IA) really does belong to a Mr. Sinner, and **SLEEZE** (IA) is sported merrily by a Mr. Sleezer. **SWEAR** (IA) goes with a Mrs. Swearingen, **STERNO** (TX) with a Mr. Stern, **TEASER** (IA) with a Mr. Teaser, **TRULY** (IA) with a Mr. Truly, **TRUMP** not with the much publicized Donald of New York, but an Iowan named Trumpold.

WEEONE (IA) is the property of a Mr. Weeces, **WELOVE** (IA) of a Mr. Love, **WISE** (IA) of a Mr. Wise, **WORKMN** (IA) of a Mr. Workman. A Mr. Kenworthy of Iowa uses **WORTHY**, a Mr. Rath **WRATH** (IA), a Mr.

Wurster **WURST** (IA). **SIN** (IA) belongs to a woman whose first name is Cynthia, **DOUBLE O** to a Texan named Outlaw whose first name also beings with the letter O.

A few of these plates have complicated stories behind them. The California plate **H HMBRT** would be meaningless unless you knew the inside joke involved — that it belongs to a middle-aged man who married a much younger woman and became a "geezer father." The plate, dreamed up by his young wife, is a reference to the protagonist in the novel *Lolita*.

Some of the plates that can tantalize us most are those that, like good poems, aren't "perfectly clear," as Richard Nixon used to say, but present us with an element of mystery. **ABLE2** (WA) is a simple example. Able to do what? Think about it and all sorts of vistas unfold before you.

The same can be said for the folksy Ohio plate **AINTEZ**. What ain't? we have to ask. **ALMOST** and **ALWAYS** are Iowa plates with the same built-in, unseen question mark, as are **ANYTIME** from South Carolina, **IBETOO** from Virginia, **IDIDIT** from Alaska, **IHOPESO** from North Carolina, and **ILIED** from Washington.

If you saw **ARUMOR** from Iowa drive by, you'd have to wonder what the rumor was about. Does **ATRAIN** (VA) belong to a Duke Ellington buff, and is **BAMBO** (IA) a deer-style Rambo?

To what do **BUYNBI** (VA) and **BYNBY** (IA) refer? Does **CRUMPET** (WA) mean the snack the English enjoy with tea, or the kind they take out for an illicit night on the town? **IASKU** (VA) makes the viewer respond, "Ask you what?" Does **IMD14U** refer to the driver or the car? Is **MRSYUK** (IA) a lady comedian? Is the owner of the plate **IAM** (AK, KY) a philosopher? And what of **NUTN2IT** (WA)? Nothing to what?

Is **OUTNMAY** (VA) the plate of a college student or of one of the prison inmates who stamps out these plates? Does **OMYEARS** (VA) belong to someone with ear trouble or to a gray panther? Is **SERVE** (IA) an altruist? A waiter? A tennis player? Are **CYNBAD** (MS) and **SINBAD** (IA) really sailors? Is **TITANIC** (IA) to be taken in a positive or negative sense? Does **TWEEDL** (AK) belong to Dum or Dee? Does **SS SUE** (VA) s-s-s-stutter?

To what does **UPN DWN** (CT) refer? What, exactly, is **AUFDWAL** (ID), and what's **UPTOU** (DE)? What is "it" in **UCRE8IT** (WA)? What's the story behind **3RDTRY** (VA)? **B4NAFTR** (IN) what?

Did the owner of **BAWANA** (IA), or **BUWANA** (MI), or **BWANA** (AR, IA) see too many old Tarzan movies? Is **SAY SAY** (VA) a Jimmy Stewart imitator?

What is **B-ONDME** (PA)? Is **DBLNKL** (IN, WA) for or against the 55 mph speed limit? What should be done **ASAP** (WA)?

To whom or what does **DRIVEL** (AK) refer? What **AINT EZ** (MS)? What is a **DNDEAL** (MI)? Why would anyone want **EARWAX** (IA) on their tag? Is the owner of **DOODAH** (AK) an old Stephen Foster fan? How on earth did anyone get **DNGLBRY** (WA)? Or **HUMJOB** (WA)? In **GSTFSN** (IA), what is being fussed about? What is the significance of **HMNRACE** (WA)? The meaning of **HOHUM** (KS)?

One wonders who and what were involved in **HE LIED** (TX), but the plate on a big South Carolina Mercedes is far more clear: **WUZ HIS**.

Does the holder of **IAMIAM** (WA) go around singing "I'm Henry the Eighth, I Am"? Why would anyone adorn their tag with **ILDUCE** (WA), the title of Europe's second most detestable dictator during World War II, not to mention **FUHRER** (WA)? Is **WE SOLY**, on a

Honda in North Carolina, intended to placate "Buy American" neighbors?

IWILL (IA)? I will what? **IWANNA** (AK) what? **IWUNDR** (IA) what? What's the scoop on **I8ABUG** (WA)? Is the owner of **MEEMEE** (DE) really that self-absorbed? Does the holder of **MSLTOE** (IA) watch where he or she stands? Is **MYCAAH** (IA) originally from Boston? What is **NEWS4U**? Or is this the plate of a journalist? Of what is **PGREEN** (AK) envious? Is **PODUNK** (IA) garaged in a small town?

Who has **PUKRPWR** (WA) been kissing? What's **UPTOU** (DE) or **UPTOME** (ID)? Who in Iowa would **RATONU**? Is **REDTAPE** (WA) a bureaucrat? What is the significance of **ROCKSOFT** (NC)? A rock group, perhaps? Is **ROLLOUT** (IA) a camp counselor or a drill sergeant? Is **SPKEZY** (IA) the plate of a bartender or tavern owner? What is **TABOO** (AK)?

One can understand the general sentiment behind **TGIF** (CT), but **TOEJAM** (WA)? Really! **TRULY** (IA)!

Why would **TUSCH** and **TUSH** (WA) apparently name their cars after their hinder parts? What's the story behind **UBOAT** (WA)?

At whom is **UBOREME** (WA) directed? To what would we **ADD H2O** (TX)? Who would need to be reminded that **URU IMI** (CT)? What sorts of people in Washington state have **WAHZOH, WAZOO, WAZOOO, WAZZOO**, and **WAZZU**?

Is **2HI2CU** (SC) on one of those ridiculous looking jacked-up pickups riding atop oversized tires? Is **2NDCAR** (AK) on the Porsche or Mercedes of a jokester?

Wouldn't you love to know the stories behind such plates as **ALIBABA** (WA), **BLEEP** (IA), **COWPIE** (WA), **GERM** (IA), **H-DMPTY** (OR), **KAMAKZI** (WA), **MOORMAN** (NC), **NIGHTY** (AK), **NODOUT** (DE), **QTIP** (CT), **SUNSET** (ND), **TARBABY** (WA), **XTINCT** (IA), **YESIDO** (IA), **YOUDOG** (IA), **ZOMBIE** (IA), and **1BADDAY** (SC)?

More complicated and just as mysterious are two North Carolina plates: **2L84U2W8** (too late for you to wait) and **2N10Z4U** (too intense for you).

In these mysterious realms there is room for sentiments of all stripes, even polar opposites, such as **1MTHE1** in Connecticut and **IAINTH1** in Washington. Having said that, let's close the text of this chapter with an Iowa plate, **THEEND**.

ABLE 2 (WA)
ABNORM (IA)
ABONUS (IA)
ACCUSED (WA)
ADEAL4U (WA)
AEIOU-Y (TX)
AFTER 5 (TX)
AFTER 6 (TX)
AFRDTE (NH)
A GIFT (NH, TX)
A GIZMO (TX)
AHCAH (NH)
AINTME (NH)
ALAMO (WA)
ALIAS (ME, VA)
ALKEMY (IA)
ALMOST (ID, MS)
ALNITE (MS)
ALWAYS (IA, ID)
ANON (MS)
ANRCHY (NS)
A NU U (MS)
ANYTYM (IA)
APOGEE (AK)
APRIL I (VA)
ARIDDL (MS)
A RIDDL (MS)
ARUMOR (IA)
ASMIL4U (PA)
A THANG (VA)
ATTA2D (KY)
A4DBLE (WI)
BBGUN (IA)
BECAUSE (ID)
BELCH VT (VA)
BEME (IA)
BLZZRD (AK)
BOPEEP (MI)
BRBDAWL (CA)
BRBDOLL (CA)
BRBEDAL (CA)
BRBYDLL (CA)
BRBYDOL (CA)
BUK O RU (TX)
B4UGO (KY)
CACH 22 (MI)
CACHET (IA)
CANCER (AK)
CIRCLES (VA)
CLUBMUD (WA)
CNORE (AK)
CRAASH (VA)
CRISIS (AK)
CZAR (TX)
DALESR (CA)
DEF I (VA)
DEJAVU (DE, IN)
DEJAVU2 (IN)
DERCAR (IA)
DETHWSH (CA)
DEVIL (DE)
DFN8LY (IA, MI)
DIRT RD (VA)
D LIGHT (TX)
D-MAIN 1 (VA)
DODADD (WA)
DOODAD (KY)
DOWNPAT (WA)
DR LOVE (MS)
DR LUV (MS)
DSCOVRY (IA)
D TAILS (CT)
EARNED (IA)
EE SUX (VA)
EGOTAG (IA)
EIN (NJ)

ELF (IA)
ENIGMA (AK, MI, TX)
EPICNTR (CA)
EPIGRAM (CA)
EPITAF (CA)
EPITAPH (CA)
EPITHET (CA)
EQANOX (CA)
EROS (AK)
EVEN ME (ID)
EXCUSE (VA)
EZ4U2C (MI)
FASN8N (VA)
FIGMNT (TX)
FIXIN2 (KY)
FLGSHP (IA)
FLU (DE)
FOREVER (IA, MI)
FOMOST (MS)
FORSALE (IA)
FREDOM (IA)
FTKNOX (AK)
GASWAR (IA)
GAYDAY (KY)
GIGGLE (IA)
GIZMO (AK, MS, SC)
GIZZMO (MS)
GOTEVN (IA)
GOTIT (IA)
GRAVY (IA)
GR8ST8 (WI)
GUMBAH (WA)
GUMWAD (TX)
GUSTO (IA)
GUTS (IA)
HAMBNE (IA)
HAMBONE (IA)
HARDER (VA)
HATSTAK (IA)
HEHHEH (IA)
HELPNU (AK)
HEPAID (OR)
HERES2U (WA)
HICKEY (AK)
HICKUP (AK)
HILTOP (IA)
HOBNOB (IA)
HOMADE (IA)
HOME TRX (VA)
HOOKONE (WA)
HOOPLA (KY, MI)
HOT DIP (TX)
HOWLIN (IA)
HRTLAND (IA)
HUBBUB (IA)
HUGS2U (NC)
HYHORSE (WA)
I AM (WY)
IAM4U (VA)
IASKU (VA)
IBPWEE (WA)
IBETOO (VA)
I CAN (MS)
I CAN 2 (MS)
I CANT (MS)
ICEBOX (AK)
ICEBRG (AK)
ICECAP (AK)
ICEMAN (AK)
ICICLE (WA)
ICYOU (IA)
IDIDIT (ID)
ID LUV2 (DE, MS, VA)
I DO (VA)
IDOIT (VA)
IDONT (OH, VA)

IDONTNO (ID)
I DNT NO (MS)
I DUNNO (AK)
IFIHADU (ID)
IFONLY (MS, WA)
IGLOO (AK)
IGO55 (WI)
IHADIT (WA)
IHAVIT (WA)
IHEARU (IA)
IHELP (DE, IA)
IHOPESO (NC)
IKARE (IA)
IKNOWUR (VA)
ILOVE (IA)
ILOVEU (AK, IA)
ILUVIT (AK)
ILUVME (IA)
ILUVU (AK, DE, IA)
ILUVU2 (AK, IA)
ILYKIT (AK)
IMD14U (ND)
I MIGHT (MS)
IMPORT (AK)
INDCNT (VA)
IN EFECT (VA)
INFNIT (VA)
I NOIT (MS)
IN SHORT (AK)
IOU NUTN (VA)
ISTLDO (VA)
I TOLD YA (IL)
I TRY TO (VA)
IUS2BE (TX)
IWAN2 (VA)
IWONIT (AK, IA, OR)
I WONT (ID)
I WUNIT (AK)
IWUVU (AK)
I WUV U 2 (AK, OH)
I 1T (VA)
I 4 GOT (TX)
JACKPOT (IA)
JACNJIL (WA)
JUNGLJM (WA)
JUSME (IA)
JUS1MOR (WA)
KEWPIE (VA)
KGB (WA)
KINGDOM (VA)
KMOSHN (TX)
LEGACY (IA)
LIBIDO (AK)
LIFSUX (AK)
LMNDROP (WA)
LONGS II (VA)
LOOGY (WV)
LOVEPAT (WA)
LOVEU (IA)
LOVEYA (IA)
LOVEYU (IA)
LST BOY (TX)
LTL BIGR (VA)
LUST (AK)
LUVSUX (AK)
LUVU (IA)
LUVU2 (IA)
LUVYOU (IA)
LUV2 (IA)
MABE ME (VA)
MAD M (VA)
MARX (IA)
MEDIUM (WA)
MEIN (SC)
MEMOIR (IA)
MEMORY (IA)

M FUQUA (VA)
MIASMA (MS)
MILADY (IA)
MINITMN (WA)
MISTER (IA)
MONSOOR (IA)
MPATHY (TX)
MRSBS (IA)
MR WHY (TX)
MR WISE (TX)
MYTIPS (WA)
N ASIL (VA)
N E FECT (ND)
NEFFECT (WA)
NEMISIS (IN)
NEURON (WA)
NEUTRON (WA)
NEVRNUF (WA)
NEW TAG (MS)
NOBODY (IA)
NOFUTR (VA)
NO QTR (TX)
NOSEEUM (VA)
NOTHIN (IA)
NOT2BD (VA)
NTRPRZ (IA)
NUFSED (IA)
N4THE (KY)
OKKIDO (VA)
ONAWHIM (WA)
ON A WIM (TX)
ON D LVL (TX)
ON LE ME (TX)
OUTHOUS (WA)
OZONE (AK)
PAID FER (WA)
PAIDFOR (IA, WA)
PAID4 (AK, IA, IL, MS, OR, WA, WI)
PARADOX (CA, IA)
PATIWGN (WA)
PATTWGN (WA)
PAYD 4 (MS)
PD FOR (MS)
PDYWGN (WA)
PEASOUP (WA)
PERHAPS (ID)
PICASSO (WA)
PIGMY (IA)
PINEER (IA)
PHARAOH (WA)
PIRATE (IA)
PLACEBO (WA)
POISON (IA)
POIZON (IA)
POOBEAR (IA)
POOPER (AK)
POPE MAN (VA)
POPTART (WA)
PROBLEE (VA)
PSEUDO (IA)
PTECOAT (WA)
QPDOLL (WA)
QUIOTE (WA)
RAINBO (AK, IA)
RAINBOW (IA)
RATED G (SC)
RATED X (SC)
RAW JEW (MS)
REB (IA)
REBEL (IA)
RIDNLO (IA)
RIPPER (MS)
ROBOT (IA)

RSTHOME (WA)
RSVP (MS)
RUBICON (WA)
SAGEBSH (WA)
SANDBAR (WA)
SANDMAN (IA)
SANMAN (IA)
SANTA (CO, IA)
SARCASM (IA)
SATAN (AK, DE, WA)
SCARAAB (WA)
SCHRADE (WA)
SCLAUS (AK, IA)
SCORCH (IA)
SCUMPAD (VA)
SEESAW (IA)
SETLMNT (WA)
SEWER (SC)
SEW4TH (IA)
SHAMROC (WA)
SHAMROX (WA)
SHATZ (AK)
SHEPAID (WA)
SITNBUL (WA)
SLAMMR (AK)
SMLWRLD (WA)
SNOJOB (IA)
SNSHINE (IA)
SOLUTION (NC)
SOS (IA)
SPITWAD (WA)
SPUTNIK (WA)
SRNDPTY (WA)
STASH (DE)
STEALTH (IA)
STELTH (IA)
STHELEN (WA)
ST8HOOD (WA)
SUM DAY (MS)
SUM THN (IA)
SUM TYM (IA)
SURREAL (WA)
SWOOP (IA)
TEAPOT (IA)
TEEPEE (AK, IA)
TEN2ONE (CA)
THXHUN (AK)
THIS YR (VA)
THE 3RD (MS)
THMS UP (TX)
TICTOC (IA)
TICTOK (IA)
TIKTOC (IA)
TIKTOK (IA)
TIP TOE (MS)
TIQTOQ (IA)
TNIGHT (MI)
TOOTOO (WA)
TOTO TOO (VA)
TOXIC (AK)
TROJAN (AK)
TROLL (AK)
TROPHY (IA)
TRULOV (IA)
TRULUV (IA)
TRUTH (IA)
TSPOON (IA)
TYMOFF (IA)
TYMOUT (IA)
U-BOAT (KY)
UBTRIPN (WA)
UBUGLY (WA)
UBUGME (WA)
UBUGME2 (WA)

UCME (IA)
UCRE8IT (WA)
UFO (AK, IA, ID, MI, MS, TX, WY)
UFOS (IA)
UGAWUGA (WA)
ULOSE (IA)
UNLISTD (IN)
UNOWHO (IN, MI)
UPCHUCK (WA)
UP N DWN (CT, TX)
URANUS (IA, TX)
URAWAY (IA)
URGONE (IA)
UR LOVE (TX)
UR ONE2 (MS)
URUGLY (MS)
UR IT (VA)
UR WHO UR (VA)
VARIETY (IA)
VETNAM (MI)
VETO (IA)
VICTIM (AK)
VIRUS (AK)
VOWELS (KY)
VRBOTN (MS)
VRRIETY (CA)
WANABE (MI)
WANAGO (IA)
WANTED (IA)
WASNTME (ID)
WAZNTME (WA)
WEEWEE (MI)
WE HAD2 (MS)
WELOVU (IA)
WELUVU (IA)
WEQUIT (VA)
WISDOM (IA)
WIZARD (IA)
WUV (NJ)
XCEDRIN (WA)
XCEDRN (WA)
XCUSEME (IA)
XCUSME (IA)
XMAS (MS)
XPDYTR (VA)
XPOSED (IA)
XXXXX'S (VA)
YESIAM (KY)
YSGUYS (VA)
YOUBET (IA)
ZERO (IA)
ZEUS (AK)
ZIGZAG (IA)
ZIPLOC (IA)
ZODIAC (IA)
1-CENT (KY)
1GUESS (KY)
1N ONLY (OH)
1N2N3N4 (TN)
1ST LOVE (IA)
1STLUV (IA)
14U (IA)
2BA LIMO (VA)
2 FOR 2 (VA)
2GONZO (TX)
2GROSS (TX)
2LIP (VA)
2L & BACK (VA)
2 NIGHT (MS)
2 THOU 2 (VA)
3RDTRY (VA)
4 EVER (AK, IA)
4 HOLLY (VA)
4KEEPS (IA)
4MYBACK (VA)
9 LIES (VA)

CHAPTER 15

No-Nos

XXX-rated and rejected.

If ever there was a book chapter that proves the adage "There's no accounting for taste," this is it. Since one driver's vulgarity is another driver's lyric, each state's department of motor vehicles has had to get into the censorship business to prevent the offensive display of plate messages that concern 1) sexual activity, 2) excretory functions, 3) racial or ethnic slurs, 4) profanity, 5) the drug culture, 6) blaspheming the Almighty, and 7) matters that might otherwise offend or mislead people.

DMV personnel take this part of their job seriously and go to great lengths to protect us from offense. California has developed a computer program that is also used by other states to flag objectionable terms, and many states' DMV officials even look up terms they're not sure of in a variety of foreign dictionaries. Some go so far as to examine suspect plate applications in a mirror to see if the message spells something untoward backwards. It has become something of a game — slyly striving to outwit the DMV, and state officials trying just as hard to catch us at it.

Gross plates do, of course, slip through from time to time; most states have received complaints from the public and have had to contact the holder of the offending plate demanding that it be turned in and replaced with a more acceptable message.

The author has read of only one actual court case involving censorship of personalized plates — the California case of Aaron Katz v. Department of Motor Vehicles in 1973. Mr. Katz requested the plate **EZ LAY**. (Was he a chicken farmer?) Whatever his reason, the First District Court of Appeals turned him down, saying the DMV's refusal served a substantial government interest and was only an incidental restriction of free expression.

Now let's get to it. First, consider the big one — sex-related plate applications that have been rejected in various states, for example **ACDC, ASTUD, BALLS, BANG, BLO, BONER, BOOBS, BUNS, BUTT, CLAP, COITUS**, and **DIGSEX**.

If you are **DUINIT**, why advertise? After all, when it comes to sex, there are two basic types of people: those who talk about it all the time, and those who are doing it. Or have at least **DUNIT** lately.

Residents of some states have wanted **EZ-MAKE** or **EZLAY**; one state rejected **EZ2LUV**, which seems innocent enough, but that's **EEEZZ** for me to say.

All references to all preferences have also been denied. Out of the closet and onto the freeway would have been **FAG, DYKE, DV 8, FAGGOT, FAIRY, FFAGUE, GABOY, FLIT, GAYGUY, GFAIRY, LXIX, MSGAY, PALGAY, RUGAY, IM1.**

DV was denied because it is **VD** backwards, **XES** because it is **SEX** reversed. An application for **2 ON 1** was turned down on the assumption that it referred to group sex. Some states have rejected **4PLAY**, but others have allowed it.

The sneaky use foreign languages, as in **BABA**, French for young prostitute; **FEMM**, French for lesbian; **FICK**, German for coitus;

JUS, French for sperm; **LOLO**, a French term meaning prostitute; **MAC**, French for a person advertising sexual availability.

MOLA is a French slang term for a homosexual, **NUE** French for naked, **PATO** a male homosexual. **PINE** and **PIPI** are French terms meaning penis, **RUTE** German slang for the same organ, **SEIN** French for breasts. Another selection assumed to refer to a body part and rejected? **BUSH**. No comment.

Plate applicants who haven't progressed past the excrement or bodily byproduct-related stage have been turned down in some states for a motley assortment of plates, including: **ANAL, AZZHOLE, BARF, BARFUP, CACA, CRAP, DUMP, FAHRT, GASPASER, KUL** (French for ''ass''), **PEE, PILES, PIS, PISANT, POOP, POOPOO, PUKEUP, TERDS, TIHS** (a reverse spelling), and **TOYLIT**.

In the racial or ethnic slur category are such rejected would-be plates as **ABIE, BLKBCH, CHINK, COON, DAGO** and **DAGOGO, FROG, GOY** (although California has accepted **NICEGOY**), **GOYIM, GOOK, HUN, IMAJAP, IZAWOP, JAPS, JIG, KYKE, MRWOP, NGGR, NIG, NIPTOY, NOJAP, NOTJAP, POLAK, SHEENE, THEJAP, THEWOP, WAP, WOP, WOPCOP, XWOP, ZEJAP,** and **1WOP**.

Profanity, too, has tried to sneak onto license plates, as in **AUFOUC, AWCHIT, BULSHT, DAMNIT, DAMN, FAWKU, FCKIT, FOKU, FQK, FQU, FRIGIT, FYOU, GODDAM,** and **HELL.**

Middle-aged men clinging to fond memories of Brigette Bardot movies may recall that when vexed, the saucy Brigitte would hiss, "Merde!" The subtitles would translate this expletive "Ouch!" — something of a loose translation. Applications for **MERD** or **MERDE** have been rejected in most states, though Oregon allowed it, reasoning that the expression is used to mean "good luck" in certain parts of France.

Other plate applications have been turned down because of their connection with the drug culture. **ACID, ADDICT, AREUHI, COKE, CRAK, DO COKE, DOPE, DRUGS, EPOD** (dope spelled in reverse), **HASH, JOINT, OPIUM, PEYOTE, QALUDE, SMAK, SMKPOT, TOKE, TOKEUP,** and **TRYPOT** — all these are familiar even to squares like myself, providing we have at least watched Miami Vice a couple of times.

Trying to interpret plate rejections has been a real education, however, as regards some of the less familiar slang terms of substance abusers. **BIG D**, I am told, means

LSD; **BIG H**, heroin. **DEXY** is Dexamyl, an amphetamine. **DUST** means angel dust, **GOMA** is a crude form of opium, **GOW** is some other form of narcotic. A **GYUE** is a marijuana cigarette; **HEMP** is also marijuana.

One state disallowed **HOLD** on the assumption that it meant holding drugs for sale. A **JOLT** apparently is a marijuana joint, **LEAF** refers to cocaine, and **LENO** is Spanish for good-quality marijuana. **LID** means an ounce of marijuana; **LOCO** also refers to that drug.

MES means mescaline, **METH** is methadrine, **MEZZ** is a marijuana cigarette, and **MOJO** refers to narcotics in general. **POD** and **RAMA** are marijuana terms, **SALT** is heroin in powdered form, and **SCAG** and **SCAT** also refer to heroin.

SNOP is marijuana, **SNOW** cocaine, **TAR** opium. **USER** has been rejected as drug related, both **WEED** and **YEDO** are marijuana, and **ZEN** is LSD. Given this level of interest, no wonder drug dealers make so much money.

Plate applications headed off because they are deemed blasphemous are infrequent but have included **IAMGOD, HEYGOD, IMAGOD, NOGSUS, OGOD, OLORD, UBGOD, UJESUS**, and

YJESUS. **DOG** has been rejected because it is **GOD** spelled backwards.

Still other applications have been turned down for a variety of reasons. **AFENCE** implies illegal pursuits, as do **DANDD**, which could stand for "drunk and disorderly," **GONUDE, HOOKER, KILLER, MAFEA, MURDER, PIMP, PIMPIN, PMP, RAPE, ROLLEM, SADIST, SKYJAC, SLAYER, STRIKUM, STRIPR, UNCLAD, WHORE,** and **WHORER**.

DMVs are reluctant, too, to approve plates that would appear to give their owners official authority they don't actually possess: **CTYCOP, FBI, FUZZ, IAMFBI, IMFBI, KOPCAR, LECOP, POLIZE, THEFUZ, THEGOV, THEPIG**, and **USGOVT**.

From all this it should be clear why the DMVs of every state feel obliged to do some censoring, yet, like all who must perform this thankless function, they sometimes go too far. If someone really wants **ATHIEST** on his plate, the First Amendment provision of freedom of (or from) religion would seem to make this plate allowable. **CAPO** implies the head of an organized crime "family" (a family with values all its own), but could have been intended to signify the head of some perfectly legal enterprise.

DIEU is French for God. As many states have allowed plates reading **GOD**, and very likely every state has a plate that reads **JESUS**, why not **DIEU**? **DOYOU** has been rejected, too, but is capable of a wealth of innocent interpretations.

If a person has been in prison and has served his sentence, he should be able to display **EXCON** if he wishes; it will harm no one but himself. **EZ LVR** was rejected, probably on the assumption that it signified "easy lover," though it just as easily could mean "easy liver."

GAGA was turned down in one state because it is French for "senile," but in English usage it means "off the deep end." **IFUCAN** was probably intended as nothing more sinister than a challenge to other motorists, as in "Try and pass me — if you can."

INLUST shouldn't really offend anyone. Many people are probably more nearly "head over heels in lust" than in love. **INUFAC** is a street-slang challenge, but nothing obscene. **IRSFOE** isn't so awful either; virtually all of us feel this way at least once a year.

Who could possibly take seriously **KGBCIA** or **KGBFBI**, given their unlikely combinations, and if a person is a **NUDIST**, why shouldn't he or she be able to say so on a license plate?

PEEOUI must have been disallowed because it begins with **PEE**. Taken as a whole, however, it appears to be a decidedly innocent nickname: Peewee. **SIRSEXY** is too ridiculous to be offensive, and **SUXGAS** must surely refer to a gas-guzzling car, just as **WINO** was no doubt proposed not by someone who drinks while lying under bridges, but by a whimsical wine-fancier more into quality than quantity.

Some judicious pruning of plate applications is clearly called for, but those who labor in this vineyard should do it gently. To head off undue offense, I have done some censoring of my own in this chapter, omitting the very most offensive plate applications in my collection — to protect the sensibilities of those readers who have active sensibilities. As for you, gentle reader, gaze upon the listing that follows and contemplate the sanity of your fellow man.

ACAT8U
ASOB
ATSTUD
AZUL
BADAS
BADSHT
BADSOB
BAMBAM
BEDMAN
BI
BICHIN
BIGSHT
BIGTIT
BOOB
BRA

BUSH
BUYME
BYECOP
CARNAL
CASHIT
CHESTY
COD
DAMMBUS
DANG
DAPIG
DIGSEX
DILDO
DIRTYME
DKRAUT
DOA
DOG POOP
DOIT
DONG
DORK
DOUCHE
DPOLACK
DPSHT
DRAG
DR COON
DRCRAB
DRGOD
DROPLSD
DRUGS4U
DUMWOP
DYKEVAN
EASYLAY
EATLEAD
EATMEUP
EEEZZZ
EEGODS
ELPIG
ELTOKE
ESEGUY
ESOBEE
ESOHBE
EUNUCH
EYEMGOD
EZCOME
EZGUY
EZ LADY
EZ LUV
EZMAKE
EZSTUD
EZSTUF
FAG
FAIRY
FATBUTT
FATFANY
FEELME
FEELNUP
FOCK
FOUK
FUC
FUGG
FUGGIT
FUK
FUTZ
FUZ
GAYLIB
GETLO
GETNIT
GETSUM
GIG
GITSUM
GOOH
HAULASS
HELLNO
HEROIN
HERPES
HIFUZZ
HITLER
HITMAN
HNYBUT
HONKIE
HORNEY
HOTDAMN
HOTLOVE
HOTMOM
HOTRODS
HOTSHT
HOT4U
HUMP
HUNGLO
HUSSIE
IBDAMN
IDOIT
I LUST
IM DRUNK
IM GOD
IM GOD2
IM HELL
IMHIGH
IM HORNY
IM HOT4U
IMKEPT
IM POLAK
IM SEXY
IM TOPLS
IN HEAT
INUTERO
IN2GRAS
IN2LUDE
IPCOORS
IPUF2
IRANSUX
IRDNECK
IREDHOT
IRSSUX
ISCREW

I SHOGUN
I SLEAZY
JERK
JUGS
KICKSS
KISMY
KMYA
KWIKE
LAY1
LOO
LORDY
LTLSHT
LUST
MAKLUV
MAKNIT
METH
MIERDA
MOON
MOONME
MORFIA
MRSTUD
NAKED
NAZI
NEWTER
NOBULL
NODICK
NOOKY
NOSHIT
NYMPHO
OBARF
OLDFART
ORGASM
ORGIE
PERVERT
PHUQUE
PICK UP
POOPER
POT
PSSSS
PSTOFF
PU55Y
RCHBTCH
RUGOOD
RUHIGH
RU14ME
SEDUCER
SEXBUS
SEXPOT
SEXY60
SLAYER
SLEZEE
SLUT
SOEASY
STUD
STUFIT
TEXASS
THEFIX
TIE1ON
TITS
TOKEIT
UDOIT
UMAMA
UPYERS
USOB
VD
WANG
WARGOD
WENCH
WMNIZR
WOMB
YAWANA
4NIK8

You get the idea.